TEACHING LANGUAGES CREATIVELY

Edited by
Philip Hood

Routledge
Taylor & Francis Group

LONDON AND NEW YORK

First published 2019
by Routledge
2 Park Square, Milton Park, Abingdon, Oxon OX14 4RN

and by Routledge
711 Third Avenue, New York, NY 10017

Routledge is an imprint of the Taylor & Francis Group, an informa business

British Library Cataloguing-in-Publication Data
A catalogue record for this book is available from the British Library

Library of Congress Cataloging-in-Publication Data
Names: Hood, Philip, 1951– editor.
Title: Teaching languages creatively / edited by Philip Hood.
Description: Abingdon, Oxon ; New York, NY : Routledge, 2019. |
Series: Learning to teach in the primary school series | Includes
bibliographical references.
Identifiers: LCCN 2018025588| ISBN 9781138699656 (hbk) |
ISBN 9781138699663 (pbk) | ISBN 9781315516332 (ebk)
Subjects: LCSH: Languages, Modern—Study and teaching (Elementary)
Classification: LCC LB1578 .T47 2019 | DDC 372.65—dc23
LC record available at https://lccn.loc.gov/2018025588

ISBN: 978-1-138-69965-6 (hbk)
ISBN: 978-1-138-69966-3 (pbk)
ISBN: 978-1-315-51633-2 (ebk)

Typeset in Times New Roman and Helvetica Neue
by Florence Production Ltd, Stoodleigh, Devon, UK

Printed and bound in Great Britain by
TJ International Ltd, Padstow, Cornwall

TEACHING LANGUAGES CREATIVELY

Teaching Languages Creatively brings together the experience of international primary language experts to explore creative teaching and learning in primary languages. Drawing on the latest research and theory and illustrated with ideas and case studies from real schools, it covers key topics, including:

- engaging students in the target language;
- celebrating bilingualism in the classroom;
- incorporating technology into modern teaching;
- integrating language learning across the curriculum;
- successful transitions;
- learning languages through singing, storytelling and dance.

Ideal for primary trainee teachers, newly qualified teachers, and established teachers looking for creative new ideas to enrich the learning experience of their students, *Teaching Languages Creatively* is an essential guide for inspiring the love of languages that is so vital for young learners.

Philip Hood works as a part-time tutor at the University of Nottingham after his retirement in 2017.

THE LEARNING TO TEACH IN THE PRIMARY SCHOOL SERIES

Series editor: Teresa Cremin, The Open University, UK

Teaching is an art form. It demands not only knowledge and understanding of the core areas of learning, but also the ability to teach these creatively and foster learner creativity in the process. *The Learning to Teach in the Primary School Series* draws upon recent research which indicates the rich potential of creative teaching and learning, and explores what it means to teach creatively in the primary phase. It also responds to the evolving nature of subject teaching in a wider, more imaginatively framed 21st century primary curriculum.

Designed to complement the textbook *Learning to Teach in the Primary School*, the well informed, lively texts in this series offer support for student and practising teachers who want to develop more creative approaches to teaching and learning. Uniquely, the books highlight the importance of the teachers' own creative engagement and share a wealth of research informed ideas to enrich pedagogy and practice.

Titles in the series:

Teaching Music Creatively, 2nd Edition
Pam Burnard and Regina Murphy

Teaching Design and Technology Creatively
Clare Benson and Suzanne Lawson

Teaching Outdoors Creatively
Edited by Stephen Pickering

Teaching History Creatively, 2nd Edition
Edited by Hilary Cooper

Teaching Geography Creatively, 2nd Edition
Edited by Stephen Scoffham

Teaching Science Creatively, 2nd Edition
Dan Davies and Deb McGregor

Teaching English Creatively, 2nd Edition
Teresa Cremin

Teaching Mathematics Creatively, 2nd Edition
Linda Pound and Trisha Lee

Teaching Religious Education Creatively
Edited by Sally Elton-Chalcraft

Teaching Physical Education Creatively
Angela Pickard and Patricia Maude

Applying Cross-Curricular Approaches Creatively
The Connecting Curriculum
Jonathan Barnes

Teaching Languages Creatively
Edited by Philip Hood

For more information about this series, please visit: https://www.routledge.com/Learning-to-Teach-in-the-Primary-School-Series/book-series/LTPS

CONTENTS

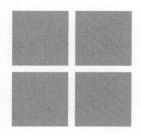

FIGURES

TABLES

CONTRIBUTORS

Colin Christie

Colin Christie is Lecturer (Scholarship) in Modern Languages Initial Teacher Education at the University of Aberdeen. Prior to this he led the PGCE Languages course at University College London Institute of Education and co-led the Modern Languages PGCE at the University of Cumbria's London base. He has held a number of advisory positions, including as a Key Stage 3 consultant and has produced teaching resources in a variety of media. He has also worked in schools and colleges in different roles, such as a Languages Development project co-ordinator in a Language College and a head of department. His PhD thesis was on the topic of spontaneous learner target language talk in the languages classroom and his academic interests include the teaching and learning of modern languages, in particular pupil use of the target language, the development of spontaneous target language talk and error correction strategies. He has been a member of the ALL ITET Steering Group linking language teaching and teacher education.

Philip Hood

Philip Hood worked in secondary, primary and higher education for 41 years before retiring in 2017. This spanned a fast-developing period of time in which communicative syllabuses and new format examinations came into being, reading moved from a mere consolidation activity to a means of meeting new language, primary languages were abandoned and restored, grammar teaching reputedly left the classroom and re-emerged, revitalised! But it is his work in the field of content and language integrated learning which best defines his beliefs about the breadth and depth that languages education should contain, with a focus on real and interesting content and authentic and purposeful tasks. He is co-author of the CUP publication *Content Language Integrated Learning*, which has successfully outlined that approach for an international audience.

Laure Jackson

Laure Jackson works at the University of Chichester as Senior Lecturer in Physical Education and leads the dance modules on the undergraduate PE and PGCE

Primary and Secondary degrees. Most recently she has developed the PGCE Secondary Dance programme. She previously worked in mainstream secondary schools in West Sussex, teaching Physical Education and Dance introducing dance to examination level. She has experience of working with both specialist and non-specialist teachers in Dance. She has led Dance CPD courses throughout her career to non-specialist primary and secondary teachers. She is a French speaker and taught PE and Dance at an International school in France. She also taught a range of classes at Gothenburg Folkuniversitet using her TESOL (Teaching English to Speakers of Other Languages) qualification.

Lynne Jones

Lynne Jones is a languages graduate and experienced primary practitioner who joined Scotland's National Centre for Languages SCILT as a Professional Development Officer in 2012. From 2013 to 2015 she was involved with the development of Education Scotland's comprehensive curricular guidance and online resources related to the 1+2 approach to language learning. Her main role is to collaborate with colleagues in SCILT and beyond to develop, facilitate and evaluate the various professional learning opportunities offered to teachers, student teachers and development officers across Scotland. She is the SCILT lead practitioner on the national 1+2 Languages Leadership Programme as well as currently being seconded 1 day a week to the Scottish College of Educational Leadership (SCEL) as a Tutor on their Teacher Leadership Programme. She has recently begun a doctorate in education (EdD) at the University of Strathclyde, Glasgow specialising in supporting teacher learning.

Susan Jones

Susan Jones is Assistant Professor at the University of Nottingham. Working with beginning teachers as well as in informal family and community-based contexts for learning, her research focuses on how language, literacies and the arts relate to the agency and identities of individuals and communities. This includes researching the ways in which young bilinguals make use of literacy practices to explore their cultural worlds and identities. Recent projects include a British Academy-funded study of the everyday literacies of families living on a Midlands council estate. She was a teacher of English in secondary schools and a tutor in Children's Literature for the Open University. She is currently Programme Leader for the Education BA and MArts and also supports postgraduate research students working for Masters, EdD and PhD.

Claudine Kirsch

Claudine Kirsch was born in Luxembourg, read Science of Education and worked as a primary school teacher in Luxembourg until 1999 when she left for Goldsmiths, University of London. There she took both her Masters and her PhD in Education and subsequently lectured on undergraduate and postgraduate programmes. During that time she published research articles and the key text for students and teachers, *Teaching Foreign Languages in the Primary School*. She joined the University of Luxembourg in January 2012 where she teaches on undergraduate and postgraduate programmes. Her research interests include multilingualism and the processes and practices of learning and teaching multiple languages in formal and non-formal educational settings.

Sarah Lister

Sarah Lister is Senior Lecturer at Manchester Metropolitan University, co-ordinating the modern foreign languages provision within the initial primary teacher education programmes. Her research and academic enterprise include motivation, early language learning, using technology in the language classroom and Content and Language Integrated Learning (CLIL). She first became interested and involved in CLIL in 2008 after attending her first CLIL conference in Tallinn, Estonia in 2008. In June 2010, she successfully secured external funding from Linked Up, a branch of the Association for Language Learning (ALL) to lead a European CLIL project. The focus of the research project was to examine the impact of CLIL on pupils' attitudes and motivation. The final project report published in 2012 along with resources and planning documentation are accessible on the Linked Up website: www.linksintolang uages.ac.uk/resources/2564.

Fhiona Mackay

Fhiona Mackay joined SCILT in 2012 as Depute Director and from October 2014 has worked in the role of Director. She previously lived and worked in Paris before qualifying as a teacher at the University of Strathclyde. She worked for several years in secondary schools, becoming Principal Teacher of Modern Languages in a large and vibrant department, offering French, Spanish, Italian and Mandarin. During her time as a Principal Teacher, she created opportunities for young people to take part in work experience placements in Europe and to learn about Chinese language and culture through study trips to Beijing, Xian and Shanghai. A passionate exponent of language learning, she spent a year at Education Scotland as a National Development Officer, where she worked with colleagues from partnership organisations such as the universities, local authorities, Scottish Government, SQA and the cultural organ-isations to promote and facilitate the learning and teaching of Modern Languages.

Elaine Minett

Elaine Minett is Senior Lecturer at the University of Chichester where she is Route Leader for PGCE Primary and Secondary Modern Foreign Languages (MFL). She taught languages in secondary schools for a number of years before her involvement in the development of primary MFL provision in a number of local schools. Her time as an advisory teacher for Primary MFL enabled her to work alongside a number of inspiring primary class teachers and develop her particular interest in how to integrate MFL in imaginative ways across the curriculum. She also had the opportunity to support non-specialists to develop confidence in delivering MFL. She was a member of the All-Party Parliamentary Group for Languages and the Expert Subject Advisory Group for Languages and has presented at a number of conferences across the country on various topics related to primary languages.

Pauline Palmer

Pauline Palmer is Primary Mathematics Subject Leader at Manchester Metropolitan University. She teaches on the undergraduate and postgraduate teaching training programmes and is the award co-ordinator for the Science, Technology, Engineering and Mathematics (STEM) Masters programme. Her research interests include change management and mathematics pedagogy. Always interested in the use of talk in the mathematics classroom, she became interested in CLIL pedagogy from working with a visiting academic from Cordoba in 2013, which led to collaboration with Sarah Lister. Their current research centres around an exciting research project, having secured funding as part of a Knowledge Transfer Partnership (KTP) project (September 2016). This is a collaborative project between the Manchester Met academics and a commercial software company, Cyber Coach. Sarah and Pauline are keen to explore the synergies between Mathematics and MFL and how CLIL can be used as an effective pedagogical tool to enhance linguistic and cognitive development in both Mathematics and MFL. The project will see the development, trialling and evaluation of a range of game-based resources designed for use in primary classrooms.

Katherine Richardson

Katherine Richardson is an experienced language teacher, teacher educator and researcher. She taught languages in primary, middle and secondary schools where she developed a strong interest in transition (particularly the academic aspect of the primary-secondary school transfer for languages). This later became the focus of her doctoral studies and she has published and presented her research in this area. Following her move into Higher Education, she taught on undergraduate and post-graduate programmes and supported the development of language teaching in primary and secondary schools. This included working with beginning teachers and experienced teachers to develop CLIL in both primary and secondary languages classrooms and supporting generalist primary teachers to teach languages. She has led a range of initial teacher education programmes at the universities of Warwick and Nottingham and has worked with teachers in the UK, Europe and China. In addition to transition, her research interests include initial teacher education, teacher development and co-teaching. She has now joined the University of Leeds where she is Academic Development Consultant.

Kristina Tobutt

Kristina Tobutt has worked throughout the education system in England from A-level to Early Years Foundation Stage since coming here from Germany in the early 1990s. This has included teaching languages in primary schools where she pioneered introducing French across the age and ability range in several East Midlands settings. Her approach was always to link language learning into the rest of the curriculum and having developed a range of such materials she co-authored with Carmen Roche the French multimodal classroom resource *A La Française*, which won a European Languages Label in 2008. She has also co-written two editions of *Teaching Languages in the Primary School* for Sage with Philip Hood. She now teaches in an Early Years setting in Newcastle-upon-Tyne.

SERIES EDITOR'S FOREWORD

Teresa Cremin

Over recent decades, teachers working in accountability cultures across the globe have been required to focus on raising standards, setting targets and 'delivering' prescribed curricula and pedagogy. In this period, the language of schooling, as Mottram and Hall (2009: 109) assert, has predominantly focused upon 'oversimplified, easily measurable notions of attainment'. They argue that this has had a standardising effect, prompting children and their development to be discussed 'according to levels and descriptors' rather than as children – as unique individuals and unique learners.

Practitioners, positioned as passive recipients of the prescribed agenda, appear to have had their hands tied, their voices quietened and their professional autonomy both threatened and constrained. At times, the relentless quest for higher standards has obscured the personal and affective dimensions of teaching and learning, fostering a mindset characterised more by compliance and conformity than curiosity and creativity.

However, creativity too has been in the ascendant in recent decades; in many countries efforts have been made to re-ignite creativity in education, since it is seen to be essential to economic and cultural development. In England, this impetus for creativity can be traced back to the National Advisory Committee on Creative and Cultural Education (NACCCE, 1999), which recommended a core role for creativity in teaching and learning. Primary schools in England were encouraged to explore ways to offer more innovative and creative curricula (DfES, 2003) and new national curricula in Scotland and Wales also foregrounded children's critical and creative thinking. Additionally, initiatives such as Creative Partnerships, an English government-funded initiative to nurture children's creativity, inspired some teachers to reconstruct their pedagogy (Galton, 2010, 2015). Many other schools and teachers, encouraged by these initiatives, and determined to offer creative and engaging school experiences, have exercised the 'power to innovate' (Lance, 2006). Many have proactively sought ways to shape the curriculum responsively, appropriating national policies in their own contexts and showing professional commitment and imagination, despite, or perhaps because of, the persistent performative agenda (e.g. Craft et al., 2014; Cremin et al., 2015; Neelands, 2009, Jeffrey and Woods, 2009).

Schools continue to be exhorted to be more innovative in curriculum construction and national curricula afford opportunities for all teachers to seize the space, exert their professionalism and shape their own curricula in collaboration with the young people with whom they are working. Yet for primary educators, tensions persist, not only because the dual policies of performativity and creativity appear contradictory, but also perhaps because teachers' own confidence as creative educators, indeed as creative individuals, has been radically reduced by the constant barrage of change and challenge. As Csikszentmihalyi (2011) notes, teachers lack a theoretically underpinned framework for creativity that can be developed in practice; they need support to develop as artistically engaged, research-informed curriculum co-developers. Eisner (2003) asserts that teaching is an art form, an act of improvisation (Sawyer, 2011), and that teachers benefit from viewing themselves as versatile artists in the classroom, drawing on their personal passions and creativity as they teach creatively.

As Joubert also observes:

Creative teaching is an art. One cannot teach teachers didactically how to be creative; there is no fail-safe recipe or routine. Some strategies may help to promote creative thinking, but teachers need to develop a full repertoire of skills which they can adapt to different situations.

(Joubert, 2001: 21)

However, creative teaching is only part of the picture, since teaching for creativity also needs to be acknowledged and their mutual dependency recognised. The former focuses more on teachers using imaginative approaches in the classroom (and beyond) in order to make learning more interesting and effective, the latter, more on the development of children's creativity (NACCCE, 1999). Both rely upon an understanding of the notion of creativity and demand that professionals confront the myths and mantras which surround the word. These include the commonly held misconceptions that creativity is the preserve of the arts or arts education, and that it is confined to particularly gifted individuals.

Creativity, an elusive concept, has been multiply defined by educationalists, psychologists and neurologists, as well as by policy makers in different countries and reserachers in different cultural contexts (Gl_veanu et al., 2015). Debates resound about its individual and/or collaborative nature, the degree to which it is generic and/or domain specific, and the differences between the 'Big C' creativity of genius and the 'little c' creativity of the everyday. Notwithstanding these issues, most scholars in the field believe it involves the capacity to generate, reason and critically evaluate novel ideas and/or imaginary scenarios. As such, it encompasses thinking through and solving problems, making connections, inventing and reinventing, and flexing one's imaginative muscles in all aspects of learning and life.

In the primary classroom, creative teaching and learning have been associated with innovation, originality, ownership and control (Woods and Jeffrey, 1996; Jeffrey, 2006), and creative teachers have been seen in their planning and teaching, and in the ethos which they create, to afford high value to curiosity and risk taking, to ownership, autonomy and making connections (Craft et al., 2014; Cremin et al., 2009; Cremin, 2015). Such teachers often work in partnership with others: with children, other teachers and experts from beyond the school gates (Cochrane and Cockett, 2007; Davies et al., 2012; Thomson et al., 2012). These partnerships offer new possibilities, with teachers acquiring some of the repertoire of pedagogic practices – the 'signature pedagogies' that artists use (Thomson and Hall, 2015).

Additionally, in research exploring possibility thinking, which Craft (2000) argues drives creativity in education, an intriguing interplay between teachers and children has been observed. In this body of work, children and teachers have been involved in immersing themselves in playful contexts, posing questions, being imaginative, showing self-determination, taking risks and innovating – together (Burnard et al., 2006; Cremin et al., 2006; Chappell et al., 2008; Craft et al., 2012; Cremin et al., 2013). As McWilliam (2008) argues, teachers can choose not to position themselves as the all-knowing 'sage on the stage', or the facilitatorlike 'guide on the side'. They can choose, as creative practitioners do, to take up a role of the 'meddler in the middle', co-creating curricula in innovative and responsive ways that harness their own creativity and foster that of the children. A new pedagogy of possibility beckons.

This series *Learning to Teach in the Primary School*, which accompanies and complements the edited textbook *Learning to Teach in the Primary School* (Cremin and Burnett, 2018, fourth edition), seeks to support teachers in developing as creative practitioners, assisting them in exploring the synergies between and potential for teaching creatively and teaching for creativity. The series does not merely offer practical strategies for use in the classroom, though these abound, but more importantly seeks to widen teachers' and student teachers' knowledge and understanding of the principles underpinning creative approaches, principles based on research. It seeks to mediate the wealth of research evidence and make accessible and engaging the diverse theoretical perspectives and scholarly arguments available, demonstrating their practical relevance and value to the profession. Those who aspire to develop further as creative and curious educators will find much of value to support their own professional learning journeys and markedly enrich their pedagogy and practice right across the curriculum.

ABOUT THE SERIES EDITOR

Teresa Cremin is a Professor of Education (Literacy) at the Open University and a Fellow of the Royal Society of the Arts, the Academy of Social Sciences, and the English Association. She is also a Trustee of the UK Literacy Association, co-editor of the journal *Thinking Skills and Creativity*, and co-convenor of the British Educational Research Association's Special Interest Group on Creativity. Teresa has been a Board member of BookTrust and the Poetry Archive, a Director of the Cambridge Primary Review Trust, and President of UKLA and UKRA.

Her work involves research, publication and consultancy in literacy and creativity. Many of Teresa's current projects seek to explore the nature and characteristics of creative pedagogies, including for example those fostering reading for pleasure, creative writing, immersive theatre, children's storytelling and story acting. Teresa is also passionate about (and still researching) teachers' own creative development and their identity positioning in the classroom as readers, writers, and artistically engaged educators and humans.

Teresa has written and edited nearly 30 books. Forthcoming and current volumes include: *Experiencing Reading for Pleasure in the Digital Age* (Sage, 2018); *Writer Identity and the Teaching and Learning of Writing; Storytelling in Early Childhood: Enriching Language, Literacy and Culture*, (Routledge, 2017, edited collections); *Teaching English Creatively* (Routledge, 2015); *Researching Literacy Lives: Building home school communities* (Routledge, 2015); *Building Communities of Engaged Readers: Reading for Pleasure* (Routledge, 2014), and *Writing Voices: Creating Communities of Writers* (Routledge, 2012).

REFERENCES

Burnard, P., Craft, A. and Cremin, T. (2006) Possibility thinking. *International Journal of Early Years Education*, Vol. 14, No. 3, pp. 243–262.

Chappell, K., Craft, A., Burnard, P. and Cremin, T. (2008) Question-posing and question-responding: The heart of possibility thinking in the early years. *Early Years*, Vol. 283, pp. 267–286.

Cochrane, P. and Cockett, M. (2007) *Building a Creative School: A Dynamic Approach to School Improvement*. Stoke on Trent: Trentham Books.

Craft, A. (2000) *Creativity Across the Primary Curriculum*. London: Routledge.

Craft, A., Cremin, T., Burnard, P., Dragovic, T. and Chappell, K. (2012) Possibility thinking: Culminative studies of an evidence-based concept driving creativity? *Education 3–13: International Journal of Primary, Elementary and Early*, Vol. 41, No. 5, pp. 538–556.

Craft, A., Cremin, T., Hay, P. and Clack, J. (2014) Creative primary schools: Developing and maintaining pedagogy for creativity. *Ethnography and Education*, Vol. 9, No. 1, pp. 16–34.

Cremin, T. (2015) Creative teachers and creative teaching and, in A. Wilson (ed.) *Creativity in Primary Education*. London: SAGE Publications, pp. 33–44.

Cremin, T., Barnes, J. and Scoffham, S. (2009) *Creative Teaching for Tomorrow: Fostering a Creative State of Mind*. Deal: Future Creative.

Cremin, T., Burnard, P. and Craft, A. (2006) Pedagogy and possibility thinking in the early years. *International Journal of Thinking Skills and Creativity*, Vol. 1, No. 2, pp. 108–119.

Cremin, T. and Burnett, C. (eds.) (2018) *Learning to Teach in the Primary School* (4th ed.). London: Routledge.

Cremin, T., Chappell, K. and Craft, A. (2013) Reciprocity between narrative, questioning and imagination in the early and primary years: Examining the role of narrative in possibility thinking. *Thinking Skills and Creativity*, Vol. 9, pp. 136–151.

Cremin, T., Glauert, E., Craft, A., Compton, A. and Stylianidou, F. (2015) Creative little scientists: Exploring pedagogical synergies between inquiry-based and creative approaches in early years science. *Education 3–13, International Journal of Primary, Elementary and Early Years Education*, Special issue on creative pedagogies, Vol. 43, No. 4, pp. 404–419.

Csikszentmihalyi, M. (2011) A systems perspective on creativity and its implications for measurement, in R. Schenkel and O. Quintin (eds.) *Measuring Creativity*. Brussels: The European Commission, pp. 407–414.

Davies, D., Jindal-Snape, D., Collier, C., Digby, R., Hay, P. and Howe, A. (2012) Creative environments for learning in schools. *Thinking Skills and Creativity*. http://dx.doi.org/10.1016/j.tsc.2012.07.004.

Department for Education and Skills (DfES) (2003) *Excellence and Enjoyment: A Strategy for Primary Schools*. Nottingham: DfES.

Eisner, E. (2003) Artistry in education. *Scandinavian Journal of Educational Research*, Vol. 47, No. 3, pp. 373–384.

Galton, M. (2010) Going with the flow or back to normal? The impact of creative practitioners in schools and classrooms. *Research Papers in Education*, Vol. 25, No. 4, pp. 355–375.

Galton, M. (2015) 'It's a real journey – a life changing experience': A comparison case study of creative partnership and other primary schools. *Education 3–13:International Journal of Primary, Elementary and Early Years Education*, Vol. 43, No. 4, pp. 433–444.

Glăveanu, V., Sierra, Z. and Tanggaard, L. (2015) Widening our understanding of creative pedagogy: A North – South dialogue. *Education 3–13. International Journal of Primary, Elementary and Early Years Education*, Special issue on creative pedagogies, Vol. 43, No. 4, pp. 360–370.

Jeffrey, B. (ed.) (2006) *Creative Learning Practices: European Experiences*. London: Tufnell Press.

Jeffrey, B. and Woods, P. (2009) *Creative Learning in the Primary School*. London: Routledge.

Joubert, M. M. (2001) The art of creative teaching: NACCCE and beyond, in A. Craft, B. Jeffrey and M. Liebling (eds.) *Creativity in Education*. London: Continuum.

Lance, A. (2006) Power to innovate? A study of how primary practitioners are negotiating the modernisation agenda. *Ethnography and Education*, Vol. 1, No. 3, pp. 333–344.

McWilliam, E. (2008) Unlearning how to teach *Innovations in Education and Teaching International* Vol 45, No.3, pp. 263-269.

Mottram, M. and Hall, C. (2009) Diversions and diversity: Does the personalisation agenda offer real opportunities for taking children's home literacies seriously? *English in Education*, Vol. 43, No. 2, pp. 98–112.

National Advisory Committee on Creative and Cultural Education (NACCCE) (1999) *All Our Futures: Creativity, Culture and Education*. London: Department for Education and Employment.

Neelands, J. (2009) Acting together: Ensemble as a democratic process in art and life. *Research in Drama Education*, Vol. 14, No. 2, pp. 173–189.

Sawyer, K. (ed.) (2011) *Structure and Improvisation in Creative Teaching*. New York: Cambridge University Press.

Thomson, P. and Hall, C. (2015) 'Everyone can imagine their own Gellert': The democratic artist and 'inclusion' in primary and nursery classrooms. *Education 3–13. International Journal of Primary, Elementary and Early Years Education*, Special issue on creative pedagogies, Vol. 43, No. 4, pp. 420–432.

Thomson, P., Hall, C., Jones, K. and Sefton-Green, J. (2012) *The Signature Pedagogies Project: Final Report*. London: Creativity, Culture and Education, available at: www. creativetallis.com/uploads/2/2/8/7/2287089/signature_pedagogies_report_final_version_11.3.12.pdf (accessed 1.6.12).

Woods, P. and Jeffrey, B. (1996) *Teachable Moments: The Art of Creative Teaching in Primary Schools*. Buckingham: Open University Press.

CHAPTER 1

REVIEWING THE LANDSCAPE

Philip Hood

INTRODUCTION

This book explores how we might structure foreign language teaching in the primary phase in a way that engages children in learning, and includes them whatever their abilities, interests or dispositions. In a study on motivating young language learners Oga-Baldwin, Nakata, Parker and Ryan (2017) looked in depth at the nature of engagement, stating (p. 140): 'The ultimate goal is to promote motivation through supporting students' behaviour, interest, and positive attitude toward the foreign language; in other words, their engagement and intrinsic motivation.' They note the importance of the three types of engagement: behavioural, emotional and cognitive, and after their detailed study conclude (p. 148) 'Engagement, influenced by the classroom environment, had a direct predictive effect on students' motivational orientations at the end of the year.' 'Creative' approaches to the teaching of any curriculum area are often held to be both engaging and motivational and we begin by exploring what this concept might mean for language learning.

'CREATIVE LANGUAGE TEACHING': SOME STARTING POINTS

We explore all our worlds through language. As Smidt (2016: 42) notes:

> we learn almost everything we know through the language or languages we understand, speak, read, listen to, write, draw, paint, sing, narrate, question, understand, appreciate, explain and use.

Our first starting point, therefore, is that all teachers are teachers of languages. In the primary classroom, this does of course include the teaching of foreign languages, and much can be learned from creative practice in this area to inform a language-rich classroom. However, our point here is that:

all teaching involves the teaching of language. We see this as a fundamental starting point because of the way it frames languages within the curriculum, and also the way it frames teachers' work and expertise.

(Jones 2017a)

It is also important for us to define what we mean by 'creative' in our discussion of teaching and learning in creative bilingual classrooms. This is a term that throughout this book can refer to both teaching in a creative way and the teaching of creativity. We argue that practice that builds effectively on the resources brought by pupils to a linguistically diverse classroom involves both of these things. Robinson (2006) has famously defined creativity as 'the process of having original ideas that have value'. This is helpful in many ways:

It emphasises that creativity is an active process, and not solely an outcome. Robinson's definition also encourages us to see the 'new' as central to creativity, whether this is new to the world (termed by Boden (2004) as 'H' creativity), or new to the person (Boden's 'P' creativity, or Craft's (2003) 'little-c' creativity). We argue, therefore, that creative classrooms encourage and celebrate different ways of encountering, exploring and expressing knowledge.

(Jones 2017b)

We might ask, 'to whom is the process of creativity 'of value'?' Robinson (2006) maintains that, too often, the value of education is defined and measured at a policy level, based on officially mandated and assessed skillsets, for example:

Creative bilingual classrooms, on the other hand, value the diverse linguistic resources represented within them, and the developing bilingual or multilingual identities of their pupils. Pope (2005: 52) emphasises that creativity is 'in(ter)ventive' and 'co-operative'.

(Jones 2017c)

Teaching and learning in creative bilingual classrooms is responsive and dialogic. Language is recognised as an asset and opportunities are sought for knowledge to be collaboratively generated and experiences to be shared. Part of this is the valuing of all the languages represented in a classroom, so providing a positive basis for learning an additional language, which is frequently new to all children.

HOW DO WE SEE CREATIVITY IN PRACTICE?

The book addresses this question in some depth, we hope. We will examine in greater detail in Chapter 8 the importance of the *classroom environment* (in that case for the youngest learners) and this needs to be kept in mind for all ages within the phase. Sometimes this means leaving behind chairs and tables and teacher 'control'; it might mean looking to other subject disciplines for content and pedagogy. For example, as part of their CPD offering, the National Centre for Excellence in Mathematics (NCETM, 2011) website features a section on the use of a role play area, not just in Early Years but also throughout primary. Their example for Y5 is a travel agent and they suggest:

Here the children could look at:

■ interpreting tables to extract information;
■ pricing up a holiday for various groups of people;
■ using percentages to calculate group discounts, sale prices etc.;
■ collecting, interpreting and using data to find out which are the most popular holiday destinations in order to inform the selection of brochures on display;
■ exploring time differences in different parts of the world and flight. durations.

(NCETM, 2011)

It is not unusual for language learners to 'do role play' of course but how much better if there is a real role-play area in the classroom that is part of everyday learning life. How much more purposeful is it to be able to take something from another curriculum subject and operate it also in a foreign language. 'Today we are having to communicate with our branch in Spain to arrange a trip for a group of people, so we need to work bilingually.' If we make our Year 3 and 4 work sufficiently progressive, both in terms of its content and in terms of its cognitive and creative challenge, our children will be ready by Year 5 to do this with confidence.

Part of the mission of this book is to ensure that across the 4 or more years of experience of primary language learning children become fired by the excitement of learning another language and accessing other cultures and so transfer to secondary schools with that enthusiasm not just intact but making a difference to their KS3 study as well. The opposite effect (of languages boredom and resistance) is the silent, often unexpressed fear of all of those engaged in primary (and secondary) language learning.

The best way of achieving the desired effect is for us as teachers to be creative in our approaches, to look constantly for fresh material, altered strategies and to fit what we offer to our group of learners. But in this book we also intend that not just the teacher but also the children work hard at this. So we must intend to develop a creativity in the learners too and to increase their independence by our careful scaffolding and encouragement of their sense of interest and enjoyment. We would like the children to have fun doing things which we seriously design for good learning; this is different from a teacher making things 'fun' as a way to get easy engagement. Because that sort of fun tends to be short-lived.

In this first chapter, therefore, we attempt to set out key issues in primary language teaching, both as a general outline and then by looking forward to the rest of the content of this book.

Through the years from around 2000 onwards a series of books emerged in the UK about primary languages teaching as the plans for the subject to become part of the National Curriculum (DfE, 2013) were shaped, briefly dashed and then restored. Building on earlier works by Frost and Driscoll (1999), Cameron (2001) and Sharpe (2001), a new set emerged in the middle of the decade, often to meet the needs of beginner teachers in training, for example: Jones and Coffey (2006), Kirsch (2008), Martin (2008) Hood and Tobutt (2009). Clearly these all have their own valuable place in the modern canon and any new volumes should take into account that they are there and should try to be 'different' in some way. By taking creativity as a central theme this book intends to look beyond the essentials of language teaching and learning and in some respects to challenge some of the assumptions that we may or may not have left behind. But we need also to be mindful of our unusual workforce. No other subject in primary schools has a less consistent provision across local authorities, chains and alliances or between even neighbouring schools. In fact no subject has a less even provision *within* schools in some cases. I recently asked a group of training teachers about what they had seen in their placement schools with regard to language teaching. Almost all had seen some, but beyond that the picture was intensely varied. Only very few had taught any language, only a few had watched their class teacher doing the role; a small number had seen a secondary teacher come in, while more had seen either a specialist teacher from their own staff or one from outside. And that is before we talked about which language! There is often talk about how vulnerable primary teachers who have received little training on top of a limited amount of post-14 language study feel when they regard the responsibility. The only truly ongoing professional development available to most of these teachers is voluntary engagement with online material in their own time or for them to work in school alongside a commercial resource which will provide the children and the teacher with a model of correctly spoken or written target language and cultural content. If the resource is good and the teacher works at this in planning and preparation as well as 'live' in the classroom, then over time the teacher will become more confident and more independent. Effective language teaching which should include as much of a creativity dimension as every other subject comes at a price which senior leaders in schools do need to pay and this should include, at an absolute minimum, resources which promote both engaging content and good, age-appropriate learning habits.

Where have we come from and where are we going? Do we do this as an isolated nation, perhaps soon to become more cut off from mainland Europe as we leave the EU, a nation which cannot look further afield as we have the 'curse' of working from a base where the first language (L1) is English, the lingua franca of the world, we are told? The journey through government policy during the post-millennium period is summarised in the first chapter of Hood and Tobutt (2015). But between the wildly optimistic signing of the Barcelona agreement in 2002 which promised *two* foreign languages for all in primary education (enacted just as the government was ending compulsory language learning between 14 and 16 years old) and the emergence of the research report 'Lessons from Abroad' in 2012 there was little obvious attention being paid to what the practice was in Europe or beyond. There was great optimism, some funding, an enormous amount of energy centred around the Centre for Information on Language Teaching (CILT) primary team and we did get a substantial and content-rich primary languages web-presence to support the KS2 Framework which emerged between 2005 and 2007 (DfE, 2005, 2007). But like much else in terms of support for teachers that evolved through the years of the Labour governments, it did not fit the curriculum and educational model of the incoming Coalition government of 2010 and it was at best archived, at worst lost completely. The sense of a hiatus from 2010 to 2012 meant that the energy that had gradually built up in the first decade of the new century was largely lost in so many schools where the forceful and ever-changing agenda had simply moved on.

CURRENT ISSUES IN LANGUAGE LEARNING

To establish a starting point for the book we should recap some of the perennial issues in language learning and teaching which need to be kept in mind when considering twenty-first century provision. These could be summarised as:

■ the rationale for using the children's own contexts and interests to determine the content of the language learning and how best to explore one's own culture and the culture of others;

■ the importance for motivation and thinking skills development of creative approaches to teaching and to teaching children to be creative in the primary language classroom;

■ the importance of authenticity and credibility in the materials we use – this includes all platforms as paper, video, audio and screen are all equally valid and each can be both creative and mundane, stimulating and restrictive;

■ the difference between learning language/s and using language to learn – both strands are important but the second has a more obvious immediate purpose which will appeal to children as it will locate what they are doing in what they know and are interested in. But for the first we need to remember the importance of creative approaches in the emergence of grammatical understanding and the use of language learning strategies;

■ the knowledge and skills of the workforce that enable all of the above to become a reality over time. This is a factor that cannot be ignored and for which we need to show as much creativity if we want teachers to feel they can be successful.

If we address some issues arising from the final bullet point first: there is clearly a need for online resources which are freely accessible and which will build confidence. These need to be at all levels and to relate to the type of language teachers will want to know for their work with children. People must decide themselves how they relate to free language learning apps such as Duolingo or subscription resources such as Babbel. They are set up in a very different way from classroom learning but will serve a purpose if teachers enjoy the way they work. At a basic more classroom-linked level the website the Spanish Experiment and sister sites for French and Italian with the parallel German version the German Project are easy to locate with a search. The site Zut (2018; www. zut.org.uk/index.html) and its parallel Spanish, German and Welsh sites are conventional word-based sites which are not especially suitable for use with children of primary age but which will be fast ways for a teacher to learn some core vocabulary in mainstream topics if less confident. For French there is a large resource at. Bla Bla Français, (2018; www.blablafrancais.com/), which offers differentiated and conversational 'lessons' with animated video sequences designed to teach you language through comprehension and production tasks which are mildly amusing.

For pedagogical professional development as opposed to language learning sites Professional Development Consortium in Modern Foreign Languages (PDC in MFL) (2015; https://pdcinmfl.com) is an authoritative and very full resource offering many links to other online materials. This has been set up in recent years precisely for the current KS2/KS3 workforce and is founded on strong research principles.

Returning to our bullet point list, the first issue is very broad and relates as much to an overall philosophy of teaching as to languages as a subject. As Chapter 8 will address in depth, the early childhood education and care (ECEC) context in many countries is centred around children's own ownership of much of what they do in an educational setting, and this phase can stretch sometimes, for example in Sweden, up to 7 years old. Teachers of children from 2 up to 5 or 6 years old work to a highly complex planning system that identifies times (often invisibly) for teacher-led, teacher-initiated and child-initiated activity. The overall routines and rules for 'co-existence' in a setting are of course never absent and through this overall guiding structure children learn how to live together in a mini-society morally and collaboratively, and how to gain agency and independence within such a framework. This may not be very familiar to teachers of children aged 7–11 who operate in a more constrained setting with the acceptance of the whole class planning framework, data-driven expectations and the beginnings of a culture where children somehow need to learn that life is sometimes boring! Notions such as 'In the Moment Planning', which are much discussed in an ECEC teaching context and even the more common child-centred topic choice, are less easily available to teachers in the middle/upper primary phases. Nevertheless, even with the content constraints of the 2013 National Curriculum (NC) for England teachers in some cases use a process of negotiation with their classes to establish the key topics they will address and then work the curriculum objectives for the range of NC subjects into those themes. Language learning can be about anything and in fact primary language teachers can respond to children's interests, if not 'in the moment' then over time if resources are available or can be created according to simple steps or formulae.

The next three bullet points involve aspects of pedagogy which turn on whether we hold a more transmission approach to teaching which picks up on lower order thinking skills or a more constructivist stance. The importance of thinking is usually linked to Bloom's taxonomy (1956) which was revised in 2001 and which is explored and explained in an accessible way by Wilson (2018) at https://thesecondprinciple.com/teaching-essentials/beyond-bloom-cognitive-taxonomy-revised/. To illustrate key aspects of these bullet point issues listed above and show how they relate to classrooms we will use a very simple example of materials and tasks. In doing so we hope to remain as realistic as possible about the fifth bullet point.

Perhaps the first question to deal with is the ways in which teachers might start or continue a unit, whether we need to teach a set body of vocabulary as an initial stage and whether any pattern of linearity exists which we should follow. Once upon a long time ago people spoke about a system or cycle called the 3Ps that had nothing to do with pigs, although they might be useful in explaining it and its limits. In that cycle the teacher first has to present new language to the class. Imagine they do not know the story of the three pigs. The teacher once might have chosen a neat set of flashcards or PowerPoint slides with images of pigs, adult and young, a wolf, straw, sticks, bricks, houses made of those materials, a chimney, a cooking pot, etc. The approach might have been that if you first teach small units of language, for example words, then it will be possible to follow a more complete text, a story. But the Three Pigs story contains a lot of repetition and with visuals would be comprehensible without any of that pre-teaching. If that story was part of a programme of learning the additional language, then it is likely that some vocabulary might already have been previously met. However, even if not, it is possible to set up children's experience of exposure to and engagement with a whole text through an enjoyable call and response activity while hearing the story. It does involve listening and repeating but in ways the children choose to do rather than as an enforced and artificial practice activity. And the new vocabulary set, whether a simple word such as pig or a more complex concept such as *I'll blow your house down* would be internalised and learned as a product of an engaging activity. This is less about teacher presentation and more about learners *meeting* new language (see also Hood 2014; Hood and Tobutt 2015). It is also about them learning language from using it rather than it being the objective for a specific part of a lesson and a detached activity.

Figure 1.1 shows how, with a simple photograph and using a relatively common topic (Healthy eating and eating in different countries), we can structure a content and language 'learning ladder' through progressive questioning. The important aspect of this process to emphasise is that we start with three open questions and a genuine 'unknown'. These questions, although simple in language terms, encourage a range of answers so can be legitimately asked more than once, allowing natural repetition. This is a vital feature of more creative classrooms as nothing closes down creativity more than a question, to which the answer is already known, being practised solely for the sake of practice. If there is the possibility of more than one answer and some new information emerging, then the question can legitimately be asked several times and the 'practice' takes place in a natural context. In this example the first opens up a whole vocabulary area so children who know different words can make different contributions and perhaps a mind map of food items can be established. The second extends that into the more personal with likes/dislikes. The third implies seeking an opinion about which meal is shown in the photo but to do this only asks for a time expression, so giving valuable practice to a less creative area of vocabulary. This notion of engendering some thinking, debate even, if only about a very simple concept should be at the heart of language learning because it is at the heart of normal life and is about using cognitive capacities not just imitative or knowledge memory faculties. The fourth question reveals the truth – i.e. it is a breakfast that for some will constitute a disequilibrium. The follow-up to that invites a recycling of the vocabulary from questions 1–3 but now with a different purpose, to explore potential cultural differences within the classroom and between countries. It is a fairly simple step to draw in the ideas around healthy eating and, depending on the stage of learning of the children, this raises another important point which will be explored in a lot more depth in the next chapter, where the lessons learned from teaching English as an Additional Language are drawn from. This is about how children can show their understanding.

Using photos and structuring stepped questions, as open as possible.

Topic: Healthy Eating

1. Qu'est-ce que vous voyez?
2. Vous aimez manger ...? / boire ....?
3. Il est quelle heure?

4. Ca, c'est un petit dejeuner – c'est normal pour vous? Pourquoi pas?

5. Un petit dejeuner qui est bon pour la santé – ça consiste de quoi? Pourquoi ...... est bon pour la santé ?

6. Qu'est ce que vous aimez manger qui est bon pour la santé / mauvais pour la santé ?

■ **Figure 1.1** Sample questions on a photograph

C'est bon pour le santé et j'aime ça! | Ca n'est pas bon pour le santé, mais j'aime ça!

C'est bon pour le santé, mais je n'aime pas ça! | C'est mauvais pour le santé et je n'aime pas ça!

■ Figure 1.2 Matrix to allow expression of facts/views on food/drink items

The link on the slide (Figure 1.1) is to a very simple Word document arranged as a matrix which is shown as Figure 1.2. This allows children (and teachers in the task setting) to differentiate the actual outcomes produced. From simply sticking culturally authentic pictures of food items under each heading (showing comprehension of the four states of fact/opinion about foods) to writing food lists, to writing complex sentences including 'because clauses', a whole range of possibilities exist, all of which demonstrate the child has understood the point of the exercise and something of the language used to express views on it.

The examples above are merely meant to begin some thinking about how we should approach language teaching and learning in the primary phase and could be used as a stimulus for discussion at a development meeting. Questions about how far the content of language lessons can and should be linked to the rest of the class curriculum and how this might be done realistically, as well as an analysis of the actual techniques used in these examples, are valuable ways to start towards a school/family of schools/local authority or chain developmental programme.

THIS BOOK AND HOW IT MEETS OUR AGENDA

The chapters in this book have been deliberately chosen to come at the theme from a variety of standpoints. Beyond the 'mission' outlined at the beginning of this chapter there is no single line of belief, no single pedagogy, no blinkered obsession about approaches in the form of 'dos and don'ts'. We outline here what is to come as readers may want to attack the text in different ways and in different orders, depending on context, interest and confidence. We try to sum up each chapter in a form that shows its 'take' on the theme of the book.

In Chapter 2 'Learning from creative bilingual classrooms' by Susan Jones and Philip Hood we show that in all classrooms children access the discourse with varying amounts of understanding because they have different amounts of their first, second or even third languages (L1, L2 or L3) at their disposal. We offer a focus on classrooms where teachers plan for pupils with English as an Additional Language (EAL) in order to portray how a language-rich classroom can be established in a concrete context that very many teachers already understand because it is part of their everyday practice. The chapter also seeks to encourage transfer from the EAL/bilingual classroom context to the primary languages teaching and learning context with the following focus points, each showing a range of creative techniques within a positive multilingual classroom:

- Supporting understanding: in what different ways and modes can teachers encourage children to access material in L2? How can teachers set tasks that engage children in constructing meaning from those input 'texts'? How can we make this a more shared and collaborative process and why might that be better for learning?
- Supporting talk: if using the language is the best way of learning the language, how can teachers best provide opportunities and scaffolding for children to negotiate meaning, make decisions and initiate both questions and answers related to the content material? Can we generate exploratory talk in an additional language?
- Supporting learners to express their own understanding: what are the alternatives to 'writing a paragraph to explain xxx'? How can teachers scaffold different learners with different language capabilities to demonstrate understanding in written, visual and oral modes? How are the effective comprehension of sources, the discussion of meaning, significance and causation and the expression of a new understanding related parts of a cycle of learning?

Chapter 3, 'Creative approaches to highlighting target language use in the primary classroom' by Colin Christie, makes the point that it is often argued that extensive target language use is not possible with younger learners at the early stages of language learning due to the limited amount of language they possess. This chapter shows how learners who might have only a small amount of target language at their disposal can use it creatively and routinely in the languages classroom. It also considers how the teacher can go about creating a climate for its use, which will be termed a 'target language lifestyle'. It also shows how carefully planned target language by the teacher can lead to confident, regular use by learners. To do this, it explores techniques for ensuring that they can access the language they need, such as through teaching with mimes, intensive repetition and practice, lesson routines and textual support. A key aspect of encouraging learners to use the target language is creative approaches to the drilling of language. This involves active repetition and memorisation techniques, competing against the teacher and fellow learners, as well as the inclusion of songs and chants. While some of these techniques might not be new, their use to teach routine and essential language of classroom interaction is innovative.

The chapter includes a focus on creating the conditions for learner target language use to flourish, such as consistent praise and the setting up of contexts for real language use like benign competition, talk about objectives, greetings, making requests and correcting mistakes. At the same time, English is not banned but is seen as a useful means for clarifying meaning and for asking for new items of language.

Discussing language learning often draws several themes together and in Chapter 4, 'Developing speaking and pronunciation skills through storytelling on the app iTEO', Claudine Kirsch combines a focus on pronunciation, creating stories and the use of computer programs and apps to offer multimodal support for language learning. The chapter explores how primary school children develop pronunciation skills in French through collaborative storytelling on the iPad app iTEO. Pupils might find it challenging to write several sentences about themselves, but conversing while using the same vocabulary may be even more daunting for some. Thus, teachers have to develop vocabulary, pronunciation skills and confidence. The chapter shows how pupils in a Year 6 class who produce stories in French with iTEO develop their pronunciation skills. The iTEO app allows users to collaboratively record and edit oral language. Each recorded item is represented by an icon on the iPad's interface. By clicking on the icon, users can listen to their recording as often as they wish. They edit text by rearranging the sequence of icons and by deleting icons. In order to structure their text, they can insert pictures taken with the iPad's inbuilt camera. One of the most important features of the App is the automatic playback that materialises the language used thereby providing opportunities for reflection. The author has previously shown that children in Luxembourg have developed language and metalinguistic skills through storytelling on iTEO. Storytelling is a leading activity because it activates cognitive, social and emotional processes and capitalises on children's resources.

Content and Language Integrated Learning (CLIL) is a sub-theme throughout the book and in Chapter 5, 'Teaching languages creatively through the context of mathematics', Sarah Lister and Pauline Palmer examine the role of language in mathematics and make connections between mathematics and second language learning, remembering that mathematics is a language in itself. It draws on work by Craft (2010) about creativity in the digital age and explores game-based learning as a creative context for CLIL. The aim of this is to increase and sustain learner motivation and engagement as well as providing a greater cognitive challenge and a stronger base for developing learners' conceptual understanding. It is entirely in harmony with the overall aim of the book to emphasise the 'value added' of a cross-curricular/CLIL approach to promote meaningful language learning in context and for a purpose. Through game-based learning, both key mathematical concepts and language as well as problem-solving skills will be enhanced, so blending once again the use of technology with other methods to offer children a rich learning environment.

Chapter 6 continues the integrated curriculum theme and in the intriguingly entitled From *empires and eruptions* to *lost worlds*: placing languages at the heart of the primary curriculum', Elaine Minett outlines a creativity-based project that was carried out in schools as part of a programme of support for primary class teachers in their role as language teachers. It aimed to integrate language learning with other curricular areas and so embed it in the school curriculum. The chapter gives a rationale for this practice but also discusses the advantages and disadvantages of the approach, all with a view to making it manageable (and attractive) for the teachers involved. Six different projects are described with the aim of creating:

■   engaging contexts: stunning starts, marvellous middles, fabulous finishes;
■   contexts where languages are the driving force;

- language learning opportunities for progression and differentiation with examples of pupils' work;
- a classroom environment where there are opportunities to enhance the international dimension and intercultural understanding;
- an enhanced role for ICT;
- greater use of the wider community/environment;
- opportunities for family learning/parental involvement;
- greater independence through promoting Knowledge About Language/Language Learning Strategies;
- meaningful celebrations of achievement.

The chapter concludes with reflection on what has been learned in terms of securing the place of languages in the primary curriculum and with regard to the role of non-specialist class teachers. Implications for transition from KS2 to KS3 are also considered, both in terms of skills' acquisition and development, and with regard to recommendations for a different approach to the new KS3 curriculum and the call for increased cross-curricular learning and improved connections between subjects.

Elaine Minett again, together with Laure Jackson explore a subject which some say is neglected in the primary curriculum and is less linked with language learning in Chapter 7, 'Ahoy there, me hearties! Combining foreign languages and dance in the primary curriculum'. They explore the mutual benefits of combining these two areas of the primary curriculum with an example scheme through the exciting theme of pirates. Based around a pack of teaching materials consisting of 12 lessons and suitable for pupils in Key Stages 1 and 2, this project sought to investigate the impact of learning languages through the context of dance and to consider pupils' responses to engaging in dance taught in the foreign language. Materials were piloted in a local primary school and used in training sessions with undergraduate trainees as well as serving teachers. The pack was then delivered in its entirety to 60 pupils in a different local school and data collected to explore the benefits of learning in this way and the potential to inform future practice. Sharing findings from the research project involving trainees, teachers and pupils, the authors present the teaching resource with activities designed to ensure engagement and progression in both subjects.

Although in England and Wales primary languages focuses on the Key Stage 2 age range, many practitioners consider that the best time to start is when children first attend school. Chapter 8, 'Teaching the youngest learners', by Kristina Tobutt and Philip Hood makes the case that children can benefit from and certainly enjoy language learning from the earliest stages of their education. This chapter focuses on the 3–7 age range and explores the use of songs and stories, games and routines and the learning of language through simple decision-making tasks, linked to the wider curriculum. From the first days in school or nurseries children can become quickly used to operating in more than one language and to responding to heard instruction. They enjoy 'making' activities (e.g. mask making) and also engaging in physical activities, e.g. following a trim trail, and all of these can be triggered by instructions in the target language that they will internalise quickly as they are applied to real actions and outcomes. In this way their exposure to language is entirely authentic and purposeful and simple but natural language can be used at all times, constituting a good model of Krashen's (1982) comprehensible input. Songs and stories should be authentic, from target language-speaking countries and, as long as they are visually supported, do not need any vocabulary pre-teaching. This is the best way to encourage children to start to use the language actively. The chapter shows the underpinning of this thinking and also offers ideas for sources of authentic materials and some short exemplar scripting for teacher language to stimulate creative activity by children. It will also show how children can start in the simplest ways to be creative with language themselves.

In Chapter 9, Creativity around transition, Katherine Richardson draws from her extensive research into the issues surrounding the move from primary schools to secondary and how this now features transition arrangements for language learning. Many schools have identified transition as a general area for development and, while they work very hard at their practices, they have been facing much more complexity recently as the links between neighbourhood families of schools have become less fixed in the new educational climate. For both primary and secondary schools languages transition is a relatively new but growing issue as the number of primary schools teaching languages in the first decade of this century expanded. There is much diversity between primary schools (and often within primary schools) even to the point where the languages taught may differ between neighbouring schools. Good practice in transition benefits both children and also teachers who can gain professionally from collaborative work throughout the transition phase. This chapter looks at what can and should happen from a language learning focus, though some consideration is given to pupil well-being. It addresses common challenges to effective transition in creative ways, both in terms of the structures that benefit the process but also through suggesting a range of exciting cross-phase projects that inspire children and show their receiving secondary schools their true capability.

In Chapter 10, 'The next stage of the journey: lessons learned from Scotland', Lynne Jones and Fhiona Mackay from Scotland's National Centre for Languages (SCILT) offer the book a positive vision for future development in early language learning. This illustrative case study explores the recent experience of primary language curriculum development in Scotland and shows how important are both government initiative and support for policy setting and enactment. Coherence is a highly needed commodity, it appears.

In the final chapter, 'The next stage of a journey: lessons learned from this book', Philip Hood concludes the volume in two ways: first the chapter synthesises the standpoints taken in other chapters in the book with a view to establishing a rationale for a range of creative approaches; second, it suggests through an acronym, DARE, a potential set of principles through which teachers and children can make language learning really their own.

REFERENCES

Bloom, B. S. (ed.) (1956) *Taxonomy of Educational Objectives*. Vol. 1: Cognitive Domain. New York: McKay.

Boden, M. A. (2004) *The Creative Mind: Myths and Mechanisms*. London: Routledge.

Cameron, L. (2001) *Teaching Languages to Young Learners*. Cambridge: Cambridge University Press.

Craft, A. (2003) Creative thinking in the early years of education, *Early Years*, 23:2, 143–154.

Craft A. (2010) *Creativity and Education Futures: Learning in a Digital Age*. Stoke-on-Trent: Trentham Books.

Department for Education (2013) *The National Curriculum in England – Key Stages 1 and 2 Framework Document*. London: DfE.

Department for Education and Skills (2005) *Key Stage 2 Framework for Languages, Parts 1 and 2*. London: DfES.

Department for Education and Skills (2007) *Key Stage 2 Framework for Languages, Part 3*. London: DfES.

Frost, D, and Driscoll, P. (1999) *The Teaching of Modern Foreign Languages in the Primary School*. London: Routledge

Hood, P. (2014) Content language integrated learning: has its time come? In P. Driscoll, E. Macaro and A. Swarbrick (eds) *Debates in Modern Languages Education*. London: Routledge.

Hood, P. and Tobutt, K. (2009) *Modern Languages in the Primary School*. London: Sage (2nd edition 2015 Teaching Languages in the Primary School).

Jones, J. and Coffey, S. (2006) *Modern Foreign Languages 5–11 A Guide for Teachers*. London: David Fulton Publishers.

Jones, S. (2017a,b,c) personal communications.

Kirsch, C. (2008) *Teaching Foreign Languages in the Primary School*. London: Continuum.

Krashen, S. (1982) *Principles and Practices in Second Language Acquisition*. Oxford: Pergamon.

Martin, C. (2008) *Primary Languages: Effective Learning and Teaching*. London: Sage.

National Centre for Excellence in Mathematics (NCETM) www.ncetm.org.uk/resources/36070. Last accessed 12 January 2018.

Oga-Baldwin, W. L. Q., Nakata, Y., Parker, P. and Ryan, R. M. (2017) Motivating young language learners: a longitudinal model of self-determined motivation in elementary school foreign language classes, *Contemporary Educational Psychology*, 49, 140–150.

Pope, R. (2005) *Creativity: Theory, History and Practice*. Oxford: Routledge.

Robinson, K. (2006) 'Do schools kill creativity?' www.ted.com/talks/ken_robinson_says_schools_kill_creativity/transcript. Last accessed 12 January 2018.

Sharpe, K. (2001) *Modern Foreign Languages in the Primary School – the What, Why and How of Early MFL Teaching*. London: Kogan Page.

Smidt, S. (2016) *Multilingualism in the Early Years: Extending the Limits of Our World*. Oxford: Routledge.

Wilson, L.O. (2018) 'The second principle' https://thesecondprinciple.com/teaching-essentials/beyond-bloom-cognitive-taxonomy-revised/. Last accessed 3 July 2018.

CHAPTER 2

LEARNING FROM CREATIVE BILINGUAL CLASSROOMS

Susan Jones and Philip Hood

INTRODUCTION

In this chapter, we focus on classrooms where teachers plan for pupils who are learning English as an additional language, in order to portray how a language-rich classroom can be established in a concrete context that teachers already understand. In doing so, we seek to encourage transfer from the context of the positive multilingual primary classroom to the teaching and learning of foreign languages. We begin by outlining some fundamental principles that underpin our approach in the chapter. These are our starting points for further exploration of teaching and learning in bilingual classrooms. We then locate the experience of teachers working with linguistically diverse pupils within a wider social, political and economic context, exploring some of the dominant ideas that influence policy and practice in this area. Moving on, we draw together what can be learned from research and good practice in teaching English language learners to inform creative foreign language learning. Each section of the chapter concludes by considering links to practice in primary languages teaching, providing reflection points for readers to relate what they have read to their own contexts.

We feel it is important at the outset to explain our own use of language in relation to creative teaching in bilingual classrooms. Definitions are important in the context of the teaching and learning of languages, as Ball argues (2011: 12), 'not least because they index the social status of languages and speech communities'. Reflecting upon the potential for hidden messages contained within the terminology commonly associated with this area of education is, therefore, vital to positive and inclusive practice. Although a common initialism within education policy and practice in England, the term 'English as an Additional Language' (EAL) does, we argue, emphasise an orientation towards the acquisition of English while implying a monolingual norm and highlighting difference as deficit. Terms such as 'bilingual' or 'multilingual', on the other hand, are descriptive, rather than evaluative. They 'acknowledge the existence of different areas of linguistic knowledge and expertise' (Yandell, 2011: 163), signalling the norm of multilingualism:

a bedrock for acceptance of the importance – for *all* children – of learning other languages. This is the basis upon which the chapter builds, and we move now to consider some other important starting points when considering what we can learn from creative bilingual classrooms.

Positive multilingual classrooms recognise the central role of the teaching of language and, rather than viewing the presence of English language learners in the classroom as an issue to be addressed *in addition to* the many existing demands of the day-to-day work of schools, this way of viewing language learning provides a focus across the whole of the classroom, and all of its learners. In the same way, we can look at the teaching of other languages as an enriching and exciting aspect of our daily or weekly work, and something that often unites all children in new discoveries.

Chapter 1 has examined briefly the nature of 'creativity' in multilingual classrooms and much of what we see throughout this book is linked strongly to practice in multi- and plurilingual classrooms, with practice in supporting English language learners and bilingual teaching leading the way. These, then, are our starting points for discussing teaching and learning in linguistically diverse contexts. Before we focus more closely on what happens within creative bilingual classrooms, however, we offer a brief overview of the wider context, and consider some of the influence this has upon the experience of teachers and learners in this area of education.

THE BIGGER PICTURE FOR TEACHING AND LEARNING OF 'ENGLISH AS AN ADDITIONAL LANGUAGE' IN THE UK

Questions about how to best support pupils newly arrived in UK classrooms and learning English have long been at the forefront of political, public and professional debates, and particularly so in recent times. In the last two decades, the numbers of pupils identified by schools as speaking English as an additional language has more than doubled. The school census of January 2017 reports that 20.6 per cent of pupils in state-funded primary schools speak a language that is, or is believed to be, in addition to English. This figure is said to represent an increase of 0.5 per cent on the previous year (Department for Education, 2017). Over the past 10 years this figure has increased from around 12.5 per cent. At the same time as this increase in numbers of pupils, schools have also seen the removal of both specific funding for specialist language support, and any statutory accountability for the use of available funding to support bilingual learners (NALDIC, 2016). A similar reduction process has seen the virtual end of primary languages funding with the previous resources such as The Centre for Information on Language Teaching (CILT) abolished and the very extensive primary languages website existing only in a reductive archived state.

Teachers in schools across the UK will recognise that effectively supporting bilingual pupils is no longer a concern that predominantly affects urban settings. The demographic of a wide range of communities is changing as a result of global migration and relocation, and public and political discourse around the issue of immigration often includes the perceived impact on education. Negative views of bilingual learners are based on an assumption that speaking languages other than English is both a disadvantage and out of the norm. Such disquiet suggests a view of education as 'domestication'

(Freire, 1972), where the reproduction and maintenance of the dominant social order is a main priority.

In fact, research tells us that, contrary to popular and political discourse, monolingual English speakers in a class with those learning English are at no disadvantage (Ohinata and van Ours, 2013). Neither are 'standards' at risk, with eight out of the ten schools with the highest proportion of bilingual learners judged to be 'Good' or 'Outstanding' by Ofsted in recent years (Monaghan, 2014). A report for the British Academy by Tinsley (2013) also emphasises the future economic need for the community languages spoken in our country in the age of the global marketplace. Indeed, elsewhere in the UK, a very different historic, cultural and political context means that bilingualism is actively promoted at a policy level in Wales as an intellectual and economic advantage. The inclusion of foreign languages across Key Stages Two and Three in both England and Wales is also based on such principles. Bilingual education policy elsewhere in the world emphasises that English language learning does not have to be perceived as a problem. A focus on bilingualism as a right, and as a resource (Ruíz, 1984), encourages the recognition of diversity of knowledge and experience as an asset to be drawn upon creatively in an inclusive classroom. This also means creating space for bilingual and multilingual pupils to be able to explore and develop all aspects of their lifeworlds (Rikkinen, 2000). It may be true that at the stage when learners are only beginning a foreign language, and therefore do not have a rich fund of content available to them, it might seem difficult to apply similar thinking. But the aim to create the language-rich classroom for foreign language learning as well as for bilingual learning is a very important part of making the subject seem real, and of encouraging children to see their potential and their progress quickly.

Kenner and Ruby (2012: 40) point out that 'if different languages and cultures are part of your life, they will contribute to multiple aspects of your identity, all of which will be important to your sense of self'. Many pupils who are labelled as EAL within mainstream schooling also attend complementary schools, staffed almost entirely by volunteers, where they learn about the languages and cultures of their families and communities, gaining knowledge that supports their bilingual literacy development. Kenner and Ruby describe the fact that there is often little awareness in mainstream schools of what happens in these complementary classrooms. However, much can be learned from the ways in which community education contexts contribute to the academic and social achievements of bilingual learners. In their homes and in community contexts, young learners have been shown to switch between languages in oral and written form, communicating with friends, family and community members in different languages through a range of media. Creative multilingual classrooms celebrate this diversity of language and its use. Kenner and Ruby remind us that monolingual learners can also share where they hear different languages, such as on holiday, TV, internet, contributing to an understanding of the breadth of languages in the daily environment of school and its and wider community.

The wider context for teachers working in linguistically diverse classrooms is complex, placing teachers at the centre of global debates. The impact of these debates on policy making at a national and local level is felt in the everyday experience of classrooms. The high profile of this issue in wider society, alongside a reduction in specialist support, adds challenge to an already complex aspect of teaching. Research also highlights the rich resources that exist in multilingual contexts, and that are drawn upon creatively in

REFLECTION POINT: LEARNING FROM THE BIGGER PICTURE

■ How do you feel as you approach the teaching of languages in your classroom? How does this relate to your feelings about teaching in other areas of the curriculum? What support is available to you?

■ What can you infer about the 'hidden curriculum' in your school as it relates to languages and language learning? What messages are suggested about languages, about speakers of other languages, and about being able to speak more than one language?

■ How are the experiences of speakers of other languages included in the classroom and across the wider school? This includes the experiences of pupils who speak languages other than English, their families and communities.

classrooms across many different communities worldwide. In the next part of the chapter, we begin to explore three principles relating to teaching and learning in these creative bilingual classrooms. In doing so, we by no means suggest that effective practice can be reduced to a simple list of techniques; rather, by drawing together what can be learned from theory and research in this area, we offer some underpinning principles which can guide the choices made by teachers to support language development in all of their learners.

SUPPORTING UNDERSTANDING

As Ball (2011: 13) acknowledges:

> it is an obvious yet not generally recognised truism that learning in a language which is not one's own provides a double set of challenges, not only is there the challenge of learning a new language but also that of learning new knowledge contained in that language.

Our focus in this part of the chapter is on the different ways and modes through which teachers can encourage children to access material in their new language. We consider the tasks teachers might set that engage children in constructing meaning from those input 'texts'. We do this in light of what the literature on language acquisition and on bilingual education tells us, including how we might make this a more collaborative process, and why that might be better for learning.

Writing about multilingualism in the context of Early Years, and the experience of very young learners from homes where languages other than English are spoken, Smidt (2016: 53) emphasises that 'there is no language that does not enable children to be able to communicate, understand, explain, question and make sense of the world'. Positive teaching of language recognises that any existing language is a basis for the development of new learning. As Davies (2009) highlights:

> learning involves integrating new information ('input') into [the learner's] existing mental model of the world (or schema). In second or additional language learning,

prior knowledge of content or language plays a major role in helping to make second language input more comprehensible.

When they arrive in a primary languages classroom, therefore, children are already making sense of the world through the languages they already use. The value of home language and literacy practices, such as songs and oral storytelling, in preparing young children for understanding the language and literacy practices of the school setting has long been recognised in the literature (e.g. Heath, 1983). Smidt (2016) reminds us that this exposure to language need not have been in the main language of schooling for it to have a positive impact on development in that language. We need to see that exposure to the new foreign language should be enabled as far as possible in a similar way to how all other languages are experienced. This will be taken up with reference to younger learners in Chapter 8.

Our first point in relation to developing understanding in a new language, therefore, is the importance of using all languages as a resource to support new understanding. This is based on theories of language acquisition such as that developed by Cummins in his 'dual iceberg model' (2005: 5). This views language, as is suggested by the name, like an iceberg that floats on water, with 'surface features' that are visible and look separate. These equate to the features of the different languages spoken by an individual, which will look and sound different, and mean different things. Like an iceberg, an individual's capacity for language has far more below the surface, however. This is what Cummins describes as a 'common underlying proficiency', and much like the main body of the iceberg, includes a foundation of features that underpins understanding of language more generally. This also includes the fact that if you learn something in one language, such as a mathematical concept, it becomes available in another, once you have learned the vocabulary to express it. Content therefore scaffolds language acquisition, as opposed to vice versa. Cummins builds on the ideas of Vygotsky, who argued that a child with 'a certain degree of maturity in the native language':

> can transfer to the new language the system of meaning he already possesses in his own. The reverse is also true – a foreign language facilitates mastering the higher forms of the native language. The child learns to see his native language as one particular system among many, to view phenomena under more general categories, and this leads to awareness of his linguistic operations.
>
> (1986: 195–196)

This model of language acquisition emphasises the ways in which 'experience in either language can promote development of the proficiency underlying both languages' (Cummins, 2005: 5). Quality stimulation in L1 can have a positive effect on processes in L2, and vice versa. If the content learned in one language is available in the other, it therefore makes sense to combine the topics for language learning in a primary school with the overall theme being used in a particular time frame. If KS1 pupils are looking at islands as a topic, for example, then material about a French- or Spanish-speaking island such as La Réunion or Tenerife can help children learn key words such as sea, beach, mountains, map, volcano, forest – adding to the depth of their learning at the same time as teaching some vocabulary.

Successful language learning can therefore be built on a foundation of direct engagement with L1, and can benefit development in both new and existing languages. For those who are new to English language learning or for those learning a new foreign language, it is therefore important to provide opportunities for them to be able to access and use their existing knowledge about language in order to develop *all their* languages successfully. How can we use existing linguistic resources to support new understanding? Here are some examples from practice related to teaching EAL, applied to foreign language learning:

Using *contexts for learning* which to draw on/enhance students' diverse experiences, such as looking to countries and cultures where the target language is spoken for examples of geographic features, stories, songs or foods. In the case of French and Spanish, which are world languages, there may be experience of a number of contexts outside France and Spain where those languages are spoken. As aspects of culture are discovered there will also be links made by children from different language backgrounds who see comparisons and contrasts which are different from those perceived by first language English speakers. All of this enriches the conversations and lays the ground for more purposeful learning of vocabulary and structures in the foreign language.

Using visual support also helps to locate new language in context. Visual support can be used to support cognitively demanding tasks, where higher-order skills are engaged in the development and consolidation of learning. If we are using some prior content knowledge to facilitate the learning of new vocabulary, then a photo or diagram or object can remind the child of what they already know and evoke curiosity about how we talk about that in another language. In other words, we are not talking just about visuals to teach single word vocabulary items in an equivalence exercise, but associations which should fix the language more firmly into the memory.

Making relationships between ideas, words, objects or processes: sorting well-chosen images into groups by ranking, matching or compare/contrast activity. This can be at the earliest stage a task using simply single words, but quite quickly they can be embedded in sentences and learning can take place through the thinking processes involved in making the connections. Two girls in Year Six once showed us how to make comparisons in French using the adverb *plus*; they had learned this by reacting to a set of sentences describing data-tables. They had never been shown this grammatical feature but had worked it out for themselves from the material they had before them. This shows how foreign language learning can be styled to resemble standard practice in teaching EAL.

Key visuals: diagrams that show relationships between content, concepts and language, such as flow charts, food chains (Pim, 2012). Interestingly at www.youtube.com/watch?v=6i22SoSLj9M there is a 10-minute film where an artist draws a food chain while commenting in Spanish. This is not easy material but the visual aspect of it would allow children to supply key vocabulary that they are familiar with and to take time to internalise both content and language if the teacher could create a parallel commentary and mute the sound.

Working walls (Pim, 2012: 55): these are a common feature in many primary classrooms. Featuring a stimulus to start off a topic, learners can contribute their own questions and ideas and make connections to their own experiences. A dedicated area of the wall can feature an explicit focus on the topic seen through the additional language, with as much visual material and key words as possible; this can contribute to establishing a positive multilingual learning environment.

Making links across new and existing languages, and talking about these links. Doing so means that metalinguistic knowledge is built across the whole class by drawing from the diverse resources in the group. For example, Kenner and Ruby (2012) describe looking at a recipe in two languages, leading a pupil at a complementary school noticing that the verbs come at the end of the phrase in Bengali. Monolingual children will notice different features of a target language compared to English, such as more grammatical marking (e.g. for gender or for case), word order issues, capitalisation of nouns in German). It is important to discuss vocabulary and structures in *any classroom language* and, where available, support staff or community members can help with this to show that languages are inherently interesting in the ways they do things differently. Pupils can be engaged in researching any new aspects of language they encounter in both their mother tongue as well as in L2 (Kenner and Ruby, 2012).

Bilingual texts: it is often possible to get the foreign language versions of familiar and popular stories and to use them as texts which raise awareness of vocabulary and grammatical features in a very natural way, especially if they have some in-built repetition (Chapter 8 features this for the younger leaners). Those with other languages can also highlight things they have noticed (Pim, 2012). Depending on the class you are working with, it is best to go for a reasonable age match and to focus on picture-based material that can be 'read' on different layers.

Performing: preparing for a performance in the foreign language for a school event – sometimes a class that has learned a particular song can teach it to other children in an assembly or can entertain parents at a consultation evening. Different children have different strengths and those with more than one language may have skills in interpreting for family members and could narrate as well as perform. Additionally, groups can work on material as a resource for learning in class, investigating meanings and examining language structures to increase metalinguistic awareness (Kenner and Ruby, 2012).

Language as part of a learning community – sometimes there are either native speakers of the foreign language or children who have lived in a country where the target language is spoken in a class or school. These children are very valuable assets (though they may appreciate some flexibility over materials). These children might wish to take some responsibility for leading learning based on their knowledge. What can children teach the teacher about their language or experience of life in another context?

Being able to relate new language to existing linguistic knowledge makes sense based on well-regarded models of language acquisition. These tell us that context is therefore vitally important in developing understanding of, and in, a new language. High levels of contextualisation should, however, work alongside high levels of cognitive challenge if we are to plan work that appropriately supports the development of understanding. Using a real concrete context for tasks which support the development of new understanding (concrete before abstract) (cf. Cummins, 1981; Gibbons, 2009; Coyle *et al.*, 2010) allows learners to manage new language and content without too much overload.

Context becomes even more important for learners when concepts become more abstract. This is, of course, the likelihood in older primary classrooms where not only is the language spoken more challenging in terms of specialist vocabulary, but the concepts covered may also be more difficult. There is a commonly held belief that young children learn languages very quickly, and lose this 'sponge-like' quality as they get older. However, research relating to the trajectory of language acquisition suggests that this is not always the case. It tells us that learning a language can take a long time, and is influenced by a number of factors.

Research into language development has identified important phases. Again according to Cummins, the first phase of language develop concerns the 'basic interpersonal communication skills' (referred to in this model of language acquisition as 'BICS'). These can be developed in 1 or 2 years, which can mean that a learner appears to be quite fluent orally. In the context of pupils labelled 'EAL', this can mean that support is reduced or withdrawn, especially where such resources are scarce and are therefore directed at learners who are at an earlier stage of acquisition. However, to develop language that allows a person to process more cognitively challenging concepts, to be able to 'think' through a language in other words, can take far longer than 1 or 2 years. Cummins' model refers to this kind of language as Cognitive Academic Language Proficiency (or 'CALP'). Gibbons (2009) helpfully describes the two phases, and the language developed within them, as 'playground language' and 'classroom language'. Support for understanding in language learning should build on an awareness of this trajectory of language acquisition.

Enabling learners to develop their understanding and eventually progress in their language learning beyond basic interpersonal communication brings us to another key principle from research into learning in bilingual classrooms: the importance of challenge. In her work on developing academic language in bilingual classrooms, Gibbons (2009) argues that we should aim for learning to take place in what she calls the 'Challenge Zone': this is where a task combines a high level of support through context with a high level of cognitive challenge. Without a clear context, a challenging task leaves a learner frustrated and anxious. Too little challenge with no support leads to boredom. High levels of support, with little challenge, leave learners in their comfort zones. Powerful learning, according to Gibbons, happens when both context and challenge are high.

REFLECTION POINT: LEARNING ABOUT PLANNING TO SUPPORT UNDERSTANDING IN PRIMARY LANGUAGES

■ What opportunities are there for drawing on existing knowledge of different languages in the classroom tasks you are planning?

■ What opportunities are there in the wider curriculum to draw attention to how language works, and to make comparisons?

■ How might monolingual English speakers be able to explore the connections across aspects of language?

■ How will you use visual support to provide a clear context for learning new language?

■ What bilingual resources, such as bilingual picturebooks, are available?

■ How can you ensure that language learning combines high levels of both context/support and cognitive challenge?

SUPPORTING TALK

Smidt (2016: 43) highlights the fact that:

> in addition to reading and writing, spoken language has an ever-present and highly significant role in schools and settings. And for younger children, not yet reading and writing, talking and listening are vital. A good learning environment is one where there is a buzz of noise as learners share and compare ideas and experiences.

In this section, we start from a premise that using the language is the best way of learning the language. We ask how teachers can best provide opportunities and scaffolding for children to negotiate meaning, make decisions and initiate both questions and answers related to the content material in their new language. We would not question that in the context of learning EAL, but what about in primary foreign language learning?

For example, in the early days of learning a new language, a period of relative silence is to be expected. This can be because of the cognitive processes involved in the production, as opposed to the receptive understanding, of language. It can also relate to the perceived status of a speaker's first language and its impact on their confidence as members of the group (Heath, cited by Smidt, 2016). To develop talk, therefore, 'linguistic and affective support is needed' (Ball, 2011: 31). However, historically, in foreign language teaching methodology, we structure the activity to get the full engagement of everyone. A devil's advocate view could be made that this creates unnatural language use, mere 'performance', or sometimes even parroting. If it does not build into connected understandings of and capacities for language content and usage, is it good enough in the long term?

Factors that facilitate second language learning include comprehensible input (Krashen, 1982) and comprehensible output (Swain, 2000). As Gibbons (2009: 133) explains:

> unlike what happens when we listen or read (activities that don't require the learner to actually produce language), speaking requires learners to pay attention to what they are saying and how they are saying it, for the benefit of their listeners. This requires them to process the language at a deeper level.

Drawing on Swain, Gibbons argues that 'using language in interactions with others is not simply an outcome of the learning that has already taken place but is itself a source of new learning' (p. 134). If there is to be new learning, Gibbons argues, this should involve 'stretched' or 'pushed' language, where speakers are outside their comfort zone. This should be supported by high levels of context, as outlined above. The theme of supporting talk will be developed more fully in the next chapter. Meanwhile, here are some ideas in brief of ways in which learners can be encouraged to use the language in order to learn the language:

Questioning: this should not be limited to closed questions. 'Extended IRF (Initiate, Respond, Feedback)', according Gibbons (p. 137), includes prompts to extend, connect to prior learning, and not just giving the answer. At its simplest level, asking why, and supporting a range of responses to the question why, enables ideas (and language) to be developed.

Time to think: allowing talk to develop with ongoing reflection, such as 'think-pair-share' before reporting back. Where there is some L2 literacy capability in the learners, possibly at Key Stage 2, mini-whiteboards can be used to capture initial responses before building to longer oral ones.

Appropriating and recasting contributions made by learners: teachers using the students' language as a basis for modelling new language, rather than correcting (Gibbons, 2009).

Talk based on classroom routines and structures: promoting everyday use of the language as part of a language-rich environment (Smidt, 2016: 67; Ball, 2011: 31)

Board games and play: this again emphasises the routines of language in a clear context. Games such as find the difference (Gibbons, 2009: 148) and enquiry and elimination (e.g. 'Guess Who' type games) involve open questions and can support wide use of vocabulary.

Prompts and sentence starters: if the teacher pauses and invites sentence-completion, this encourages the language known to be shared and for language needs and interests to be identified.

Collaboration through drama and role play provides a context-rich opportunity for practising language with peers and, as far as possible, situations should invite more open, improvised language rather than pre-learned formulaic turns.

To summarise what we have covered in this section, we share a list of criteria for tasks which are well-designed for supporting the development of talk in learners of an additional language, developed by Gibbons (2009: 149–150):

- There is a real need to talk.
- Language is used for an authentic purpose.
- The task is embedded in a curriculum topic.
- The task is engaging and relevant to what the students are learning.
- The task is cognitively demanding, at a level appropriate for the grade.
- The task requires participation by all members of the group.
- The task requires learners to use stretches of language.
- There is often a built-in 'information gap', since the students hold different information or opinions.
- There is a clear outcome for the task, such as the solving of a problem or the sharing of information.

REFLECTION POINT: LEARNING ABOUT SUPPORTING TALK IN THE PRIMARY LANGUAGES CLASSROOM

- What can you expect from pupils in the early stages of learning a new language? How can you respond to support their continued development as confident language learners?
- How can classroom routines and structures support talk in a new language?
- How can you plan to support learning of both 'BICS' and 'CALP' through activities that have high context/high support?

SUPPORTING LEARNERS TO EXPRESS THEIR OWN UNDERSTANDING IN CREATIVE WAYS

In the context of learning an additional language, we always need to consider the alternatives to 'writing a paragraph to explain xxx', and the opportunities for teachers to scaffold different learners with different language capabilities to demonstrate understanding in written, visual and oral, or even in multimodal forms. If we are learning content, and not just some language phrases/structures, we need to scaffold a straightforward and effective way for learners to show their comprehension of sources, meaning, significance, causation and the expression of a new understanding of related parts of a cycle of learning. We need to be creative about this to avoid generating frustration when learners understand but cannot show that they do.

This can be done by use of:

- ■ *Visuals*, such as tables, charts and diagrams.
- ■ *Talk* to accompany the above.
- ■ *Writing frames* to allow learners to focus on the key language rather than all of the language.
- ■ *Thinking time* – using the language to think, and learners 'talking their writing'.
- ■ *Planning answers and longer responses* in the form of a shared writing task.
- ■ *Arts-based responses* – exploring language through drama, dance, art, poetry (Anderson and Chung, 2011; see www.gold.ac.uk/clcl/multilingual-learning/creativity/).

In recent years, researchers in bilingual education in Canada have been exploring one particular form of response that enables learners to powerfully demonstrate their learning of and in a new language while drawing creatively on their existing experiences to produce 'identity texts' (Cummins and Early, 2011). These are longer, creative and often collaborative responses that can take many forms, but are all based on a pedagogic premise that 'children have to see themselves in every aspect of their work at school' (Leoni *et al.*, 2011: 46). We devote some time to exploring this kind of response in a bit more detail here, including its potential as an aim in a primary languages context. Identity texts illustrate how supporting the development of a new language can creatively build on each of the areas we have already outlined: they can support understanding by locating new learning within a highly contextualised task; they support collaborative talk for a real purpose; and can provide creative means of expressing understanding, including how new learning relates to a student's existing knowledge and experience. There may be potential in your classroom to develop such longer projects, and to allow all learners to explore how the learning of a new language relates to their existing lifeworlds.

In the words of Cummins and Early, identity texts are:

> the products of students' creative work or performances carried out within the pedagogical space orchestrated by the classroom teacher. Students invest their identities in the creation of these texts – which can be written, spoken, signed, visual, musical, dramatic, or combinations in multimodal form. The identity text then holds up a mirror to the students in which their identities are reflected back in a positive light.
>
> (2011: 3)

For those who use more than one language in their daily lives, the recognition of these languages in mainstream schoolwork through their inclusion in identity texts has powerful consequences for learning. Cummins and Early (ibid.) suggest that these include connecting new information and skills to their background knowledge, increased students' awareness of the specialised language of school subject areas, and their awareness of relationships between L1 and L2, leading to students being enabled to produce more accomplished literacy work in the school language. Like the many other examples we have shared of good practice in creative bilingual classrooms, and based on the theoretical contexts for language learning that we have outlined, identity texts offer much potential for primary language learning.

An example of an identity text, 'Flying Home', can be found at the Digital Story Books site.

In this example, pupils have collaboratively created a digital storybook that brings together their learning about the migration patterns of Canada geese with illustrations based on their own experiences of moving to live in a new country. They also recorded multilingual audio versions to accompany a hardback version. Chapter 4 in this book also looks at children using an app independently for the development of language skills including pronunciation.

An important aspect of identity text production is that they 'affirm students' identities as intelligent, imaginative and linguistically talented' (Cummins and Early, 2011: 4). This is powerfully illustrated by the experience of one student, Madiha, who reflected on the impact of being involved in creating an identity text as part of a unit on the theme of migration. Madiha was in the early stages of acquiring English when she worked with two friends, Kanta and Sulmana, both of whom had been learning English for a little longer. Together, they created a 20-page book illustrated by another friend, Jennifer, which 'describes how hard it was to leave our country and come to a new country' (Leoni *et al.*, 2011: 46). Madiha compared the experience of creating her identity text with what she'd been asked to do when she was newly arrived in her new country and 'the teachers didn't know what I was capable of' (ibid.: 50). As a result, Madiha had been given a colouring book and crayons and told to get on with colouring. With her identity text, however, she reflects that 'I could actually show the world [. . .] I'm not just a colouring person [. . .] I can show you I am something' (ibid.: 50).

REFLECTION POINT: LEARNING FROM CREATIVE APPROACHES TO EXPRESSING UNDERSTANDING IN PRIMARY LANGUAGES

■ How are learners' responses in a new language encouraged and celebrated? (visual? multimodal? across school?)?

■ What opportunities are there for pupils to draw on the wide range of resources and prior knowledge that they bring to learning in demonstrating their understanding of new concepts and how these relate to their own experiences?

■ How might longer projects, such as the examples given above of 'identity texts', support the integration of language learning into the wider primary curriculum, and a student's developing identity as a learner?

These are examples of learners who are exploring their new language in relation to who they already are, and communicating their understanding so that their teachers, peers and others in the learning community may learn about the role of language in the lives of others. In the primary languages classroom, where the new language may not be dominant in wider society, and may be new to all rather than to a small number of individuals, there is still potential to offer students the opportunity to make creative connections with their own experiences and the meanings they are making through their encounters with the new worlds represented by their language learning.

CONCLUSION

The changing social context in the UK means that, even if they have no experience already, most teachers can, at some point in their careers, expect to work with learners who arrive in their classrooms with little or no prior knowledge of the main language of learning. This means that the teaching of English to new speakers of the language is something that is a feature of classrooms across a range of different communities. Positive practice in this area, informed by theories of language learning and underpinned by approaches that recognise and celebrate the language resources brought by learners to the classroom, provides a helpful basis upon which to build language-rich classrooms for creatively teaching other languages on the curriculum. This is not to say that foreign language learning is exactly the same as teaching learners new to English but it is to say that it should resemble those practices far more than it often does.

REFERENCES

Anderson, J. and Chung, Y-C. (2011) Finding a voice: arts-based creativity in the community languages classroom. *International Journal of Bilingual Education and Bilingualism* 14 (5) 551–569.

Ball, J. (2011) 'Enhancing learning of children from diverse language backgrounds: mother tongue-based bilingual or multilingual education in the Early Years'. Paper commissioned for UNESCO.

Coyle, D., Hood, P. and Marsh, D. (2010) *Content Language Integrated Learning.* Cambridge: Cambridge University Press.

Cummins, J. (1981) *Bilingualism and Minority Language Children.* Ontario: OISE Press.

Cummins, J. (2005) 'Teaching for cross-language transfer in dual language education: Possibilities and pitfalls', available at: www.tesol.org/docs/default-source/new-resource-library/symposium-on-dual-language-education-3.pdf. Last accessed 12 January 2018.

Cummins, J. and Early, M. (2011) 'Introduction' in Cummins, J. and Early, M. (eds) *Identity Texts: The Collaborative Creation of Power in Multilingual Schools.* London: Institute of Education Press.

Davies, N. (ed.) (2009) 'The distinctiveness of EAL pedagogy', NALDIC, available at: www.naldic.org.uk/eal-teaching-and-learning/outline-guidance/pedagogy/. Last accessed 12 January 2018.

Department for Education (2011, updated 2013) 'Teachers' standards', Guidance for School Leaders, available at: https://assets.publishing.service.gov.uk/government/uploads/system/uploads/attachment_data/file/665520/Teachers__Standards.pdf accessed 03/07/2018

Department for Education (2017) https://assets.publishing.service.gov.uk/government/uploads/system/uploads/attachment_data/file/650547/SFR28_2017_Main_Text.pdf. Last accessed 4 July 2018.

Digital Story Books website: https://digitalstorybooks.wikispaces.com/file/detail/Flying+Home+ebook+English.wmv.

Freire, P. (1972) 'Education: domestication or liberation?' *Prospects* 2 (2) 173.

Gibbons, P. (2009) *English Learners, Academic Literacy and Thinking: Learning in the Challenge Zone*. Portsmouth, NH: Heinemann.

Heath, S. B. (1983) *Ways with Words: Language, Life and Work in Communities and Classrooms*. Cambridge: Cambridge University Press.

Kenner, C. and Ruby. M. (2012) *Interconnecting Worlds: Teacher Partnerships for Bilingual Learning*. Stoke on Trent: Trentham Books.

Krashen, S. (1982) *Principles and Practices in Second Language Acquisition*. Oxford: Pergamon.

Leoni, L., Cohen, S., Cummins, J. Bismilla, V., Bajwa, M., Hanif, S., Khalid, K. and Shahar, T. (2011) ' "I'm Not Just a Coloring Person": Teacher and Student Perspectives on Identity Text Construction' in Cummins, J. and Early, M. (eds) *Identity Texts: The Collaborative Creation of Power in Multilingual Schools*. London: Institute of Education Press

Monaghan, F. (2014) 'Drop the negative spin on kids who start school bilingual – they are a rich resource for the future', *The Conversation*, available at: https://theconversation.com/drop-the-negative-spin-on-kids-who-start. Last accessed 5 January 2018.

NALDIC (2016) 'EAL funding', available at: www.naldic.org.uk/research-and-information/eal-funding/. Last accessed 12 January 2018.

Ohinata, A. and van Ours, J. C. 2013 How immigrant children affect the achievement of native Dutch children. *Economic Journal* 123(570) 308–331.

Pim. C. (2012) *101 Ideas for Supporting Learners with EAL*. London: Bloomsbury.

Rikkinen, H. (2000) 'Children's Life-Worlds' in Robertson, M and Gerber, R. (eds) *The Child's World: Triggers for Learning*. Melbourne: ACER Press.

Ruíz, R. (1984) 'Orientations in language planning'. *NABE: The Journal for the National Association for Bilingual Education*, 8 (2) 15–34.

Smidt, S. (2016) *Multilingualism in the Early Years*. Abingdon: Routledge.

Swain, M. (2000) 'The Output Hypothesis and Beyond: Mediating Acquistion Through Collaborative Dialogue' in Lantolf, J. (ed.) *Sociocultural Theory and Second Language Learning*. Oxford: Oxford University Press.

Tinsley, T. (2013) 'Languages: the state of the nation. Demand and supply of language skills in the UK'. Report commissioned by the British Academy available at: www.britac.ac.uk/sites/default/files/State_of_the_Nation_REPORT_WEB.pdf. Last accessed 5 January 2018.

Vygotsky, L. (1986) *Thought and Language* (Translated and edited by Alex Kozulin). Cambridge, MA: MIT Press.

Yandell, J. (2011) 'English and Inclusion' in Davison, J., Daly, C. and Moss, J. (eds) *Debates in English Teaching*. London: Routledge, pp. 157–168.

CREATIVE APPROACHES TO PROMOTING TARGET LANGUAGE USE IN THE PRIMARY CLASSROOM

Colin Christie

INTRODUCTION

In the primary languages classroom, while learners may be used to practising and using language at discrete moments in a lesson, during set activities, it is relatively rare to hear them speak spontaneously, without prompting. This type of spontaneous talk is, however, possible to achieve through the application of a series of principles. This chapter aims to demonstrate that it is possible for primary school learners of languages to develop a limited repertoire of confident, fluent target language talk. It will show that this language need not be restricted to separate topics, but that through a focus on transferable structures, learners can speak in a range of contexts.

Target language talk is difficult to maintain, especially in a primary classroom, for a number of reasons. First, there is a list of well-rehearsed arguments as to why extensive teacher target language use might be unhelpful for the learners themselves: it may adversely affect the behaviour of pupils (Franklin, 1990; Chambers, 1992); it can deprive learners of the 'language of thought' (Cohen, 1998; Pachler, 2000); it creates mis-understandings (Butzkamm, 2003); it stands in the way of positive teacher-pupils relationships, makes the setting of objectives and teaching of grammar difficult and is inefficient (Cook, 2001); it prevents pupils from understanding classroom instructions and asking questions (Chambers, 1992).

Second, there is the concern that the teacher may not have sufficient subject knowledge to be able to respond to a less topic-bound approach to language.

These two concerns are certainly valid ones but ones that can be addressed through a carefully structured approach which works in favour of learners and teachers alike. Arguments in favour of extensive teacher and pupil target language use are as follows: learners receive additional input, which is crucial to the process of language acquisition (Ellis and Shintani, 2014); the status of the target language is maintained, i.e. it is shown that important messages need not be transmitted in English (Littlewood, 1981); it develops the ability to produce output which helps learners to process language for form and not just meaning (Swain, 1995); learners can experience the feeling of being able to communicate for real purposes, or 'communicative success' (Ushioda, 1996); pupils can experience 'communicative pressure' (Doughty and Varela, 1998) which helps them draw on their communicative resources and recycle known language.

The author has previously promoted a 'target language lifestyle' (Christie, 2016), namely an ethos or way of being in the classroom where the target language is the accepted means of communication. This ties in with the Ofsted guidelines for classroom target language talk (Ofsted, 2013) (although these have recently been archived by the organisation without a replacement). Such an ethos can seem daunting even to a secondary school modern foreign languages (MFL) teacher, but it will be shown that this can be built up gradually and in a manageable way. The following principles will help ensure a successful approach to promoting target language use:

■ planning the language;
■ presenting the language;
■ practising the language;
■ praising the language;
■ progressing the language.

These will now be considered in turn.

PLANNING THE LANGUAGE

Often the language taught to learners at primary school level, and indeed beyond, is very topic based and relates to specific groupings of words. More often than not, these are groups of nouns that are perceived to be concrete and contextualised enough for the younger learner to process easily. Topics can include numbers, colours, pets and parts of the body, for example. Such language is clearly bounded and enables learners to relate to it immediately. At the same time, for the non-specialist, it is language that can be prepared and taught in carefully packaged sections. One of the drawbacks of this approach to the selection of language, however, is that the focus can often be on the nouns and not on the language structures (Driscoll, 2014). As the Key Stage 3 languages framework (DfE, 2003) demonstrated, high-frequency language, that is language that is transferable to a number of different contexts, is particularly useful to learn. One could argue, in fact, that this is all the more important for the beginner as it enables them to be able to communicate across the range of topics fairly quickly. The capacity to communicate early on in the language-learning process can be considered an important factor in terms of motivating learners. Communicative language teaching (CLT) is based on the premise that learners should be taught contextualised, authentic language that they can put to use almost immediately. This contrasts with the grammar translation (GT) method that prioritises the development of grammatical understanding. While it is now understood that both grammatical knowledge and a communicative context are important, a focus on topics can mean the learner is unable to adapt language outside of any particular topic.

One of the objections often raised to extensive target language use by the teacher is that this can result in a monologue that is not comprehensible to learners. If learners switch to English, English then quickly becomes re-established as the language of the classroom (Macaro, 2000). In addition, learners are left with the feeling that they cannot access the target language and can quickly become demotivated. One way to avoid this is for the teacher to plan carefully the language to be used in the classroom. Ideally, this should be language that has a dual purpose: not only is it used by the teacher but can be appropriated in the same form for pupil use as well. An example of this is the following phrase:

Stop! There's a problem!	*Stop! Il y a un problème!*
Halt! Es gibt ein Problem!	*Para! Hay un problema!*

This is a phrase that the teacher can use repeatedly but at the same time it is one that learners can reuse in exactly the same form. In this way, the teacher talk becomes pupil talk.

The learning and use of chunks of language is particularly useful to developing communicative ability in the early stages of language learning (Ellis, 2008; Myles, Mitchell and Hooper, 1999). Learners can learn chunks as set phrases and this can give them the ability to put together sentences of their own more easily without necessarily having a very detailed understanding of the grammar of the language. This ability to use chunks is particularly helpful for younger learners as it gives them an accelerated start into use of the target language. One of the demotivating factors about learning a language can be the realisation that one can say very little and the use of chunks helps overcome this. Indeed, it has been shown that one relies quite heavily on the use of predetermined chunks in one's own language in the course of native speaker fluency (Pawley and Syder, 1983).

There is no suggestion that the learning of chunks is sufficient for learning a language. If one is only able to regurgitate chunks of language, one never has the ability to manipulate it fully to one's own ends. Indeed, it is now generally recognised that formal grammar does play an important role in the learning of a language as Jones points out:

> It is no longer a question of whether grammar is taught but of how, why and furthermore where it fits into the broader curricular landscape of literacy and language, across and as an underpin of the whole curriculum.
>
> (Jones, 2000, p.142)

Chunks can however form a stepping stone between a basic regurgitation of the chunks and a more creative manipulation of language. If learners understand the precise meaning of each chunk and are shown clearly how to adapt it for their own purposes, chunks can enable learners to use language in a more creative way. An example might be with the use of the set phrase 'Est-ce que je peux . . .?' 'Darf ich . . .? '¿Puedo?'[Can I . . .?]. Learners quickly realise through exposure that they can vary the infinitive that follows this phrase for example:

> 'Est-ce que je peux . . . m'asseoir/marquer les points/cliquer/écrire . . .?'
>
> [Can I . . . sit down/put up the points/do the clicking/write . . .?]

NB We are supplying just the French equivalents where there are longer utterances to avoid making the example boxes too unwieldy. There are many online classroom language resources available at low or no cost, for example through the *Times Educational Supplement* resources.

The author observed a lesson with the following sequence of events:

> Teacher: (in a competition with the class, awards himself an extra point)
> Pupils: Ce n'est pas juste! Vous trichez!
> *[It's not fair! You are cheating!]*
> Teacher: Je suis le professeur. Je peux tricher.
> *[I am the teacher. I can cheat]*
> Pupil: Est-ce que je peux tricher?
> *[Can I cheat?]*

The above shows a pupil manipulating language by borrowing the phrase 'je peux tricher' from the teacher and adapting it to the set phrase he knows, 'est-ce que je peux . . .?' and combining the two. This could be followed up by the teacher's pointing out that 'est-ce que je peux' is followed by an infinitive and by learners' making a list of possible infinitives to use.

It will be suggested here that using the classroom as a context for language use will enable learners to encounter language which is both contextualised and transferable. The classroom, in essence, becomes the topic. As Harris points out:

> there is surely no more real communicative context than the classroom itself.
>
> (Harris, 1996, p.264)

Such an idea may at first seem quite daunting, particularly for the non-specialist. The classroom-as-context may seem less definable and more open-ended than more traditional topics, posing the danger that language and lessons can be less easily prepared. However, it will be shown here that by developing set classroom routines, language can be planned and allow the learner to develop a repertoire of spontaneous talk.

There are a number of frequently occurring contexts in the classroom that can form the basis of routines for using the target language. In the primary school context, these routines can be particularly powerful because they can be short and thereby fit into shorter slots available for language learning, for example at the beginning or end of other timetabled sessions.

Possible routines are as follows:

Seating routine

> P: Est-ce que je peux m'asseoir?
> [*Can I sit down?*]
>
> T: Pourquoi?
> [*Why?*]
> P: Parce que je suis cool/fantastique/super
> [*Because I am cool fantastic/super*]

It will be noted in the example above that the reasons given are not entirely authentic and communicative as one can argue that being fantastic is not a logical reason to be allowed to sit down. However, this may be a good example of how communication and authenticity need to be adapted to the classroom setting. This slightly contrived communication is a price worth paying as a building block towards more authentic communication. It is contrived because it is communication in a pedagogical context. As Widdowson (1990, pp. 46–47) points out: 'Pedagogy is bound to be a contrivance. That is precisely its purpose.' This section and the subsequent one on progression will show how language needs to be built up gradually if learners are to internalise it to such an extent as to be able to use it spontaneously.

Second, the language used when giving the reasons above is significant. The words used are cognates. The origin of the word cognate means 'born together' and these are words very similar in form to the English. This makes them more easily accessible to the learner in the early stages of the routine. Furthermore, in French, they are words that have the same form in both the masculine and feminine, so do not require changing. A development of this routine would be to use another cognate which simply requires the addition of an '-e' in the feminine form, for example:

> T: Pourquoi?
> [*Why?*]
> P: Parce que je suis intelligent (e)
> [*Because I am intelligent*]

Third, it can be seen that the springboard phrase 'Est-ce que je peux . . .?' can be applied to a whole number of infinitives as will be seen below.

Requesting routine

This routine is similar to the seating routine, and the same reasons can be used. This helps reinforce the language of justification and adjectives in the masculine and feminine forms. The requests here are not the usual rather transactional ones which are often used in languages classrooms, for example asking to take off the sweatshirt, go to the toilet, borrow a pen and so on. However, these are not precluded and can be used with the springboard phrase 'Est-ce que je peux . . .?'

Pupils can request to take on a number of classroom roles, depending on what the teacher feels comfortable delegating. If there is a team competition in place, a pupil could take responsibility for recording the points on the board. A pupil can also take the role of the teacher, for example by clicking to advance PowerPoint slides or by pointing to images on the board in a repetition activity. The language could be as follows:

Est-ce que je peux faire les points?
[*Can I do the points?*]

Est-ce que je peux cliquer?
[*Can I do the clicking?*]

Est-ce que je peux faire le prof?
[*Can I be the teacher?*]

Justifications and reasons can be added as per the seating routine above.

Objectives routine

This routine need not set out formal, measurable learning objectives (although this is also possible in the target language) but can begin by setting out activities for the lesson. An example is given below in the form of a song, set to the tune of London's Burning:

Qu'est-ce qu'on va faire? x 4
Aujourd'hui? x 2
Qu'est-ce qu'on va faire? x 2
On va mimer x 2
On va parler x 2
En français! x 2
On va chanter x 2
[*What are we going to do?/today? We are going to mime/speak/sing/in French!*]

The advantage of this routine, as with the others, is that learners will have frequent exposure to this language if the routine is reinforced every lesson. This means the language will become embedded and part of their repertoire. A likely scenario, for example, is that learners will spontaneously ask at the beginning of their (French) lesson: Qu'est-ce qu'on va faire aujourd'hui? [*What are we going to do today?*]. This will be even more likely if such spontaneous talk is rewarded as we shall explore later. It is at this point that the teacher's own persistence with target language talk and routines is also rewarded. To the onlooker (or inspector!) such spontaneous pupil talk will appear very impressive and totally unplanned, whereas is in fact it has been carefully nurtured by the teacher.

The objectives routines above is also a good introduction to the near future tense. It can be exploited further through a paired oral translation activity as seen below.

This heightens grammatical awareness by breaking down the language into its constituent parts but also allowing learners to put it back together to make meaning.

The language below can be added to the bottom of the above objectives routine:

1. we are going to; 2. to speak; 3. to mime; 4. to sing
5. what are we going to do?; 6. today; 7. to play; 8. in French

A: Comment dit-on numéro un en français?
[*How do you say number one in French?*]
B: A mon avis, c'est. . . .
[*In my opinion, it is . . .*]
A: Oui, c'est correct/non, ce n'est pas correct
[*Yes, that's correct, no it's not correct*]

The dialogue above has the added advantage of introducing more useful transferable language: 'in my opinion it is . . .'; 'it is . . ./it is not . . .'

Number 7 (to play) will allow learners to draw on memory if they have seen the verb before, as this verb is not featured in the song.

Dismissal routine

A dismissal routine, where the language learning stops at a break in the day, can be a gentle introduction to the past tense. The way this works is that students have to ask for permission to leave the classroom, in the target language. An example is as follows:

P: Est-ce que je peux partir?
T: Pourquoi?
P: Parce que j'ai participé/parlé français

Evaluation routine

This routine can be used in context, for example the class can be divided into two halves to sing a song. Each half can then evaluate the other half's singing. This has the advantage of introducing pupils to the language of opinions at an early stage. The routine can start with the following language:

C'était comment?
A mon avis, c'était   excellent
                        bien
                        comme ci, comme ça
                        nul

[*How was it?*
In my opinion, it was excellent/good/ok/rubbish]

PRESENTING THE LANGUAGE

A key element in getting pupils to speak spontaneously in the target language is that the language of classroom interaction needs to be taught, rehearsed and practised. This needs to be done in exactly the same way as topic language and needs to be reinforced constantly.

A common assumption is that pupil classroom talk will take care of itself while the language associated with clearly defined topics is taught. In fact, the language of the classroom needs to be taught specifically, in exactly the same way as the topic language does. This means that learners need to be presented with the meaning and pronunciation of each structure or language item, especially in the early stages.

If language can be presented interactively, it is more likely to be retained by learners and also extend opportunities for target language use. One technique for presenting language is whereby the teacher displays (or preferably flashes up) an image, for example of a pupil sitting down and with a question mark. It is important that the picture is flashed as this adds in an element of competition and challenge for the pupils. It is surprising how quickly young learners can recognise the flashed image. Pupils then ask for the target language for the image for example:

Comment dit-on [Can I sit down?] en français?

[How do you say 'Can I sit down?' in French?]

Clearly, learners may not land upon the target phrase immediately from just an image but the teacher can guide them along the way. It may take several attempts by pupils to arrive at the target phrase in English but this is all part of the challenge and probably they are more likely to remember it. The teacher can steer learners towards the target phrase through prompting, for example in English or in the target language 'C'est une question'.

It is proposed that new language is always presented with a contextualising question. Questions are often neglected forms, meaning that learners are able to provide answers but very often do not understand the question posed to them. Furthermore learning a series of responses alone means that learners cannot have an authentic, interactive conversation. Second, a key structure, or *stem*, can be taught, to which subsequent items can be attached. Third, these subsequent items should be presented. This is illustrated below with topic language (free time activities):

Contextualising question (CQ):
Qu-est-ce que tu aimes faire le week-end?
[*What do you like doing at the weekend?*]
Stem:
J'aime . . .
[*I like . . .*]
Subsequent items:
J'aime aller au parc
[*I like going to the park*]

It is advisable to categorise the subsequent language items so that learners build up an understanding of the pattern being presented. In this example, it is infinitives of verbs relating to free time activities that are being presented. In French, they can be divided into -er verbs, and activities with faire, for example:

> J'aime . . . aller au parc/écouter de la musique/jouer des jeux
> [*I like . . . to go to the park/listen to music/play games*]
>
> J'aime . . . faire du vélo/faire les courses/faire mes devoirs
> [*I like . . . to cycle/go shopping/do my homework*]

This enables learners to spot, practise and internalise patterns more easily. Indeed, if the infinitives are colour-coded green for example, learners can begin to talk about grammar in the target language using the following formula:

> Teacher: Pourquoi c'est vert? [*Why is it green?*]
> Pupils: Parce que c'est l'infinitif. [*Because it's the infinitive*]
> Teacher: Pourquoi c'est l'infinitif? [*Why is it the infinitive?*]
> Pupils: Parce que c'est 'I like **to** go' [*Because it's 'I like **to** go'*]

This innovative way to present new language is one, then, which involves interaction with the learners. Traditionally, learners are simply presented with items of language and told their meaning. This following technique allows learners to draw on their existing knowledge of English rather than simply be passive recipients of language.

The above phrase 'Comment dit-on en français?' can be supplemented by 'Comment dit-on . . . en anglais?' and this has been called a 'linguistic lifebelt' (Christie, 2016) as it stops pupils drowning in a sea of language they do not understand. It means that at any point a pupil can ask if he/she does not understand. Either the teacher can provide translation or explanation or, better still, can ask one of the class to do so. Such a question could be rewarded as this encourages learners to be active participants in the comprehension of the target language rather than passive recipients of it. One does of course have to guard against pupils' constantly asking this question in order simply to gain points, but this can be achieved through careful explanation to the class. It is harder for the non-specialist to encourage use of the question 'Comment dit-on . . . en anglais?' as he/she may be put on the spot. However, depending on the age and nature of the class, dictionary use could be encouraged.

Mimes are a good way of introducing language and it might be a good idea to establish set mimes for common high-frequency structures such as:

> C'est [*it is*]
> Ce n'est pas [*it is not*]
> Il y a [*there is*]
> Il n'y a pas [*there is not*]
> Est-ce que je peux . . .? [*can I . . .?*]

A further way of presenting new language is to give several target language options on the board for an English phrase, or vice versa, and pupil discuss in pairs in the target language which option they think is correct:

A: A mon avis, c'est numéro un.	[*In my opinion, it's number one*]
B: Je suis d'accord.	[*I agree*]
Je ne suis pas d'accord. A mon avis, c'est numéro deux.	[*I disagree. In my opinion, it's number two*]

When presenting language for the first time there is often disagreement among practitioners as to whether textual support should be presented from the outset. It is argued here, however, that text to support that is presented straightaway reinforces the sound-spelling link (or grapheme-phoneme correspondence) particularly important in a language like French (Erler, 2004). The argument against giving textual support is based on the idea that learners will simply pronounce words as they are written. Strong oral input and repetition can overcome this. The case against textual support also stems from the audio-lingual method of the 1970s, where exposure to the written word was discouraged until it had been thoroughly drilled orally. This method focused very much on oral proficiency and communication, and suppression of the written word can be seen as unhelpful in a context where reading and writing are also important.

PRACTISING THE LANGUAGE

An essential element to develop fluent talk among learners is that language needs to be sufficiently repeated and rehearsed in order for it to be internalised. As Johnson (1996) points out, there are two types of language knowledge, declarative and procedural, and both are important for language learning. Declarative knowledge describes the ability to talk about language and understand the rules. Procedural knowledge is that ability to speak fluently without particularly thinking about it. The latter is dependent upon practice and rehearsal as with any other skill such as driving for example. This develops automaticity and the ability to speak confidently without too much cognitive processing and makes spontaneous talk possible.

As Johnson notes, language that can be used spontaneously has to be language which has been rehearsed and practised by the learner. In other words it needs to be proceduralised:

Hence, for tasks such as spontaneous conversation where immediate access to knowledge is required, procedural knowledge is important.

(Johnson, 1996, p. 85)

This means that plenty of repetition of the language is necessary so that the use of certain structures and phrases becomes second nature to the learners. This repetition phase can, however, be rather tedious for learners so some interactive techniques can make this more interesting and engaging. Some possible ones are set out below.

Ping pong

Here a phrase is segmented into syllables or words and chorally repeated by the teacher and the class in turns. At the same time, they mime as if playing a game of ping pong.

Mexican wave

Here the same segmentation takes place but pupils are divided into groups and each group says their segment in turn around the class. At the same time they make a Mexican wave.

Pistons

In this activity there is the same segmentation. Learners work in pairs sitting next to each other and standing up when they say their segment. As such, learners move up and down in sequence like a vertical piston.

Mime and guess

In this activity, learners work in pairs. Person A mimes the phrase and Person B says it. Mimes can be devised in a number of ways. They can relate to the meaning (for example pointing to self and miming swimming for 'I swim') or to sound (for example miming shape of an 'eel' for 'il').

Test your partner

This activity has a similar accompanying dialogue to the translation activity seen above. Learners have on the board six numbered images, for example, and test each other on them. The textual support in the target language should be provided under each image. The tester looks at the board and the partner being tested tries to answer without looking.

> A: Comment dit-on numéro un en français?
> [How do you say number one in French?]
> B: A mon avis, c'est . . .
> [In my opinion, it is . . .]
> A: Oui, c'est correct/non, ce n'est pas correct
> [Yes, that's correct, no it's not correct]

Stop! Commence!

Learners work in pairs. One starts reading the language item/s, the other controls the partner saying, in the target language, 'Stop! Start!'

> Stop!   Commence!

Sergeant major

Again, learners work in pairs. One starts reading the language item/s, the other controls the partner saying:

'Louder! Quieter!'
'Faster! Slower!'

> Plus fort! Moins fort!
> Plus vite! Moins vite!

Chef d'orchestre

A series of sentences is displayed on the board, one below the other. A pupil is chosen to wait outside. With the teacher, the rest of the class chooses a pupil who will give a secret sign and also what that sign should be. This sign should not be too obvious but might be something like scratching one's nose.

The class then begins repeating the sentences in order and changes to the next sentence every time the secret sign is given. The pupil who was outside enters the room and has to guess who is giving the sign. The pupil has three goes at this using the target language:

Pupil: In my opinion, it is (name)
Class: Yes, that's right/No, that's not right

> A mon avis, c'est . . .
> Oui, c'est correct/Non, ce n'est pas correct

Treasure hunt

This is like a game of hot/cold. A pupil goes outside and a flashcard is hidden around the classroom. As the pupil comes back in, the class repeats the language item/s, getting louder as the pupil approaches the flashcard and quieter as the pupil moves away from it.

Mouthing

The teacher mouths a language item (i.e. says it without sounding it) and pupils guess which item it is. This can then be replicated in pairs.

Beep

This is like an oral cloze. The teacher 'beeps out' a word and pupils have to say which word it is. Again, this can be replicated in pairs.

Standing up game

The class is divided into two teams and then, in pairs, pupils are numbered on each team. So, in a class of 32 there would be 8 pairs in each team. The teacher then says a word or phrase in English and gives the class time to work out what it is in the target language. The teacher then says a number one to eight and the first pair to stand up and say the phrase correctly in the target language wins each time.

Rolling flashcards

The teacher holds a pack of flashcards with images on them to represent given words or phrases. She then rolls one of the cards and pupils have to say the word/phrase.

Songs

These can be used to great effect to reinforce language, as seen in the objectives routine song above. There are a number of familiar tunes to which songs can be set:

Happy Birthday
Frère Jacques
She'll be coming round the mountain
London's Burning
A marching rap
The national anthem
TV tunes, e.g. The Flintstones, Match of the Day theme, the Adams Family

PRAISING THE LANGUAGE

A particularly effective way to encourage target language talk in the classroom is to ensure that it is rewarded each time it occurs. Reward is particularly important in the languages classroom and speaking out loud in a foreign language in front of others and with the potential to make pronunciation errors can be quite daunting for learners. If they see that the effort to speak is rewarded, regardless of the accuracy, then this type of talk is more likely to take place. It is also important to create an environment where learners are willing to take risks and where errors are not viewed negatively. This is not to say that accuracy is not important and it is necessary to correct learners when inaccurate forms appear. This can, however, be done in a sensitive and productive way in an environment where learners understand the importance of error correction as a way to learn rather than as a technique to highlight their own shortcomings.

One way to promote spontaneous learner talk is, then, by ensuring that any pupil talk in the target language is rewarded. This can perhaps best be achieved through a team competition. The class is divided into two teams and a pupil can be appointed to score the points on the board. The teacher can reward the speaking in the target language with one point for example, with additional points awarded for accuracy and originality. The language of the requesting routine can be used for this as seen above. To avoid having one pupil scoring the points for a whole lesson, a series of pupils can be appointed, perhaps in 10-minute slots. This focus on the reward of target language talk demonstrates to learners that it is valued by the teacher. Competition also generates its own set of language, for example:

> Est-ce que je peux avoir un point?
> [Can I have a point?]

This request for a point can be followed up with the teacher asking 'why?' and the pupil giving a justification.

Teams can be given culturally relevant names. They might be for example French- or Spanish-speaking countries, football teams or cities. One may also adopt a model where there are several teams in one class, grouped on tables.

Competition also generates teacher-pupil and pupil-pupil talk such as:

> Tu triches! [You are cheating]
> Il/elle triche! [He/she is cheating]
> Ce n'est pas juste! [It's not fair!]

The teacher can also make deliberate mistakes, for example writing up the wrong date or misspelling a word. Pupils can be rewarded for using a correction routine such as:

> Stop! Il y a un problème. ce n'est pas . . ., c'est . . .
> [Stop! There's a problem. It's not . . ., it's . . .]

Obviously, this would need teaching and drilling, just like the language for any other routine.

PROGRESSING THE LANGUAGE

The Key Stage 2 National Curriculum (DfE, 2013) emphasises the need for pupils to make substantial progress in their language learning. This means developing the complexity and the accuracy of their language. Language routines that use set phrases but that do not develop over time would hinder this progress.

It is sometimes argued that giving over lesson time to routines and classroom interaction language means that there is less time for topic language and therefore language development. This makes it important to develop the language of the routines and of the classroom interaction over time so that it does not stagnate and so that learners are encountering new structures that they put to use. Below are some examples of how language might develop.

A greetings routine might start as follows:

> Comment ça va? *[How are you?]*
> Très bien merci, et toi? *[Very well, thanks, and you?]*
> Très bien merci.

It can then develop to include a justification, which can include a number of elements of progression, such as tenses and negatives:

> Parce que . . . [Because . . .]
> Present tense: . . . c'est le week-end/. . . j'aime le français *[. . . it's the weekend/. . . I like French]*
> Perfect tense: . . . Arsenal a gagné *[. . . Arsenal won]*
> Future tense: . . . je vais aller au cinéma *[. . . I'm going to go to the cinema]*
> Negatives: . . . je suis . . . mais je ne suis pas . . . *[. . . I am . . . but I am not . . .]*

An objectives routine can include time markers:

> D'abord on va . . .
> Ensuite on va . . .
> Finalement on va . . .
> *[First of all, then, finally we are going to . . .]*

Routines such as the evaluation routine can be expanded by adding justifications that include different tenses and conjunctions, for example.

A WORKED EXAMPLE: *THE HUNGRY CATERPILLAR*

Here is an example, in French, of how some of the techniques shown above can be incorporated into teaching around the topic of *The Hungry Caterpillar* story.

Learners are taught the phrase 'Comment dit-on en français?' and this phrase is displayed for learners to use.

The following items can be taught:

> une saucisse *[a sausage]* une sucette *[a lollipop]*
> un cup-cake un cornichon *[a gherkin]* la chenille a faim
> *[the caterpillar is hungry]*

As described earlier, flash an image of the item and learners ask for the target language item, for example, 'Comment dit-on 'a lollipop' en français?'

The teacher then displays and models the French. Mimes can be used here and then pupils can do the mime and guess activities in pairs.

A good drama activity is fruit salad (or musical chairs). Pupils sit in circles with one pupil in the middle. Pupils are allocated a word from the list of four nouns above. The pupil in the middle says a word and all the pupils with that word have to swap chairs, with one ending up in the middle. This is then repeated. If a pupil in the middle says 'la chenille a faim', everyone has to move.

Next, the contextualising question can be taught:

Qu'est-ce que la chenille a mangé?

This can be practised using one or more of the following techniques: ping pong, Mexican wave, pistons and mime and guess.

The response can be taught as follows:

Elle a mangé

une saucisse	une sucette	une glace
un cup-cake	un cornichon	
du melon	du gateau	

Repetition and practice techniques that can be used are: stop! commence!, sergeant major, chef d'orchestre, treasure hunt, mouthing, test the teacher, beep, standing up game and rolling flashcards.

Days of the week can be added to the beginning the sentence for example:

Lundi elle a mangé . . .
Mardi elle a mangé . . .

The days of the week can be rehearsed using a song to the tune of 'Nice one Cyril':

Lundi, mardi, mercredi,
Jeudi, vendredi
Samedi, dimanche

Writing can be introduced giving learners a clearly structured and categorised writing frame:

lundi			**un**	Cup-cake cocon cornichon trou
mardi			**une**	pomme sucette saucisse glace feuille verte
mercredi	**elle**	**a mangé**	**du**	fromage melon
jeudi	**il**	**a grignoté**	**de la**	tarte pizza
vendredi			**deux** **trois**	poires prunes
samedi			**quatre** **cinq**	bananes oranges
dimanche			**six** **sept**	cerises fraises

Il était une fois . . .				Une . . . . . . grenouille un . . . . . . hamster . . . souris . . . rat . . . tortue . . . serpent
et	il elle	avait	très faim	
Lundi Mardi Mercredi Jeudi Vendredi Samedi	Il a mangé Elle a mangé	une . . . un . . .	. . . poire . . . cornichon . . . fraise . . . hamburger . . . patate . . . gateau . . . pizza . . . banane . . . ananas . . . carotte . . . melon . . . tomate	Mais il/elle avait toujours faim!
Et finalement, Dimanche, il/elle n'avait plus faim!				

CONCLUSION

This chapter has focused on creating the right environment where learners appropriate carefully planned, set structures for their own fluent, and often spontaneous, use. This, coupled with a focus on increased grammatical awareness and manipulation of language, will give learners the tools to communicate confidently in the target language. It has also been shown that the development of such confident use by pupils need not be beyond the reach of the non-specialist teacher. In fact, the very planned nature of the classroom talk and frequent recycling of it, coupled with the use of textual support, allows the teacher to be in control of the language that pupils use.

Thanks to Marian Carty for some of the examples given above, in particular the writing frames.

REFERENCES

Butzkamm, W. (2003). 'We only learn language once. The role of the mother tongue in FL classrooms: death of a dogma', *The Language Learning Journal*, Volume 28, Number 1, pp. 29–39.

Chambers, G. (1992). 'Teaching in the target language', *The Language Learning Journal,* Volume 6, Number 1, pp. 66–67.

Christie, C. (2016). 'Speaking spontaneously in the modern foreign languages classroom: Tools for supporting successful target language conversation', *The Language Learning Journal*, Volume 44, Number 1, pp. 74–89.

Cohen, A. D. (1998). *Strategies in Learning and Using a Second Language.* Boston: Addison Wesley Longman.

Cook, V. (2001). 'Using the first language in the classroom', *Canadian Modern Languages Review*, Volume 57, Number 3, pp. 402–423.

Department for Education (DfE). (2013). Languages programme of study: Key Stage 2. National Curriculum in England. London: DfE. [Online]. Available at: www.gov.uk/government/uploads/system/uploads/attachment_data/file/239042/PRIMARY_national_curriculum_-_Languages.pdf. Last accessed 12 January 2018.

DfE (2003). Framework for teaching modern foreign languages: Years 7, 8 and 9. [Online]. Available at: http://webarchive.nationalarchives.gov.uk/20130401151715/http://www.education.gov.uk/publications/eOrderingDownload/0289-2003PDF-EN.pdf. 12 January 2018.

Doughty, C. and Varela, E. (1998). 'Communicative focus on form'. In C. Doughty and J. Williams (Eds), *Focus on Form in Classroom Second Language Acquisition* (pp. 114–138). Cambridge: Cambridge University Press.

Driscoll, P. (2014). 'A new era for primary languages'. In P. Driscoll, E. Macaro and A. Swarbrick (Eds), *Debates in Modern Languages Education* (Chapter 19, pp. 259–272). Abingdon: Routledge.

Ellis, R. (2008). *The Study of Second Language Acquisition.* Oxford: Oxford University Press.

Ellis, R. and Shintani, N. (2014). *Exploring Language Pedagogy through Second Language Research.* Abingdon: Routledge.

Erler, L. (2004). 'Near-beginner learners of French are reading at a disability level', *Francophonie*, Number 30, pp. 9–15.

Franklin, C. E. M. (1990) 'Teaching in the target language: Problems and prospects', *The Language Learning Journal*, Volume 2, Number 1, pp. 20–24.

Harris, V. (1996). 'Developing pupil autonomy'. In E. Hawkins (Ed.), *30 Years of Language Teaching.* London: CILT.

Johnson, K. (1996). *Language Teaching and Skill Learning*. Oxford: Blackwell.

Jones, J. (2000). 'Teaching grammar in the Modern Foreign language classroom'. In K. Field (Ed.), *Issues in Modern Foreign Languages Teaching* (p. 142). London: Routledge Falmer.

Littlewood, W. (1981). *Communicative Language Teaching*. Cambridge: Cambridge University Press.

Macaro, E. (2000). 'Issues in target language teaching'. In K. Field (Ed.), *Issues in Modern Foreign Languages Teaching* (pp. 171–189). Abingdon: Routledge.

Myles, F., Mitchell, R. and Hooper, J. (1999). 'Interrogative chunks in French L2: a basis for creative construction?', *Studies in Second Language Acquisition*, Number 21, pp. 49–81.

Office for Standards in Education (Ofsted) (2013). 'Judging the use of the target language by teachers and students'. [Online]. Available at: www.gov.uk/government/uploads/system/uploads/attachment_data/file/383328/Judging_the_use_of_the_target_language_by_teachers_and_students.pdf. Last accessed 12 January 2018.

Pachler, N. (2000). 'Re-examining communicative language teaching'. In K. Field (Ed), *Issues in Modern Foreign Language Teaching*. Abingdon: Routledge.

Pawley, A. and Syder, F. H. (1983). 'Two puzzles for linguistic theory: Nativelike selection and nativelike fluency'. In J. C. Richards and R. W. Schmidt (Eds), *Language and Communication* (pp. 191–226). Harlow: Longman.

Swain, M. (1995). 'Three functions of output in second language learning'. In G. Cook and B. Seidlhofer (Eds), *Principle and Practice in Applied Linguistics* (pp. 125–144). Oxford: Oxford University Press.

Ushioda, E. (1996). *Learner Autonomy: The Role of Motivation* (Vol. 5). Dublin: Authentik.

Widdowson, H. G. (1990). *Aspects of Language Teaching*. Oxford: Oxford University Press.

DEVELOPING SPEAKING AND PRONUNCIATION SKILLS THROUGH STORYTELLING ON THE APP iTEO

Claudine Kirsch

INTRODUCTION

> They are confident children but they are not confident at speaking. They are happy to have a go but they are quite self-conscious. Pronunciation is a weakness.
>
> (Ms Smith, teacher, interview 2015)
>
> We want to pronounce correctly but it is hard.
>
> (Mike, 10)
>
> Pronunciation is important because you could be saying a completely different word in French if you don't pronounce it right.
>
> (Lucy, 10)
>
> Sometimes I go on my mom's phone and do translator.
>
> (Sarah, 10)
>
> When we use iTEO, I pronounce something and then they (peers) pronounce it. We listen and see where we can improve.
>
> (Tom, 10)

This short vignette, with quotes from a Year 6 teacher in London and some of her 10-year-old pupils, raises several questions. Why is pronunciation important? What is its place in the curriculum? What problems do English-speaking pupils encounter when learning French? How can pronunciation be taught and what role might technology play?

The quotes indicate that this teacher and these children relate pronunciation to communication and perceive it as important though challenging to learn. The children wish to pronounce accurately and use digital technologies to assist them. In school, the app iTEO, an oral text recorder and editor, enables them to listen to their recorded text and encourages them to give each other feedback. This chapter attempts to find answers to some of the above-mentioned questions by discussing what we know about the teaching of pronunciation and linking this to the findings of a case study on the use of iTEO in this Year 6 class in London.

THE TEACHING OF PRONUNCIATION: FROM AUDIOLINGUAL PROGRAMMES TO THE AFFORDANCES OF NEW TECHNOLOGIES

Teachers and learners feel that *correct* pronunciation is important. Students have consistently asked for instruction, guidance and feedback on pronunciation (Gilakjani and Ahmadi 2011). Teachers are aware that pronunciation is crucial for communication, but they do not give the same importance to pronunciation as to other aspects of language learning (Wahid and Sulong 2013). According to Munro and Derwing (2011) and Nilsson (2011), *correct* pronunciation is not an issue addressed in the majority of language classrooms. Furthermore, explicit guidance on how to teach pronunciation is rare in textbooks and there is little training in initial teacher education. These factors may explain the teachers' lack of confidence (Derwing and Munro 2005).

In his review of methods of language teaching, Morley (1991) observed that pronunciation has not always been marginalised. From the 1940s to the 1960s, audiolingual programmes drew on articulatory phonetics to teach about sounds and their articulation, stress, intonation and rhythm. Periods of explicit instruction preceded drills where learners practised and memorised pronunciation. The aim was to achieve native-like pronunciation, understood as an aspect of linguistic competence (Lewis 2005). This practice was soon at odds with research findings that showed that the isolated drilling of phonemes and lessons in phonology and phonemic transcriptions did not improve pronunciation. With the rise of Communicative Language Teaching (CLT) in the 1970s came a change in the approach to the teaching of pronunciation. Articulatory phonetics was abandoned in favour of a comprehensive framework that focused on functional language. One of the aims of CLT is the development of communicative competence. Researchers, teachers and students alike found it unrealistic and difficult to achieve native-like pronunciation (Derwing and Munro 2005, Foote, Holtby and Derwing 2011, Saito 2011). Their aim was to develop 'intelligible' and 'comprehensible' speech. *Intelligibility* is often defined in relation to how well particular words can be understood. In order for an utterance to be intelligible, or clear, the listeners need to pay attention to the articulation of sounds, stress and intonation. They may then be able to transcribe this oral message and yet be unable to understand it. *Comprehensibility* is related to the meaning attached to the words. In order to render an utterance comprehensible, speakers need to focus, among others, on socio-linguistic, socio-cultural and pragmatic aspects (Smith and Nelson 1985). With CLT, pronunciation came to be taught alongside vocabulary, grammar and communication strategies. Teachers addressed *segmental* features (i.e. the production of sounds) and *suprasegmental* ones (i.e. stress, rhythm, intonation). Studies of the effectiveness of CLT reported, among others, that beginners acquired basic communicative skills but were unable to develop these to an advanced level (Lightbown and Spada 2013). Most could fluently produce high-frequency words such as greetings but not necessarily accurately. Researchers explained that many teaching programmes had neglected to focus on pronunciation.

Today, teachers and researchers call for the explicit teaching of pronunciation but still within a meaning-based approach. Teachers focus on form when and if necessary. In the last decades, advances in technology have facilitated the teaching and development of pronunciation skills. Some computer programmes visualise the way sounds are articulated by showing the correct position and shape of the tongue. Speech analysis applications transform speech into sound waves and help learners assess how their pronunciation differs from a model. Many online dictionaries come with audio files that model correct pronunciation. Some translators are based on automatic speech recognition programmes and offer audio files of the translations. Sarah, the 10-year-old girl introduced in the vignette, used a translator on her mother's mobile phone to record words in French. When the utterance was unintelligible or wrong, the device could not translate it into English. Sarah noticed she had made a mistake. To correct her pronunciation of the French word, she entered the English word and listened to the translation. In general, these digital tools are helpful to develop and improve pronunciation skills as learners receive both opportunities for imitation and practice, and feedback.

While applications specialised in developing pronunciation (and oral skills) may be beneficial, still other affordances of new technologies have been reported; they increase learner autonomy, allow for personalised and contextualised learning, connect formal and informal learning contexts, and widen opportunities for interaction (Lee 2014, Thompson and Derwing 2014). Pearson (2006) illustrated how students used digital speech recorders and editors in their Spanish dialectology classes. They interviewed native speakers, compiled sound files of people speaking different dialects, recorded their own speech and analysed the recordings. Applications that allow for the creation and sharing of audio files and podcasts are generally perceived to be promising for the development of speaking and pronunciation skills. Sze (2006) observed that students who created podcasts tended to rehearse a text before recording it. He concluded that this practice contributed to their improved pronunciation. Ducate and Lomicka (2009), however, warned that podcasts by themselves do not improve pronunciation. An explicit focus on pronunciation is necessary for this to happen.

In sum, this section has shown that the attention paid to pronunciation changed with the teaching methods: important in audiolingual programmes, less so in CLT and important again today. The goals shifted from native-like pronunciation to the production of intelligible and comprehensible speech. The methods moved from transmitting knowledge on phonics and practising sounds in isolation to developing communicative competence with minimum or no attention paid to pronunciation. While 40 years ago there was little material or advice on how to teach pronunciation, today new technology is a real asset, particularly so because it helps design authentic, social, meaningful and interactive learning environments. As such, learners have opportunities for additional practice and can receive individualised feedback from programmes, teachers, peers or native speakers.

In the following sections I will present the content-free app iTEO developed in Luxembourg to encourage nursery and primary school children to collaboratively produce stories in a range of languages (Kirsch 2017, Kirsch and Bes 2017). Next, I will show how storytelling can promote language learning. Storytelling with iTEO addresses the methodological issues raised above and offers learners opportunities to focus on form within a Task-Based Approach. The children's desire to be understood by an audience makes them pay attention to the way they record text on iTEO.

THE APP iTEO AND DIGITAL STORYTELLING

The app iTEO

In the 1990s Gretsch drew on social-constructivist language learning theories to design the computer application TEO, an oral text recorder and editor. Twenty years on, Gretsch and Kirsch, researchers at the University of Luxembourg, drew on TEO to produce the app iTEO. The aim was to promote innovative and mobile language teaching. The app is easy to use. Learners record a word, phrase, sentence or a longer stretch of text that appears as a numbered icon on the user interface. This item is automatically replayed but users can also choose to listen to selected items or the entire text. The replay materialises the language used and provides learners with opportunities for revision, analysis, negotiation of meanings and interpretations of discourse. Learners can insert pictures with the iPad camera and edit their text by rearranging and/or deleting the icons on the screen. Kirsch and Gretsch researched the use of the app among others in language lessons in primary schools in Luxembourg and showed how children developed language and metalinguistic skills (Kirsch and Gretsch 2015). Of particular relevance for this chapter is Gretsch's (2014) analysis of the way in which a 7-year-old boy helped a girl pronounce 'de rien' (you're welcome). The boy began by repeating the phrase and asking her to copy it. When he noticed that she was unable to correct herself, he segmented the phrase into syllables 'de', 'ri' and 'en' and wrote it on the board. He listened to her pronounce the phrase and realised that she pronounced 'en' incorrectly. He said 'un' and raised his thumb (alluding to counting) to make her think of the number 1 in French. She understood. She put the syllables together and pronounced the word correctly. Thanks to the imaginative and lengthy tutoring, she remembered the word, recorded it and recalled it weeks later.

Language learning through digital storytelling

Kirsch and Gretsch encourage the use of iTEO within the framework of storytelling. Stories appeal to our emotion and imagination, harness our creativity, and transport us beyond the limits of time and space (Wajnryb 2003). Their content, repetitive structure and rhythm invite learners to participate (Sneddon 2008). The nature of the stories and the listeners' engagement together facilitate memorisation and language learning. Researchers showed that storytelling has the potential to increase the learners' confidence in speaking a foreign language and contribute to the development of oral skills (Tsou, Wang and Tzeng 2006, Kirsch and Bes 2017). Kirsch (2012), for instance, demonstrated that English primary school children consolidated vocabulary and acquired new words and phrases through listening to a story with repetitive structures. The children were tested after 6weeks and were shown to have retained the new vocabulary.

Using stories in language learning classes can be daunting because beginners may lack the vocabulary to follow the plot. It is important, therefore, that teachers choose appropriate stories and scaffold the learners' comprehension using mime, gestures and actions, modulating the tone of voice, pointing to pictures and repeating key phrases (Heathfield 2014). Teachers promote comprehension by asking learners to retell stories with or without props. Morrow (2001) found that the practice of retelling stories encouraged language use, furthered comprehension and increased the syntactic complexity of the learners' productions. Looking at studies on digital storytelling, Di Blas and Paolini (2013), Flewitt, Messer and Kucirkova (2014) and Pellerin (2014) reported that the storytelling apps investigated involved the children in playful and collaborative activities that motivated them to record and edit text. The learners improved their listening and speaking skills. Kirsch and Bes (2017) showed that the joint construction of stories on the app iTEO and the discussions of these oral texts enabled primary school children in Luxembourg to develop oral skills in the target languages German and French, learned from Year 1 and Year 2 respectively. For instance, Lina, Aaron and Lee pointed out wrong agreements and mistakes in pronunciation both during the recording of a French text and after its replay.

Would primary school pupils learning foreign languages in other countries use iTEO as productively? Kirsch asked a primary school teacher in London to use the tool in the classroom. Unlike the teachers in Luxembourg, Ms Smith, who decided to take part in this brief study, did not attend a professional development course on the implementation of the tool.

THE USE OF iTEO IN FRENCH LESSONS IN LONDON

The following section describes how the English teacher in the vignette and her class used iTEO in four French lessons. The section will raise questions about the teaching of pronunciation that will be addressed in the final section.

A brief investigation of iTEO in England

In September 2015, Ms Smith, a young and enthusiastic teacher of a Year 6 class in London, implemented iTEO in her weekly half-hour French lessons. Her class was attended by 25 children of which 16 were bilingual with 2 who spoke French at home. Ms Smith, who had taken a degree in French and spent a year in France, aimed at developing positive attitudes and some basic skills in French. Her syllabus was based on stories and songs. She also liked project work as it helped her embed French in the wider curriculum. The children in Year 6 were beginners but had learned some French with Ms Smith in Year 5. They had, for example, covered topics such as food, sports and clothes. During the project on clothes they learned some basic vocabulary, made some clothes and organised a catwalk where they presented their collection in French. The written notes helped them remember what to say. Ms Smith hoped that iTEO would encourage the pupils to speak, make them aware of pronunciation and improve their skills. As explained in the vignette, the pupils had good listening skills and were eager to write but hesitated as soon as it came to speaking. She feared that pronunciation was holding them back.

From September to December 2015 a student assistant and I collected data. We video-recorded three lessons where the teacher and the pupils used iTEO, interviewed Ms Smith once, and interviewed Alice, Sarah, Lucy, Mary, Mike, Tom, the six focus children, on four occasions. In total, we collected 4 hours of audio- and video-recordings. These data offer a glimpse into the use of iTEO and the affordances of the tool for developing speaking and pronunciation skills. At this point it is important to note that iTEO was not developed specifically to improve pronunciation.

Using iTEO in the French lessons

During the first two sessions Ms Smith introduced phrases enabling the pupils to introduce themselves, that is, give their name, mention their age and the name of their home town, and indicate their likes and dislikes. They also learned to describe locations. Excerpts of model texts on the whiteboard read *Bonjour. Je m'appelle Marie. J'ai 10 ans. J'habite à Paris. J'aime lire. Je n'aime pas le foot. Il y a des fleurs, des arbres, des forêts, des montagnes.* In each lesson, Ms Smith read the text aloud to model pronunciation, gestured and mimed, actioned, and pointed to pictures to aid comprehension. She then asked for translations. Once the pupils understood the meaning, she asked them to produce a written text based on the model seen in her lesson. The pupils made use of a word bank and supported each other. They worked enthusiastically and drafted up to five sentences in a few minutes. Alice, for example, wrote *Bonjour Je m'appelle Alice. J'habite à London. J'ai onze ans. J'adore les croissants. J'aime le foot.* Sarah composed *Je aussi habite dans une village. Il y a des maisons et des arbres.* Next, the children read the text aloud to a peer or the class. Having noticed some mistakes, Ms Smith drilled some of the mispronounced words. She had the class repeat these in chorus after her. In the third lesson, the pupils wrote a French story. Many began to write a text in English that they intended to translate later into French. Others worked on their text at home using the internet to find translations. Three of the focal children explained in an interview that they used their parents' mobile phones and computer websites to learn new words. They depicted these as helpful learning devices.

Ms Smith used iTEO in two lessons. She recorded herself twice reading a text. She then asked the pupils to listen carefully to the replay, thereby providing more input. She had the text displayed on the whiteboard so that the pupils could listen to her and read at the same time. Once, she asked the pupils how they could improve their pronunciation skills with the help of iTEO. Mike suggested listening carefully to himself and Sarah explained she could record the native French-speakers in the class and listen to them. The focus children offered further ideas during the interviews. Five of them declared that iTEO was helpful because it encourages feedback and allows repeated listening which enabled them to notice mistakes. Ms Smith commented similarly:

> For them to hear their text back helps with pronunciation, with accuracy. And they can hear themselves back and correct their work. I think it helped their pronunciation and it will continue to.
>
> (Ms Smith, interview 2015)

Ms Smith had many ideas of how to implement iTEO in her class and within the school. She thought of recording the beginning of a text and have the pupils continue it. She also intended to put audio files with the recordings of her class on the school blog in order to provide pupils with additional opportunities to listen to texts and practise at home. She planned to play some iTEO stories to younger learners in assemblies and have the Year 6 pupils create visual props to help the audience understand. Furthermore, she envisaged recording model texts in French and giving these to colleagues less confident in teaching French.

The pupils' use of iTEO

In each of the lessons, the focus children recorded a text they had written. When unsure about the pronunciation of a word, they asked their peer or the latter assisted without being asked to do so. Sarah, for example, pronounced *arbres* in an unintelligible way and Mary modelled it correctly. Tom stumbled over the words *et* and *j'aime*. Alice offered a translation and modelled the pronunciation. Once the pupils had recorded their text, they listened attentively to its replay. At first, not being used to hearing their voice, they laughed. But they quickly stopped and turned their attention to the recorded text. While they listened, they sometimes pointed at the corresponding written word on the text in front of them. At other times, the children read their text silently, mouthing it, along with the audio file. On occasions, they seemed to be aware that there was an issue with pronunciation but no child knew how to correct it. When Tom was unsure about the pronunciation of a name, he and Alice listened several times to the replay before they agreed it was correct. Some pupils used the replay function to listen to the recordings of peers. They did not, however, choose to listen to the model texts recorded by Ms Smith.

Pronunciation difficulties

Before looking in greater detail at ways of teaching pronunciation, it is useful to examine some of the pupils' mistakes. The following are Alice and Sarah's sentences. The first column in the table is their written text, the second its transcription using the International Phonetic Alphabet (IPA), and the third the oral text. Bold indicates that a syllable is stressed and the italics refer to grammatical mistakes. The incorrect words and the mispronounced sounds are underlined and represented in IPA in the fourth column.

Written text	IPA version	Alice's spoken text	Mistakes in IPA
Bonjour	[bɔ̃ʒuːʁ]	Bonjor	[vbɔ̃ʒɔ̝ː]
Je m'appelle Alice	[ʒə mapɛl alis]	Je m'appelle Alice	
J'habite à London	[ʒabit a lɔ̃dɔ]	Ji habite à London	[ʒi habit]
J'ai onze ans	[ʒe ɔ̃z ɑ̃]	J'a onze ans	[ʒeɪ ʌnz]
J'adore les croissants	[ʒadɔʁ le kʁwasɑ̃]	J'adore les croissants	[kʁwasɑ̃z]
J'aime le foot	[ʒɛm lə fut]	J'aime le foot	
Je suis un chat	[ʒə sɥiz– ɛ̃ ʃa]	Je suisse un chat	[sɥis ʃat]

Written text	IPA version	Sarah's spoken text	Mistakes in IPA
Je aussi habite dans une village. Il y a des maisons et des arbres	[ʒabit osi dɑ̃ ɛ̃ vilaʒ yn mɛzɔ̃ dɑ̃. il j amɛzɔ̃ e dez aʁbʁ]	Je aussi **habit**at dans une **vill**age. Il y a des **ma**sson et des arb**res**	[ʒabitat dʌnz] [mazɔ̃n] [aʁbʁz]

These texts present some of the typical pronunciation mistakes the focus children made during the lessons. *At the segmental level*, they pronounced some vowels or consonants incorrectly, at times because they were influenced by the English pronunciation. Many pupils, for example, pronounced the letter 'e' in the word *je* like they would in English, thus producing [ʒi] instead of [ʒə]. In the excerpt above, the diphthongs [uː] as in *bonjour* and [ɛ] as in *maison* were mispronounced. The six focus children also frequently pronounced letters that are 'silent' in French, in particular 's', 't' and 'e'. They would, for example, articulate the 's' in *Paris*, *les*, *ans* and *suis,* as well as the 't' in *chat* and *forêt*. Some pupils aspirated the 'h' like Alice in *habite*. When words were similar in English and French, pupils used the English word. Thus, they said London, habitat and rivers instead of *Londres*, *habite* and *rivières*. When pupils had heard words only a few times or never (e.g. *natation* and *maison*) they tended to mispronounce them. Apart from mistakes at the *segmental level*, they tended to stress the wrong syllables. In her first sentence Sarah stressed a wrong syllable twice and she emphasised two rather than one word. The syntax was also incorrect leaving the sentence incomprehensible.

Having a record of the pupils' text on iTEO allowed Ms Smith to analyse their oral productions. A detailed analysis can help teachers select appropriate exercises as well as reflect on the teaching approach. Ms Smith, for example, was able to notice that a large number of mistakes occurred because the pupils recorded words they had chosen from a vocabulary list but had not practised yet. Additionally, they were reading their text, and in doing so encountered letter combinations that were at times unfamiliar to them. Ms Smith was able to improve the children's pronunciation by focusing more on their speaking skills and less on writing. She could have chosen some of the exercises presented below.

TEACHING PRONUNCIATION

Reviewing classroom-based studies on pronunciation, Thompson and Derwing (2014) found that 52 per cent of the teachers focused on segmentals, 30 per cent on supra-segmentals, and 30 per cent on both. The authors reported that teaching about pronunciation can be successful. Studies investigating the efficiency of phonological instruction showed that learners improved their pronunciation (Derwing and Munro 2005, Saito 2011). Thompson and Derwing (2014), however, warned that these studies are often based on a limited set of pronunciation features and, therefore, questioned the extent to which the learners' speech became more intelligible and comprehensible. By contrast, this does appear to be the case in studies focusing on suprasegmental features or both segmental and suprasegmental ones (Derwing, Munro and Wiebe 1997, Derwing, Munro and Wiebe 1998).

The teaching approaches reviewed in the literature differ widely but whatever the approach, researchers and practitioners would agree on a number of principles for teaching pronunciation. The latter are not language-specific. In my examples, however, I will only refer to French because this was the language taught in the case study. The readers will need to apply their subject knowledge in the language they will teach and find similar examples.

Guiding principles

1   The teaching of pronunciation needs to take place in a supportive learning environment where pupils have opportunities to engage in meaningful interactions.

The focus can shift from meaning to form, here pronunciation, when needed. Celce-Murcia (1983) suggested that teachers identify frequent pronunciation mistakes of their students, find words or phrases including the problematic words, design communicative tasks that encourage the use of these words and develop drills to practise and consolidate.

2   Learners should have access to models, including native speakers. Listening to these provides them with opportunities to imitate, practise the language and get feedback.

3   Feedback is a driving force in improving pronunciation (Saito and Lyster 2012). Therefore, teachers as well as peers should give constructive feedback thereby focusing both on positive aspects as well as those requiring modifications.

4   Teachers should raise the learners' awareness of phonetic rules but this should not happen in isolation. Pronouncing sounds in a new language is not only a physical phenomenon: pupils must also learn to conceptualise sounds differently. They may, for example, erroneously believe that they need to pronounce every single word in a sentence, and, therefore, do so. In reality, a speaker produces one stream of sounds that the listener subsequently segments into isolated words to make sense of the message. Pronouncing every single word in French is a mistake. Some sounds, like in Sarah's utterance *il y a*, need to be contracted. Pupils must also learn which syllables to stress. Unless they know, they may adopt the same pattern as in their home language and create unintelligible phrases in the target language. In the English language, for example, there is no rule that explains which syllable of a word needs to be stressed. In French, the final syllable of a word or group of words is stressed. In English, one can stress any word in a sentence, depending on what one wishes to emphasise. By contrast, a French speaker stresses the final syllable of a word or word group in a sentence if these are connected and if there is no pause. These examples show that teachers need to have a good understanding of the phonetic system of the target language.

5   Learners need to learn how to monitor their speech. Listening to one's own utterances while speaking is difficult but this skill can be learned in activities of 'critical listening' which Gilakjani and Ahmadi (2011) consider key to improving pronunciation. As seen above, computer programmes and apps such as iTEO that allow users to record speech and listen to it can play an important role. The language is materialised, projected into distance, and learners can discuss and analyse it. Studies on digital storytelling demonstrated that pupils rehearsed oral text, monitored speech and corrected themselves. With practice, the pupils learn to notice particular aspects of pronunciation and monitor speech.

Practising segmental and suprasegmental elements

With regard to segmental elements, several textbooks suggest teaching phonetic transcriptions, the most common type being the IPA used in the transcripts of Alice and Sarah's sentences. Beginners learn this unfamiliar system as well as the meaning and spelling of a word and its use in sentences. However, the isolated practice of phonology and pronunciation rules does not improve pronunciation. It is more beneficial to teach pupils about sound articulation and discrimination. Some examples follow. Using simple diagrams or computer programmes, teachers can visualise the position of the tongue and lips when articulating particular sounds. English pupils learning French may benefit, for example, from seeing the mouth position of the sound [u], a rarity in English. They will notice that the tongue is situated high and towards the front of the mouth as if they produced the sound [i] (as in 'to see'). They need to round their lips to produce [u] and stretch them to articulate the sound [i]. They can practise these sounds while observing their mouth position in a mirror. Learners may also find it useful to touch their vocal cords when producing particular sounds. The latter vibrate with voiced sounds (e.g. the English [g]) but not with unvoiced ones (e.g. [k].) Depending on the language learned, beginners may also like to work on aspiration. Aspiration refers to the gentle airstream produced with the articulation of a sound. Learners can feel the airstream by placing a hand in front of their mouth. In English, the voiceless sounds [p], [t] and [k] are aspirated when they come before a stressed vowel and are not preceded by an [s]. Examples are pot [pʰat], top [tʰap] and cot [kʰat]. The English language has more aspirated sounds than the French and this may explain why some pupils in the Year 6 class aspirated several words including those beginning with [h]. Among the most popular exercises are sound discrimination activities, especially those including minimal pairs (Mukhtar 2013). Minimal pairs help learners distinguish sounds and practise them. This is particularly useful for sounds found in one language but not another. Working on the phonemes [i] and [u], such pairs could include the words *dit – du* and *nid – nu*. As always, drills should be meaningful, brief and embedded in a meaningful context.

Websites, programmes and practitioners suggest a number of ways of developing the learners' awareness of stress, rhythm and intonation. Pupils can practise syllable stress by clapping the syllables of a word softly or loudly depending on the stress. The word *téléphone*, with three syllables and the stress on the last one, would sound soft-soft-loud. When clapping words in French, pupils will soon notice that the stress is always on the last syllable unlike in the English language where the stress can vary. Examples are *grand-mère, Paris, parisien, Méditerranée* and **grand**mother, **Pa**ris, Parisian, Mediterranean. A similar exercise can be carried out with sentences. Teachers can progressively lengthen sentences in French and the pupils will notice that the stress remains on the last syllable. An example illustrates the case:

Je visite ma grand-**mère.**
Je visite ma grand-mère dans sa mai**son.**
Je visite ma grand-mère dans sa maison à Pa**ris.** (I'm visiting my grandmother. I'm visiting my grandmother in her house. I'm visiting my grandmother in her house in Paris.)

Once the pupils have recognised a pattern, the teacher may mention the rule.

Regarding intonation (the varying pitch levels of speech), a beginner in French needs to learn the 'melody' of declarative, exclamative, imperative and interrogative sentences. Imperatives, for instance, are pronounced with a sharp fall at the end (*Ouvrez le livre!*). Pupils can learn about intonation through tapping the rhythm of an utterance or humming its melody.

Songs and stories are ideal when focusing simultaneously on segmental and supra-segmental features. Both are characterised by repetitive speech, rhythm and, at times, rhymes, which make this text genre enjoyable and memorable. Songs and stories familiarise learners with sounds, rhythm and intonation patterns and help them notice that oral speech is connected. When working on pronunciation, teachers can ask pupils to discriminate between specific sounds, find rhyming words and clap the rhythm.

This chapter has shown that storytelling on iTEO can encourage pupils to collaboratively produce texts in foreign languages and contribute to the development of language skills. Pupils learn to monitor and analyse their speech owing to iTEO's replay that materialises the language used. They learn to modify their speech with the support of more knowledgeable peers and teachers. Teachers help pupils by setting meaningful tasks, giving them the space to explore and produce texts, and focusing their attention on form when productions are unintelligible or incomprehensible. They can improve pronunciation with specific exercises at the segmental or suprasegmental level following some key principles outlined in this chapter.

REFERENCES

Celce-Murcia, M., (1983). 'Teaching pronunciation communicatively', *MEXTESOL Journal* 7(1), 10–25.

Derwing, T.M. and Munro, M.J., (2005). 'Second language accent and pronunciation teaching: A research-based approach', *TESOL Quarterly* 39(3), 379–397.

Derwing, T.M., Munro, M.J. and Wiebe, G., (1997). 'Pronunciation instruction for fossilized learners. Can it help?, *Applied Language Learning* 8(2), 217–235.

Derwing, T.M., Munro, M.J. and Wiebe, G, (1998). 'Evidence in favor of a broad framework for pronunciation instruction', Language Learning 48(3), 393–410.

Di Blas, N. and Paolini, P., (2013). 'Beyond the school's boundaries: PoliCultura, a large-scale digital storytelling initiative', *Educational Technology & Society* 16(1), 15–27.

Ducate, L. and Lomicka, L., (2009). 'Podcasting: An effective tool for honing language students' pronunciation?', *Language Learning and Technology* 13(3), 66–86.

Flewitt, R., Messerand, D. and Kucirkova N., (2015); 'New directions for early literacy in a digital age: The iPad', *Journal of Early Childhood Literacy* 15(3), 289–310.

Foote, J.A., Holtby, A.K. and Derwing, T.M., (2011). 'Survey of the teaching of pronunciation in adult ESL programs in Canada, 2010', *TESL Canada Journal* 29(1), 1–22.

Gretsch, G., (2014). 'iTEO as a Tool-and-Result in dialogical multilingual language learning. Storytelling at home and at the nursery school: A study of bilingual children's literacy practices', in N. Morys, C.Kirsch, I. de Saint-Georges and G. Gretsch (eds), *Lernen und Lehren in multilingualen Kontexten: Zum Umgang mit sprachlich-kultureller Vielfalt im Klassenraum*, pp. 183–219, Frankfurt: Peter Lang Verlag.

Gilakjani A.P. and Ahmadi, M.R., (2011). 'Why is pronunciation so difficult to learn?', *English Language Teaching* 4(3), 74–83.

Heathfield, D., (2014). *Storytelling with Our Students. Techniques for Telling Tales from around the World*. Guildford: Delta ELT Publishing.

Kirsch, C., (2012). 'Using storytelling to teach vocabulary in language lessons–does it work?', *Language Learning Journal*, 1–20. Available online at https://doi.org/10.1080/09571736.2012.733404. Last accessed 4 July 2018.

Kirsch, C., (2017). 'Young children capitalising on their entire language repertoire for Language Learning at School?. *Language, Culture and Curriculum*, doi: 10.1080/0790 8318.2017.1304954.

Kirsch, C. and Bes, A., (2017), 'Emergent multilinguals learning languages with the iPad app iTEO: a study in primary schools in Luxembourg'. *Language Learning Journal*, doi:10.1080/09571736.2016.1258721.

Kirsch, C. and Gretsch, G., (2015). L`apprentissage langagier avec l`app iTEO, Multilinguisme: enseignement, littératures et cultures au Luxembourg, Synergies pays germanophones, *Gerflint* (8), 37–48.

Lee, L., (2014). 'Digital news stories: Building language learners' content knowledge and speaking skills', *Foreign Language Annals* 47(2), 338–356.

Levis, J.M., (2005). 'Changing contexts and shifting paradigms in pronunciation teaching', *TESOL Quarterly* 39(3), 369–377.

Lightbown, P.M. and Spada, N., (2013). *How Languages Are Learned*, 4th edn. Oxford: Oxford University Press. Original edition awarded first prize (1993) in the Applied Linguistics division of the English Speaking Union's Duke of Edinburgh Award.

Morley, J., (1991). 'The pronunciation component in teaching English to speakers of other languages', *TESOL Quarterly* 25(3), 481–520.

Morrow, L.M., (2001). Literacy Development in the Early Years, Boston, MA: Allyn and Bacon.

Mukhtar, E.A., (2013). 'The effect of using communicative approach on developing pronunciation sub-skills', *Educational Research* 4(3), 294–308. Available online at www.interesjournals.org/ER/march-2013-vol-4-issue-3. Last accessed 12 January 2018.

Munro, M.J. and Derwing, T.M., (2011). 'The foundations of accent and intelligibility in pronunciation research', *Language Teaching* 44(3), 316–327.

Munro, M.J. and Wiebe, G., (1998). 'Evidence in favour of a broad framework for pronunciation instruction', *Language Learning* 48(3), 393–410.

Nilsson, M.W., (2011). 'Better a railing at the top of the cliff than a hospital at the bottom! The use of Edward Lear's nonsense ABC as a didactical tool in the development of pronunciation skills in young learners of English', Kristianstad University-Sweden.

Pearson, L., (2006). 'Teaching Spanish dialectology with digital audio technology', *Hispania* 8(2), 323–330.

Pellerin, M., (2014). 'Language tasks using touch screen and mobile technologies: Reconceptualising task-based CALL for young language learners', *Canadian Journal for Learning and Technology* 40(1), viewed 5 June 2015, from www.cjlt.ca/index.php/cjlt/article/view/26295/19477. Last accessed 12 January 2018.

Saito, K., (2011). 'Examining the role of explicit phonetic instruction in native-like and comprehensible pronunciation development: an instructed SLA approach to phonology', *Language Awareness* 20(1), 45–59.

Saito, K. and Lyster, R., (2012). 'Effects of form-focused instruction and corrective feedback on L2 pronunciation development of /ɹ/ by Japanese learners of English', *Language Learning* 62(2),595–633.

Smith, L.E. and Nelson, C.L., (1985). 'International intelligibility of English', *World Englishes* 4(3), 333–342.

Sneddon, R., (2008). 'Young children learning to read with dual language books', *English Teaching: Practice and Critique* 7(2), 71–81.

Sze, P., (2006). 'Developing students' listening and speaking skills through ELT podcasts', *Education Journal* 34(2), 115–134.

Thomson, R.I. and Derwing, T.M., (2014). 'The effectiveness of L2 pronunciation instruction: A narrative review', *Applied Linguistics* 26(3), 326–344.

Tsou, W., Wang, W. and Tzeng, Y., (2006). 'Applying a multimedia storytelling website in foreign language learning', *Computers and Education* 47(1), 17–28.

Wahid, R. and Sulong, S., (2013). 'The gap between research and practice in the teaching of English pronunciation: Insights from teachers' beliefs and practices', *World Applied Sciences Journal* 21, 133–142.

Wajnryb, R., (2003). Stories. Narrative Activities for the Language Classroom. Cambridge: Cambridge University Press, http://assets.cambridge.org/97805210/01601/sample/9780521001601ws.pdf. Last accessed 12 January 2018.

CHAPTER 5

TEACHING LANGUAGES CREATIVELY THROUGH THE CONTEXT OF MATHEMATICS

Sarah Lister and Pauline Palmer

INTRODUCTION

This chapter aims to provide a creative insight into how practitioners might explore the synergies between mathematics and second language learning. We will draw upon some current and relevant theories to underpin the practical examples we present in an attempt to illustrate the theory in context/practice.

As teacher educators, we are mindful of the time constraints and pressures facing our school-based colleagues, with an already overloaded curriculum. The vignettes included within this chapter offer time efficient but pedagogically sound practical suggestions of how to effectively combine mathematics and second language learning, without jeopardising or 'watering down' either the mathematical or linguistic content.

It is important to stress at the outset that the practical suggestions offered here with the aim of supporting and facilitating practitioners' practice, knowledge and understanding of how languages can be used as an effective and meaningful context to explore and develop mathematical concepts.

Restricting the amount of language required is a fundamental aim of these practical suggestions and the success of these teaching activities lies in the fact that the teaching activities involve a significant amount of repetition and reusing of language for both teacher and learner, affording opportunities to consolidate and revisit key concepts and language in a variety of different contexts. This emphasis on repetition and approach to language use helps to ensure there is minimal or no linguistic expertise is required.

It is the aim of this chapter to demonstrate how effective mathematical learning can be ensured with relative small amounts of second language. It is our firm belief, based on both our own classroom experiences and ongoing research, that language can often act as a barrier to children's learning. This is a particularly pertinent point in ever increasingly multilingual classrooms where, for many children, English is not their first language. Furthermore, we suggest that locating the teaching and learning of some mathematical concepts in a second language creates a more equitable environment for all children's learning, minimising the risk of misconceptions resulting from a lack of language not subject knowledge.

From a linguistic perspective, situating children's second language learning within mathematics, we argue, has the potential to boost learner engagement and motivation as it provides opportunities for them to hear, see and apply the language for themselves in a meaningful and purposeful context. This links well with Anna Craft's (2000) view of creativity and enabling creative learners, whereby there are four key elements/characteristics required: Imagination, Purposeful, Original and of Value. We believe that creative teachers can foster creativity in learners.

The activities suggested within the context of this chapter are intended for children aged seven to eight, working in Years 3 and 4, aimed at combining mathematics and the target language. The practical examples presented within the vignettes, have all been tried and tested in school settings.

THE MATHS MAT

Prepare a large grid – this can be one already in place on your playground or you can make one, perhaps using tarpaulin, readily available from your local DIY suppliers – mark this out using electrical tape (you will need space and time to make this, but it can be used in so many ways, it is worth thinking about).

Buy the largest piece of tarpaulin that you can get. The one illustrated is 8 metres × 5 metres.

The grid strips are made out of white and red electrical tape, cut to lengths of 40 cm each, allowing for a circle at each intersection of 7.5 cm in diameter. Having tried various ways of marking these circles, we find that using black permanent marker works the best.

The mat illustrated has been set out in four quadrants, which can allow you to work with negative integers. Having these four sections also means that children can work in small groups, using one quadrant each to create their own story, treasure hunt etc.

Vignette 1: maths mat

These activities work best in a large space, so use the hall for the mat, if you can.

Once you have your grid, you can use this to retell a well-known story. Pick something like the Three Little Pigs. Use props to illustrate the story (models or masks). The pigs go to grid references to build their houses. Initially, the teacher gives these grid references though, having once modelled this, children could then give these. Enter the wolf. The children must instruct the wolf on how to get to each of the houses, using terms such as, 'forward two steps, turn to the left, forward one step . . .'

You could also try a slightly more complex idea using the children's story *Six Dinner Sid* by Inga Moore (Hodder Children's Books, 2004). We are grateful to our colleague at Manchester Metropolitan University, Fiona Haniak-Cockerham, from whom this idea originated.

■ **Figure 5.1** Maths mat

■ **Figure 5.2** Street map mat

You can set out the street with the various families (you could use colour names or various properties, for example, Monsieur Maigre ou Madame Formidable). Once more, the children must instruct 'le chat' to visit all the houses, using directional vocabulary. There can be some dialogue if he becomes a talking cat who asks for food. You can add in rules such as he must find the shortest route without crossing the same grid points again.

The suggested activities above are examples of how stories can be used effectively to explore mathematical concepts through a second language. Key mathematical concepts are being revisited within a different context and the second language (L2) is being used in a meaningful and purposeful way to access the mathematics. The children are also afforded opportunities to apply previously acquired language (e.g. colours) in a new context and for a new end goal.

THE ROLE OF LANGUAGE IN MATHEMATICS

Mathematics is a universal language (National Numeracy Review Report, Council of Australian Governments, 2008). No matter where we are or who we are, regardless of culture, gender, race or even religion, certain mathematical principles remain true (Poulshock, 2014). The 'mathematical register' is unique to mathematics, is highly formalised and includes symbols, pictures, words and numbers (Kotsopoulos, 2007). As with any other language, mathematics has its own lexis, with both specialist words and non-specialist words used in specific ways, its own syntax and grammar and children need to be able to decode this language for themselves. Many children view mathematics as a 'foreign language'. The symbols and expressions provide a formidable barrier to understanding of mathematical concepts.

Understanding is crucial in mathematics and one way to gain this understanding is through practical experiences. Learners need to talk about their practical experiences and share ideas in order to forge meaning and have opportunities to connect ideas. As teachers, we sometimes have to translate the highly compressed and abstract mathematical language for learners, taking it back into contexts that learners can access and understand. Stripping back the language and giving careful consideration to the core language required by learners to access and make sense of the mathematical content, can be an effective way to ensure all learners can access the content.

■ **Figure 5.3** Barrier game

Vignette 2: barrier games

The children work with a partner. Partner A uses a small number of interlocking cubes of different colours to make a model behind a barrier and out of sight from Partner B. Partner A instructs Partner B as she does this. The aim is for Partner B to build the same model. You may need to model this first, using the target language. It can be helpful to go through the relevant vocabulary first and you may want to leave this visible during the activity. If the children are tempted to revert to their first language, then you could have them working in groups of four, where two are acting as observers and 'linguistic advisors' for Partner A.

SYNERGIES BETWEEN LANGUAGES AND MATHEMATICS

Common to both disciplines and a factor that can have a significant impact on teachers is their own emotional responses to them. Mathematics can provoke anxiety and negative attitudes in the same way as foreign language learning. Teachers can lack confidence in their own ability. Within a second language context, teachers often cite a lack of subject knowledge and confidence as key factors in their unwillingness and difficulty to plan and teach languages effectively. Williams (2008) also reports that a lack of subject content knowledge in mathematics is an issue for some teachers. Likewise, pupils can have negative feelings about their own capabilities and may see the subject as irrelevant and of no practical use. They may be reluctant to participate actively in lessons and lack the motivation or confidence to contribute.

Both mathematics and second language learning are concerned with enabling learners to understand and express ideas for themselves and in communication with others. The way in which learners communicate their understanding not only influences the way this knowledge and understanding is communicated, but also can actually lead to deeper conceptual understanding. As a learner seeks to articulate their own understanding in order to communicate this unambiguously to others, they begin to understand the need for precision. Moreover, as they seek to do this, they can begin to question and challenge the ideas that they are seeking to make transparent. Thus, they think at a deeper level. There is always a linguistic connection to knowledge expressed because concept building requires more than knowledge. Conceptualising and communicating are inseparable and lead to deep learning. The use of a second language can support this process as children draw upon and connect ideas, actively looking for patterns and relationships.

Teaching mathematical content and concepts through the medium of another language can offer an opportunity to revisit key ideas and concepts and consolidate their understanding in a different context. This can be particularly valuable for children who have become disengaged in their conventional subject lessons. Using the teaching strategies frequently deployed in foreign language lessons, such as the use of visual images, resources and gesture, the emphasis on vocabulary and developing talk, is generally also regarded as good practice in mathematics lessons.

SOME IMPLICATIONS FOR PRACTICE

When questioned, learners reported that they had to listen hard and concentrate and that they drew on cues, seen or remembered. Learners also worked hard to identify similarities and connections:

- the need for visual prompts – use of images/diagrams/tables and charts to support the teaching input;
- the need for and value of repetition;
- the need for the teacher to slow down;
- less 'vocal distraction', less teacher talk – less is more;
- the idea of making things practical and/or visual links with learning a language and to help consolidate key mathematical concepts;
- opportunities to see, hear and use the language in a range of different mathematical contexts;
- scaffolding helps students access prior/previously acquired knowledge/learning, analyse it and use it to help them process new knowledge/language;
- students need their language and content contextualised;
- scaffolding – categorisation and classification – language and concepts;
- shortening sentences;
- breaking down materials/resources/content into manageable chunks – 'chunking the learning'.

SECOND LANGUAGE LEARNING: SOME THEORETICAL CONSIDERATIONS

Learning another language helps children to become more aware of their own. This awareness can lead to improvements in literacy across the curriculum. Language learning continues throughout our lives, particularly our educational lives, and as we acquire new areas of knowledge, we acquire new areas of language and meaning. However, Swain (2000) advocates greater emphasis on form in content-driven contexts, providing learners with problematic grammatical forms that they can then use in meaningful situations and supporting learners in dealing with and communicating more complex knowledge and concepts. She also argues that content teaching needs to ensure that learners have full use of the functional range of language and understand how form is related to meaning in relation to content and stresses the importance of careful monitoring and planning to ensure successful integration of language, subject knowledge and thinking skills.

A social constructivist view of learning places the learner at the heart of the experience and active rather than passive learning or acquisition of knowledge is encouraged (Cummins, 2005). Consequently, social constructivist learning champions interactive, mediated and student-led learning. This requires social interaction between learners and teachers where the learning is scaffolded by the teacher or someone more knowledgeable. When learners are more able to cope with the cognitive challenge or new knowledge, and possess the linguistic tools to communicate this newly acquired knowledge, it is likely they will interact with others and their peers to develop their individual thinking. Vygotsky (1978) refers to the 'zone of proximal development' to describe this kind of learning that is challenging but always achievable. Within this socially constructivist approach, the teacher's role is one of facilitator to ensure there is appropriate balance between cognitive challenge and support. Nisbet (1991:27) states 'if learning is to be retained and to be readily available for use, then learners must make their own construction of knowledge – make it their own – and must learn to take responsibility of their own learning'. For construction of knowledge to occur, for it to become embedded and for learners to be able to make it their own, they need to be able to access, acquire, manipulate and make sense of the language. It could therefore be argued that using language to learn is as important as learning to use language. We propose that learning only becomes meaningful when learners are able to understand and learning is conceptualised. For learning and knowledge to become embedded, learners need to be able to use language appropriately, because it is through language that learning is made visible. By this, we mean that learners are able to put learning into their own words. Therefore, learners are not just required to use any language but rather the language of the subject content and/or discipline in a range of different contexts. An issue that we have frequently observed in classrooms is the difficulty many learners have in transferring language skills and vocabulary to demonstrate content knowledge and conceptual understanding between subject disciplines.

Vignette 3: making flags (this can fit in nicely with events such as the Olympics or the World Cup)

Prepare a short PowerPoint (or similar) presentation, showing a series of different flags. Using the target language, talk about horizontal, vertical and diagonal lines and the shapes made between these and, possibly, what fraction of the whole flag these sections take up.

■ **Figure 5.4** Flag 1

■ **Figure 5.5** Flag 2

Have a selection of small laminated versions of these flags. Children work in groups of four. Each group receive a small pile of flags and must take it in turns to describe these to the others. One child acts as the scorekeeper and records the number of statements, in the target language, that each child makes about their flags in each round.

Building on this, children could construct their own flags – drawing, painting or collage. These could be displayed with captions describing them, in the target languages, attached. Links could also be made to a large world map and the French or Spanish speaking countries around the world, for example 'la Francophonie'.

CONTENT AND LANGUAGE INTEGRATED LEARNING (CLIL)

Content and Language Integrated Learning (CLIL) can be defined as 'integrating language with non-language content, in a dual-focused learning environment' (Marsh, 2002) where there is 'the use of languages learnt in the learning of other subjects', (Lang, 2002), or as 'a dual-focused educational approach in which an additional language is used for the learning and teaching of both content and language' (Coyle, Hood and Marsh, 2010). CLIL is often perceived to be an umbrella term to refer to any learning that involves using the foreign language as the tool in the learning of a non-language subject and where the language and the curriculum content have a dual and equal role. (Marsh, 2002). CLIL is also often described as an educational approach in which a second language (L2) or language that is not the mother tongue is used as the medium of instruction to teach content in mainstream curriculum subjects. Therefore, CLIL is about using languages to learn in order to use languages, so in a way it is more about language learning, not language teaching. According to Graddol (2006), it differs from simple English-medium education in that the learner is not necessarily expected to have the English proficiency required to cope with the subject before beginning to study.

The last two decades have seen a rapid engagement with and implementation of CLIL methodology across Europe and elsewhere. (Coyle, Hood and Marsh 2010; Dalton-Puffer and Nikula, 2006). Graddol (2006:86) describes CLIL as the 'ultimate communicative methodology'. He identifies a significant difference between the communicative language teaching methodology of the 1980s and the emergence of CLIL in the 1990s. For Graddol (2006), CLIL classroom practice provides a more holistic, purposeful and authentic way of teaching and learning languages. This view of CLIL requires an integrative approach whereby topics, texts and tasks are taken from content or subject matter classes with a focus on the cognition and academic language skills required to enable learners to participate effectively in the content instruction (Crandall and Tucker, 1990). It can be argued that placing the emphasis on content rather than language has the potential to be mutually beneficial for both the content subject and the language – a view supported by Marsh (2002). It can also be said that the dual purpose and focus of CLIL pedagogy (ibid.) provides a more cognitively challenging and more authentic platform for language acquisition and use, while providing meaningful and new contexts for learners to revisit key concepts and subject content. Learning using a CLIL approach gives opportunities for the learner to think about and develop how they communicate in general, even in their first language (L1).

Key benefits/advantages of a CLIL approach

■ supports language within a meaningful context;
■ allows learners more contact with the target language in an authentic context;
■ embeds language within a task(s);
■ increases motivation as language is used in meaningful contexts for real purposes;
■ improves language competence and oral communication skills in both L1 and L2;
■ develops multilingual awareness, interests and attitudes;
■ introduces learners to the wider cultural context – puts culture back on the agenda;
■ encourages/promotes a positive 'can do' attitude towards language learning;
■ builds intercultural knowledge and understanding;
■ develops intercultural communication skills;
■ increases learners' motivation and confidence in both the language and the subject being taught;
■ develops teachers' skills and knowledge about the subject specific language and strategies/approaches to provide opportunities for learners to access this language;
■ raises linguistic competence and confidence;
■ raises teacher and learner expectations;
■ involves risk-taking and problem solving;
■ motivates and encourages independence;
■ takes students beyond reductive topics;
■ encourages linguistic spontaneity;
■ develops learners' thinking and problem-solving skills;
■ puts culture back on the agenda;
■ increases vocabulary learning skills.

Vignette 4: Kahoot quiz

Create a Kahoot quiz for your class (https://kahoot.com) on a mathematical topic of your own choice, using the target language (children will need some practice in the specific terms first). There are some Kahoot quizzes already created and are open access to the public. To access these quizzes or to create your own you simply need to create an account with log in details and password that is also free. You can then either use the quizzes already available, adapt these to suit the needs of your own class or create your own quizzes. These could include number, geometry, statistics and algebra.

Why this is good for developing language?

Specific vocabulary can be introduced, including the prepositional terms such as 'horizontal', 'vertical', shape names, basic fractions (for example, a quarter) and properties of shape.

This vocabulary is incorporated into a meaningful context: 'Voici un . . .'

A key benefit of contextualising both subject and language content within a gaming context is the potential for significant gains in pupil motivation and engagement. This is in line with William and Burden's (1997:120) view of motivation as 'a state of cognitive and emotional arousal which leads to a conscious decision to act and give rise to a period of sustained intellectual and/or physical effort'. There is significant evidence to suggest that computer-based learning both initiates and sustains learners' motivation and interest. Teaching content through a second language, in this case, mathematics, can be argued is linked to the authenticity of the learning activities and the appropriate level of challenge (Lasagabaster and López Beloqui, 2015).

Vignette 5: exhaustive thinking – find all the possibilities

Set a scenario, telling a simple story in the target language of the ice cream shop owner who wants to sell a new range of ice creams (perhaps new fruit flavours). The children are to advise him on combinations, if he can use two scoops/three scoops/four scoops of ice cream. You could also add different toppings or cones into the combinations. They can create these pictorially but they must use the target language to describe what they have drawn. They need to find ways to be systematic, ensuring that there are no duplications or omissions.

Why this is good for developing language?

Vocabulary related to ice cream combinations is incorporated into a meaningful context: 'Il y a . . .'

Research suggests the opportunities for the regeneration of content teaching afforded by CLIL fosters greater cognitive development and flexibility in the way learners approach, access and process this content (Coyle, Holmes and King, 2009 and 2010, Dalton-Puffer, 2008, Lyster, 2007), and in turn, recognising the central role language plays in this learning process. Exponents of CLIL also extol the potential cognitive benefits of bilingualism (Baetens-Beardmore, 2008; Coyle, Hood and Marsh, 2010) as well as the opportunities CLIL presents to promote creative thinking (Baker, 2006; Meehisto, 2008) through CLIL, and what Marsh (2002) refers to as broadening 'thinking horizons'. While there remains limited research into the potential positive impact on learner's cognition and conceptual understanding, there is growing evidence to suggest that learners develop more precise concepts when another language is involved (Lamsfuss-Schenk, 2002). Moreover, there is significant evidence within CLIL research circles to suggest that not only does CLIL promote potential cognitive gains and greater L2 proficiency but also that learners' L1 appears to benefit from this bilingual learning experience (Nikolov and Djigunović, 2006).

■ **Figure 5.6** Ice cream game

Vignette 6: problem solving – a version of a 'Cluedo'-type game in which children need to solve a mystery by being detectives

The original game was developed in England by Anthony Pratt. First manufactured in the UK by Waddingtons, it is now owned and produced by Hasbro. You may find the following link helpful: www.wikihow.com/Play-Cluedo/Clue.

Ou sont les ciseaux?

Preparation:

You will need to prepare a simple map of the school showing four classrooms plus two offices and various connecting spaces that will show as a series of squares for counters to be moved along during the game.

You will need to create the cards listed below:

Cards:

- ■ Six room cards – four named classrooms (perhaps using year group or teacher names) plus two named offices.
- ■ Six character cards with names of your choosing to reinforce desired vocabulary/ language – Monsieur carré/Madame Sphere etc.
- ■ Six location cards (these should have simple pictures plus captions as follows: on top of a cupboard, under a table, inside a drawer, next to the window, behind a chair, in front of the computer).

You will also need two dice and six counters.

Begin by reading Alan Ahlberg's poem 'Scissors' in *Please Mrs Butler* (Puffin, 1984).

Set the scene – a big box of scissors has been lost somewhere in the school. There are six suspects, six rooms to search and six places within the rooms.

■ **Figure 5.7** Preparation

Game instructions: the cards are put in three separate piles labelled 'Rooms', 'Locations' and 'Characters'. The teacher takes one card from each pile and puts them in an envelope.

Step 1 – Children play the game in groups of up to six.

Step 2 – All the cards from each pile are put back together and shuffled then shared between the children equally. Children turn their own cards over.

Step 3 – Children take it in turns to throw the dice to move around the board. The object is to enter each room.

Step 4 – Children must make one suggestion about the 'crime' each time they enter a room related to character, room or location – e.g. 'Je pense que c'est . . .'.

Step 5 – The child on the left reveals one of the cards identified. If he/she does not have any of the cards they must state they don't have the card – e.g. 'Je n'ai pas . . .'.

Step 6 – If the child on the left does not have the card, the next child in the circle must do the same thing until every child in the group has been asked and responded appropriately.

Step 7 – play moves on to the next child who throws the dice and the process begins again until children are able to work out what the missing cards are and therefore what room, what location and what character cards are in the envelope.

PROBLEM SOLVING

The Cockcroft report (1982) re-established problem solving at the heart of effective learning and teaching in mathematics. The most recent version of the National Curriculum (DfE 2013:3) requires that children are expected to 'solve problems by applying their mathematics to a variety of routine and non-routine problems with increasing sophistication, including breaking down problems into a series of simpler steps and persevering in seeking solutions'. A general definition of a problem (not just from mathematics) is given by Kahney (1993 cited in Barmby, Bolden and Thompson, 2014:15): 'whenever you have a goal which is blocked for any reason – lack of resources, lack of information . . . you have a problem. Whatever you do in order to achieve your goal is problem solving'. Parallels can be drawn with game-based learning resources whereby children are presented with a range of different obstacles and scenarios that they must navigate in order to proceed through the game. Similarly, from a language perspective, when faced with difficulties in communicating information or articulating ideas, language learners need to find a solution and/or alternative ways to make themselves understood.

Vignette 7: code cracking

This activity is based on pattern recognition, an important element in both mathematics and language learning.

You could begin with reading the children a story such as *Eric the Red* by Caroline Glicksman (Red Fox, 2003), in which the hero, Eric, works in a bank and is responsible for creating the code for the safe each day. However, one day, something happens which causes him to forget part of the pattern. Luckily, his new friend can help . . .

This is another place where you can use your 'maths mat'. Create a series of cards on which you have written a series of instructions. Make these big enough to put one in each square. It is worth laminating these cards for future use if you can.

Put each card into a separate square on your maths mat, if you are using one. Otherwise, these can be laid out on the floor. The layout should be as follows:

Ouvrez le coffre-fort	Allez trois pas à droite	Descendez deux pas	Allez deux pas à droite	Allez un pas à gauche	Descendez deux pas
Montez un pas	Allez un pas à gauche	Descendez deux pas	Allez deux pas à droite	Allez un pas à gauche	Allez trois pas à gauche
Allez un pas à droite	Montez deux pas	Allez un pas à droite	Descendez un pas	Allez quatre pas à gauche	Descendez un pas
Descendez un pas	Allez trois pas à droite	Descendez un pas	Allez deux pas à gauche	Montez deux pas	Allez cinq pas à gauche
Allez trois pas à droite	Montez trois pas	Allez trois pas à droite	Allez deux pas à gauche	Montez deux pas	Allez un pas à gauche

If you do not want to play this large version, you could also use an A3 card version of this with groups or share with your class via a visualiser or Smart board.

Setting the scene

You could tell the children a story about inheriting a huge amount of money that you do not want to put into 'Eric's' bank. You have hired a company to install a security system in your home instead. There is a pressure pad on the floor and you have to press every button only once in the correct order to open the safe. Each button has an instruction on it that you need to follow to press the next button, but you cannot remember which button to start from (you only get two chances to open the safe).

Ask a volunteer to go and stand on a square of their choice. The child turns over this card and follows the clue to the next card. Will they get to be the one who opens the safe? If not, the cards are turned back up again, showing the clues, and a second child tries (one of the children could act as a recorder of starting points, so that repetition is avoided). As they become more familiar with the lay out and the moves, children may be able to predict which square or card would be a good starting point and explain why.

The children then work in small groups to make up their own version of the game, making cards in the target language.

The directions could also include North, South, East and West.

CONCLUSION

We trust our suggested activities will prove to be useful and successful and that your children will find them interesting and engaging. We are both discovering there is immense pedagogical value in finding creative and meaningful ways to make links across the curriculum that enhance the learning of the content subject and the second language. We hope that you can see that combining subject content and language learning simultaneously need not be as daunting or as scary a concept as you might have first perceived and the tremendous potential this creates for the children we teach.

REFERENCES

Baetens-Beardsmore, H. (2008) Multilingualism, Cognition and Creativity. *International CLIL Research Journal*, 1 (1), 4–19.

Baker, C. (2006) *Foundations of Bilingual Education and Bilingualism*. Bristol: Multilingual Matters.

Barmby, P. Bolden, D. and Thompson, L. (2014) Understanding and Enriching Problem Solving in Primary Mathematics. Northwich: Critical Publishing.

Cockcroft, W.H. (1982) *Mathematics Counts: Report of the Committee of Inquiry into the Teaching of Mathematics in Schools under the Chairmanship of Doctor W.H. Cockcroft*. London: HMSO.

The Council of Australian Governments (2008) *The National Numeracy Review Report*. Canberra: Commonwealth of Australia.

Coyle, D. Holmes. B. and King, L. (2009) *Towards an Integrated Curriculum: CLIL National Statement and Guidelines*. London: The Languages Company.

Coyle, D., Hood, P. and Marsh, D. (2010) *CLIL: Content and Language Integrated Learning*. Cambridge: Cambridge University Press.

Craft, A. (2000). *Creativity across the Primary Curriculum: Framing and Developing Practice*. London: Routledge.

Crandall, J. and Tucker, R. (1990) *Content-based Instruction in Second and Foreign Languages*. Newbury Park, CA: Sage.

Cummins, J. (2005) Language Issues, Education and Change in Hargreaves, A., Lieberman, A., Fullan, M. and Hopkins, D. (Eds) *Handbook of Educational Change*. London: Kluwer Academic.

Dalton-Puffer, C. (2008) Outcomes and Processes in Content and Language Integrated Learning (CLIL): Current Research from Europe in Delanoy, W. and Volkmann, L. (Eds) *Future Perspectives for English Language Teaching*. Heidelberg: Carl Winter, 139–157.

Dalton-Puffer, C. and Nikula, T. (Eds). (2006) Current Research on CLIL. Vienna English Working Papers (VIEWZ). 3 (special issue).

Department for Education (2013) *Mathematics Programmes of Study: Key Stages 1 & 2 – National Curriculum in England*. London: DfE

Graddol, D. (2006) English next: Why global English may mean the end of 'English as a Foreign Language'. The British Council. Retrieved from http://vigdis.hi.is/sites/vigdis.hi.is/files/images/einangrun_enskumaelandi_folks.pdf. Last accessed 12 January 2018.

Kotsopoulus, D. (2007) Mathematical Discourse: 'It's like Hearing a Foreign Language', *Mathematics Teacher, The National Council of Teachers of Mathematics*, 101 (4), 301–305.

Lamsfuss-Schenk, S. (2002). Geschichte und Sprache: Ist der bilinguale Geschichtsunterricht der Königsweg zum Geschichtsbewusstsein? In Breidbach, S., Bach, G. and Wolff, D. (Eds). *Bilingualer Sachfachunterricht: Didaktik, Lehrer-Lernerforschung und Bildungspolitik zwischen Theorie und Empirie* (pp. 191–206). Frankfurt/Main: Peter Lang.

Lang, D. (2002). Foreword by Minister of Education, France in *TIE-CLIL Professional Development Course*. TIE-CLIL: Milan.

Lasagabaster, D. and Beloqui, R.L. (2015) *Porta Linguarum*, 23, 41–57.

Lyster, R. (2007) *Content and Language Integrated Teaching: A Counterbalanced Approach*. Amsterdam: John Benjamin.

Marsh, D. (2002) *Using Languages to Learn and Learning to Use Languages*. TIE-CLIL: Milan.

Meehisto, P. (2008) CLIL Counterweights: Recognizing and Decreasing Disjuncture in CLIL. *International CLIL Journal*, 1 (1), 93–12.

Nikolov, M. and Mihaljevic Djigunović, J. (2006) Recent Research on Age, Second Language Acquisition, and Early Foreign Language Learning. *Annual Review of Applied Linguistics*, 26, 234–260.

Nisbet, J. (1991) Projects, theories and methods: the international scene. In Coles, M. and Duckworth, W. (Eds). *Teaching Thinking: A Survey of Programmes in Education*. London: Routledge Falmer.

Poulshock, D. (2014) (Writer) Mathematics Illuminated. Episode: 101 Scripts accessed at www.learner.org/resources/transcripts/MathIlluminated/1_PRIME_TRANSCRIPT.pdf. Last accessed 12 January 2018.

Swain, M. (2000) French Immersion Research in Canada: Recent Contributions to Second Language Acquisition and Applied Linguistics. *Annual Review of Applied Linguistics*, 20, 199–212.

Vygotsky, L.S. (1978) *Mind in Society: The Development of Higher Psychological Processes*. Cambridge, MA: Harvard University Press.

William, M. and Burden, R.L. (1997) *Psychology for Language Teachers*. Cambridge: Cambridge University Press.

Williams, P. (2008) *Independent Review of Mathematics Teaching in Early Years Settings and Primary Schools*. London: DCSF.

CHAPTER 6

FROM *EMPIRES* AND *ERUPTIONS* TO *LOST WORLDS*

Placing languages at the heart of the primary curriculum

Elaine Minett

Comment es-tu, monsieur Loup?
Comment es-tu, monsieur Loup?
Je suis blanc comme l'hiver
Beau, poilu et immobile.
Je suis gracieux, rapide et féroce
Puissant, doux et brillant.
Je suis grise comme le brume
Aussi blanc fantôme, petit et lisse.
Voci comment je suis. Comment es-tu? (sic)

(Year 5 pupil, 'Who are you Mr Wolf?' project)

. . . exceptional individual achievement . . . is more likely to emerge from a system
of education which encourages the creative capabilities of everyone.

(National Advisory Committee on Creative and
Cultural Education (NACCE), 1999:32)

BACKGROUND

The introduction of a foreign language as a statutory part of the primary National
Curriculum in 2014 (Department for Education (DfE), 2013a) will undoubtedly have led
to considerable discussion surrounding the best model of delivery in schools. Given that,
in 2016, primary schools cited the lack of curriculum time and the low priority accorded
to the teaching of a foreign language as major challenges to the successful implementation

of foreign languages into the primary curriculum (Tinsley and Board, 2017), approaches that improve the status of languages and free up curriculum time may hold particular appeal. Seven primary schools in the South of England adopted a different method to planning their languages input; already incorporating a cross-curricular approach where possible, teachers explored further ways in which the foreign language could be the driving force behind their curriculum for a term.

All Our Futures: Creativity, Culture and Education (NACCCE, 1999) emphasised the need to develop the skills of all young people to equip them to meet the challenges of the future. It also recommended a balanced approach to the experiences offered in school: 'Conventional education tends to emphasise verbal and mathematical reasoning. These are vital to the intellectual development of all young people but they are not the whole of intelligence' (1999:38). While acknowledging the importance of literacy and maths, this report suggested that a balanced curriculum could enable some young people to realise their talents in other areas. In a series of creative curriculum projects in one local authority, attempts were made to reassert the relevance of the wider curriculum. Resuming control of the curriculum, teachers aimed to re-establish breadth and variety. Although thinking creatively can be challenging given the constraints of external pressures both on the curriculum and with regard to monitoring, assessing and reporting (as recognised by Thorne, 2007), teachers were nevertheless encouraged by the messages from *Excellence and Enjoyment* (Department for Education and Skills (DfES), 2003) that they should feel able to adapt their approach to the curriculum: 'We may not be in charge of the curriculum but we are in charge of our classrooms and schools' (Fisher and Williams, 2004:2). Furthermore, in these projects teachers were encouraged to apply approaches traditionally associated with Early Years or Key Stage 1 settings to their work with older pupils:

> Traditionally, infant schools have developed very imaginative and creative learning experiences and themes . . . but the concept of cross-functional creativity tends to die out as the child progresses through the different levels of schooling.
>
> (Thorne, 2007:55)

As one teacher involved in the project commented: 'Just because pupils are in Key Stage 2, why does creativity have to stop?'

Other projects in this local authority had committed to placing subjects such as art, history or geography at the forefront of planning; for this group of schools, languages became the driver. In promoting the development of pupils' capacity to tolerate other 'races, religions and ways of life' and 'understand the world in which they live' (NACCCE, 1999:75) there appears considerable scope for justifying the place of language learning. In addition to the generic targets shared by participants in these projects, which aimed to develop a relevant, exciting curriculum for all pupils, the languages cohort had particular aims: to raise the status of language learning within school and increase curriculum time spent on language teaching (Minett, 2008). It was hoped that making languages a central part of planning would raise the profile of language learning (as recommended in the *Key Stage 2 Framework for Languages*, DfES, 2005), enabling it to become an integral part of the primary curriculum.

> I think the cross-curricular creativity approach with foreign language should really help raise the status of languages within the school. If it is incorporated into

topic-based planning it will help with the problem of having enough time to teach languages and it will have more relevance for the children.

(Year 2/3/4 teacher)

Without dwelling in particular on the issues of ensuring an adequate weekly entitlement for pupils in Key Stage 2 to learn a language, it is nevertheless worth noting that schools were struggling to deliver this provision. Without this it is hard to see how schools will achieve the 'substantial progress' required by the National Curriculum (DfE, 2013a:2). When asked to articulate the main obstacles to the successful introduction of foreign languages in Key Stage 2, one Year 5 teacher summarised thus: 'Time – to deliver, to plan, to prepare resources. Other subjects are on our School Improvement Plan and often take priority.' These challenges match those reported by Tinsley and Board (2017) who refer to 'the difficulty of fitting everything into a crowded curriculum and the recent prioritisation of literacy and numeracy over all other subjects' (p.25).

At the start of the project most schools provided a discrete lesson of 30–40 minutes each week, with some additional provision through drip-feed activities, such as register time or Information Communication Technology (ICT) lessons; this time allocation reflects the recent findings of the *Languages Trends* survey on Key Stage 2 languages provision (Tinsley and Board, 2017). Acknowledging the difficulty of creating adequate time for languages, the teachers involved in the project were keen to find a solution. According to Barlow and Brook (2009), cross-curricular approaches may provide a way forward:

Essential to any consideration of a more thematic or cross-curricular approach towards curriculum opportunity is the idea that one theme may offer wide opportunities for quality learning in several subject areas, thus supposedly saving time and repetition, while allowing for wider and more cohesive learning experiences, with greater consideration of how children learn.

(Barlow and Brook, 2009:52)

Integrating languages into the whole school curriculum, as advocated by Martin (2000a), seemed a logical – if at times challenging – way forward. The *Key Stage 2 Framework for Languages* suggests that integrating language enables us to increase both exposure and relevance for pupils, recommending that languages should not be seen as a bolt-on extra (DfES, 2005:8) and providing clear guidance for mapping primary languages against other curricular areas. In these projects, teachers aimed for 'a more cross-curricular approach, making it integrated into the school week rather than discretely taught and always seen as something separate' (Year 6 teacher). Such linking was advanced as a key factor of good practice in the DfES research report (Driscoll, Jones and Macrory, 2004:90) and again in *Modern Languages: Achievement and Challenge 2007–2010* (Ofsted, 2011), which indicated that the curriculum in outstanding primary schools was characterised by the integration of languages into other subject areas.

In these projects baseline assessments were carried out before and after the cross-curricular teaching, to measure the impact in various areas: pupils' attitudes towards learning the language; the integration of language into the school curriculum; and the development of key skill areas – listening, speaking, reading and writing. Additionally, pupils were asked to evaluate the opportunities they had to learn about the country or countries where the language was spoken. Through contact with native speakers and aspects of culture from the foreign country, each project aimed to increase opportunities for pupils to develop their intercultural awareness.

In addition to the particular aims of raising the profile of language and increasing provision, teachers were keen to develop pupils' enjoyment of the language; this chapter will explore how each project achieved this. By increasing the appeal and relevance of the learning experience, it was hoped that pupils would be more likely to absorb and retain key information (Thorne, 2007:38). These projects also aimed to engage parents in their children's language learning through a variety of means: opportunities to observe their children performing; homework tasks stimulating collaboration and discussion; puppets linking school and home language experiences.

RATIONALE FOR THE SIX PROJECTS

The seven schools involved were at different stages of delivering primary languages – most had been teaching it for 2 or 3 years although one school was in its first year of provision. None of the schools had specialist teachers but all had access to planning support and two had fortnightly in-class support from a languages specialist. Contexts for learning included: *Empires and Eruptions, Lost Worlds, Paris – City of Light, Hidden Forest, Into the Unknown* and *Who are you Mr Wolf?*

Integration of language became possible in two distinct ways: first, **enhancing** what was already happening in the curriculum through meaningful links (for example, in the *Eruptions* focus, in *Underwater Worlds* and *Who are you Mr Wolf?*); second, by actually **influencing** what was happening in other areas of curriculum planning, as was the case in *Lost Worlds*, the Paris topic and the *Empires* focus. Clearly such freedom in planning would not be possible if the Programme of Study for Modern Languages (DfE, 2013a) dictated content; lack of prescription enables teachers to ensure linguistic progression and skills development within a context of their own choosing. Crucial to all projects was the support of the headteacher, as recognised by, among others, Thorne (2007:13), Powell *et al.* (2000:62) and Sharpe (2001:17); indeed, in listing 'critical factors for success' of cross-curricular approaches, Barlow and Brook (2009:72) cite 'shared ownership from within the school (commitment of all concerned)' as well as 'dedicated support from school management'. In these projects the willingness of school leaders to explore the contribution language learning could make to the wider curriculum and to offer *carte blanche* with regard to curriculum planning enabled creativity and encouraged innovation.

The need for support in innovation quickly became evident. Teachers were planning not only the language element of the term's focus, but also rethinking the curriculum for other subject areas. In some schools, combining year groups or sharing the load with teachers of parallel classes provided support, encouraging 'cross-school communication and coordination' typical of creative organisations (Thorne, 2007:14). Two small schools pooled resources and expertise, collaborating on the same project: 'creative partnerships add to your creative power' (Fisher and Williams, 2004:16).

In addition to the language learning aims of the projects, the starting point was to explore the kind of learning experiences teachers wanted to create for pupils. Rather than a subject content focus, teachers considered essential life skills: communication, collaboration, ICT skills, an openness to and tolerance of difference. There was a consensus that children should have opportunities to investigate, to experience first-hand wherever possible, to make use of the environment both within school and in the wider school community, to make meaningful connections between subjects and to reflect on their learning. Starko describes a 'stretching of patterns' (2014:8):

> Students think about content from different points of view, use it in new ways, or connect it to new or unusual ideas. These associations strengthen the connections to the content as well as the habits of mind associated with more flexible thinking – and thus build understanding.

In making connections, teachers stressed the need for these to be in-depth and relevant, and to offer possibilities for pupils to develop appropriate skills for their age and stage of learning.

In linking languages to other curriculum areas, teachers did not set out to deliver Content and Language Integrated Learning (CLIL), to teach for example science or history through the medium of the foreign language. However, Edelenbos, Johnstone and Kubanek (2006) suggest that CLIL is 'an umbrella term with many definitions . . . which can be interpreted very broadly' (p.93); although these projects did not immerse children fully in the foreign language, nevertheless there were occasions when subject content was delivered primarily through French. The primary school environment facilitated this approach, with the same teacher delivering all subject areas and able to make both planned and spontaneous links wherever possible. In this respect languages provision in the primary school can differ considerably from the experience provided in secondary, reflecting the varied contexts (DfES, 2005:61). Indeed it would seem somewhat illogical not to take advantage of the potential natural links that exist in the primary curriculum, as suggested by Martin (2000b), Cameron (2001) and Jones and McLachlan (2009) among others.

Not only does such an approach offer status to the language and increase the time allocation, it also offers benefits for pupils, providing natural opportunities to re-encounter language in new contexts (DfES, 2005:31). Additionally pupils may benefit from opportunities to over-learn concepts encountered in other curriculum areas, possibly at a 'deeper level' (Kirsch, 2008:82) – this approach is described by Hood and Tobutt as 'learning *in* or *through* the language' (2009:19). Tierney and Hope (1998:3) explore the potential benefit of such an approach for pupils as it provides opportunities for more natural acquisition of language – 'immersion in the language to the point where it is absorbed without conscious effort'.

Empires and eruptions

This project involved two mixed-age classes, one of pupils in Years 2, 3 and 4, and one of pupils in Years 4, 5 and 6. In the launch of the term's focus, 'Dr Who' arrived in assembly complete with tardis, sharing his most recent time-travelling experiences to Vesuvius; pupils were immediately motivated to discover more about volcanoes and were tasked with finding out if it was safe for him to return. In literacy pupils focused on creative writing to describe the eruption of Vesuvius; they re-enacted the eruption through dance, drama and music and explored the science through creating eruptions them-selves. Their French lessons enabled them to explore both the volcanic region of the Auvergne in France and the still-active volcano of Soufrière on the island of Guadeloupe;

older pupils' work on different types of volcanoes (*actif*, *endormi* and *éteint*) provided rich opportunities for consideration of cognates and near-cognates. Pupils learned and performed an invented French poem about a volcano (see Figure 6.1).

Having learned the poem, pupils then experimented creating their own versions: younger pupils created simple acrostic poems using key nouns, verbs and adjectives (see Figure 6.2), while older pupils made effective use of dictionaries to write independently. This early focus on free writing enabled pupils to use language quickly for their own purpose, rather than simply manipulating it at the request of the teacher.

The second half of this project's focus, *Empires*, transported pupils back in time, prompting them to discover what life would have been like for the Romans in Pompeii. Pupils visited a local Roman villa, created mosaics, costumes and chariots, and designed menus for a Roman banquet. Without forcing an unnatural link, the French for this half term focused on Astérix, enabling pupils to experience first-hand some of the French

---

Le volcan . . .

Un jour calme,
Pas de bruit:
Un volcan rouge ou un volcan gris?

Un jour calme,
Pas de bruit:
Ce n'est pas actif, un volcan endormi.

Mais . . . Regardez! Ecoutez!
Le volcan se réveille . . .
Des tremblements de terre!
Le volcan en colère!
Le cratère s'ouvre,
la lave coule . . .
Des nuées ardentes,
Une éruption violente.

Un monstre noir, orange,
Un géant jaune et rouge.
Allez, vite! Partez, courez!
Ah oui, ça bouge!

Un jour calme,
Pas de bruit:
Un volcan rouge ou un volcan gris?

Un jour calme,
Pas de bruit:
Ce n'est pas actif, un volcan endormi.

■ **Figure 6.1** Volcano poem

■ **Figure 6.2** Acrostic poem

fascination with this fabled character. All pupils were in their first year of learning the language and the focus was appropriate to their age and competence, initially on key nouns but also quickly on adjectives. Once again, presented with new text, children were encouraged to develop their skills in decoding and perseverance; the engaging context and opportunities for collaborative approaches in deciphering meaning saw pupils tackling and understanding key language such as *le héros de ces aventures*, *très intelligent*, *sa force surhumaine* and *potion maqique*. In a logical link to art pupils explored cartoons and created their own characters. Pupils wrote letters in both English and French to persuade Astérix to allow them to join his army (see Figure 6.3).

In this example several key approaches to the projects are made clear. It was the teachers' intention at all times to develop pupils' awareness of effective strategies for learning language.

> Metacognitive awareness is gained through reflection about how the learning has occurred, enabling children to achieve deeper understanding of what is involved. It helps them to be consciously aware of how to think about similar challenges in the future, so that their thinking becomes more self-directed.
>
> (Williams, 2004:31)

Pupils' letters to Astérix exemplified how they moved swiftly through what is referred to by Hood and Tobutt as the three Ms: Meeting Language, Manipulating

Compendium
Gaul
50BC

Cher Astérix

Je suis fort et je suis rapide.
Je de'teste les Romains. Je suis
courageux and j'adore le combat.

Meilleurs voeux!

Steven.

■ **Figure 6.3** Year 5 letter to Astérix

Language, Making the Language my own (2009:194). Edelenbos, Johnstone and Kubanek (2006:29) highlight the importance of the meaningfulness of a topic for the child, and Cameron (2001) stresses the need to choose topics which engage the interest of the pupils – creating an appropriate Astérix-style identity for themselves and encountering authentic French text were highly motivating factors in this context.

Into the unknown

In this project based on outer space, Year 5 pupils arrived in the school grounds on the first morning of the new term to discover various parts of what appeared to belong to a spacecraft fallen from the sky. Among the debris pupils found a French advert for '*jeunes astronautes*' – improving their fitness levels assumed real significance that term! French complemented work from English, Maths and Science; through a focus on sentence and short text-level activities pupils were provided with numerous opportunities to revise key concepts from their science work such as the names of the planets, their distinctive features and their distance from the sun.

A particular strength of this project was the links promoted with home and the wider community; the importance of fostering links with both the school and wider local community is advocated by the Modern Languages in Primary Schools Initiative (2012). Local French speakers brought authenticity to the classroom and demonstrated the potential sources of support for primary languages from within the community; pupils also took home an astronaut puppet to teach parents and carers key language that had been introduced in lessons. Puppets may be used as a means of encouraging young learners to speak without inhibitions; additionally in these projects pupils considered puppets a link between school and home, extending their learning by demonstrating their understanding of new language and concepts. This is a link that, according to Kirsch (2008), is something that does not exist naturally but which needs to be actively encouraged. Rowley (2009:121) recognises the 'importance of children being given the motivation of passing their findings on to others, both in the school and at home'. Pupils began trying to use language autonomously, writing simple phrases and sentences to describe what the puppet was doing outside of school.

Lost worlds

As Year 4 pupils prepared to spend a day in the local woods learning survival techniques, a letter arrived in school from a French boy (Figure 6.4).

Not only were pupils engaged by the authentic handwriting and unfamiliar stamp, they were also intrigued to discover that Luc was setting off on his own survival expedition. Working in groups with dictionaries, they deciphered the meaning of the items listed from his rucksack – unexpectedly, they also insisted on replying to Luc to inform him of a few key things he had forgotten! This highlights an important aspect of working in such a way, namely the need to leave space in planning to respond to the interests of the learners and to involve them actively in the planning process (Greenwood, 2013). Rowley (2009:121) also refers to the scope for 'opportunities for redirection through flexible planning' and the 'opportunities for children to contribute to the direction of the theme'.

After their encounter with life in the 'wild' that enabled them to participate in challenges in unfamiliar environments and to recognise risk, pupils focused on an

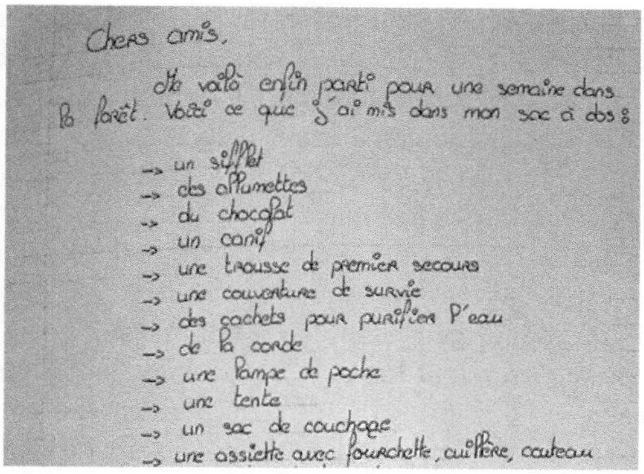

Chers amis,

Me voilà enfin parti pour une semaine dans la forêt. Voici ce que j'ai mis dans mon sac à dos :

→ un sifflet
→ des allumettes
→ du chocolat
→ un canif
→ une trousse de premier secours
→ une couverture de survie
→ des cachets pour purifier l'eau
→ de la corde
→ une lampe de poche
→ une tente
→ un sac de couchage
→ une assiette avec fourchette, cuillère, couteau

■ **Figure 6.4** Letter from Luc

exploration of prehistory. All areas of the curriculum were based around the story of the startling discovery of the Lascaux caves in 1940. Initially, pupils worked with a French translation of the key text *Boy* (2004) by James Mayhew, based on a cave boy's attempts to find somewhere warm to sleep, learning key language for weather and different geographical locations. The frequent repetition in the story enabled pupils to memorise key phrases that they used in a presentation to parents combining both the storyline of *Boy* and the Lascaux caves' discovery. This provided considerable motivation to speak with both fluency and accuracy. Interestingly, the outdoor context for this term's learning combined with the exciting story of Lascaux encouraged boys in particular to engage with language learning – several boys volunteered to take a principal role in the performance to parents, many for the first time.

Pupils engaged in a web-based scavenger hunt to research the discovery of the caves (www.lascaux.culture.fr). Combining atmospheric music and virtual tours, this website recreates some of the awe and wonder that the first visitors to the caves must have experienced. This led to creative writing based on cave settings and to an original approach to art – pupils learned about the roles and purposes of artists in prehistoric times, creating paintbrushes from twigs and moss and crushing chalk for paint. A memorable moment came when pupils spontaneously began to sing one of the songs from their French performance while recreating outdoor wall paintings in the style of prehistoric art. In the initial evidence collected at the start of the projects, the teachers admitted to using spaces outside the classroom for languages lessons only rarely. These projects showed both teachers and pupils that language has a real purpose; it has a history, and a life beyond the classroom. In this particular project all subject areas were underpinned by the exploration of the discovery of the Lascaux caves: French was the driving force behind the entire curriculum approach and for this reason, it mattered. 'Activities undertaken in pursuit of a meaningful goal offer more fertile ground for learning than activities undertaken without an obvious cause' (Starko, 2014:7).

Paris – city of light

The Paris project was launched with a simulated flight abroad and a return to school on 6 January, with opportunities to explore how Epiphany is celebrated. Pupils in Year 6 were in their second year of learning French; they began by researching famous monuments in Paris, learning adjectives to describe them and verbs to persuade tourists to visit them. The context of Paris provided a wealth of natural connections with maths, science and ICT; pupils were engaged in converting currencies, problem-solving, creating information leaflets, testing upthrust on home-made *bateaux mouches* and investigating friction through the rollerskating *gendarmes*.

Barlow and Brook (2009:72) talk of a 'time for curriculum bravery and risk-taking' – certainly this was epitomised by the approaches to the Year 6 curriculum in their key revision period prior to their Standard Attainment Tests. The decision to use a French picture book as the principal literacy text was indeed a brave one; *Une nuit, un chat* by Yvan Pommaux (2002) proved to be a perfect choice as the themes of emerging independence and friendship matched the preoccupations of this age group. Whereas the choice of *Boy* in the *Lost Worlds* project was governed largely by its simple, repetitive language, *Une nuit, un chat* provided intellectual challenge for pupils: groups worked collaboratively to become language detectives and decode meaning through context and cognates. They learned to use visual clues from pictures and to read meaning in the author's use of colour and line. Dictionaries promoted independent learning. In exploring the potential of quality stories in the teaching of primary languages, Cameron (2001) refers to the importance of characters and plot to engage learners, and to artwork that is 'as important as the text in telling the story' (p.166). Pupils understood Groucho the cat's desire to go out on his own on the roofs of the city for the first time, and relished his parents' reluctance to permit this freedom.

Une nuit, un chat (Pommaux, 2002) makes engaging use of light and shade in its pictures and this provided a further science focus for the project, along with opportunities for art work by pupils. Figure 6.5 shows how the front and rear covers of the book were recreated in the classroom, providing a backdrop for pupils' landscape pictures. In English, pupils wrote a sequel to the story and also adopted persuasive writing skills to ensure Groucho would be allowed out again. Using animation programmes pupils animated the story and added narration.

The photographs in Figure 6.5 exemplify the steps taken in all schools towards creating an environment where the foreign language and culture played a leading role.

When asked to gauge the impact of this particular project, pupils' responses to final questionnaires showed an increase in the integration of language into school life (see Figures 6.6 and 6.7 on p. 86). Interestingly, although not asked specifically, pupils reported that French was now used in the playground, in homework, and at home with parents and carers. In a pressured curriculum, encouraging pupils to see value in personal use of the language constitutes important additional provision.

Hidden forest

This project, shared by two small schools working in close collaboration, explored the hidden world beneath the sea. A collection of diving equipment greeted pupils on their arrival in school; among the wetsuits and aqualungs pupils discovered a French poem describing a young boy's experiences under the sea. In groups, they worked with dictionaries to decipher meaning. The repetition of *'Je vois', J'entends'* and *'Je touche'* provided pupils with a clear, simple structure that enabled them to create their own French poems. Within the context of whales and the environment, pupils used a French translation

■ **Figure 6.5** Classroom displays

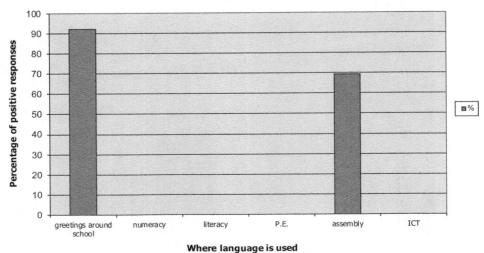

Figure 6.6 Where language is used (questionnaire 1)

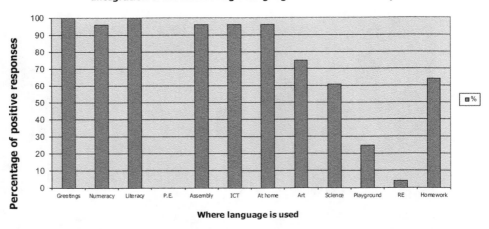

Figure 6.7 Where language is used (questionnaire 2)

of a simple text – *Dear Greenpeace* (1991) by Simon James – to explore and compare letter-writing conventions in the two languages and to identify nouns, gender and verbs. Although in Year 5 and 6 pupils were at an early stage of language learning, their work on higher numbers assumed a very real purpose as they designed and created *Top Trumps* playing cards to show key facts about sea creatures such as length, weight, life expectancy and speed.

Pupils built on their understanding of verbs to create a dance based on a healthy and unhealthy sea. The text *My Friend Whale* (2003), also by Simon James, inspired a drama presentation in French, again shared with parents. All six projects culminated in performance of some kind, partly to celebrate pupils' achievements and thereby raise the

Skills covered - questionnaire 1

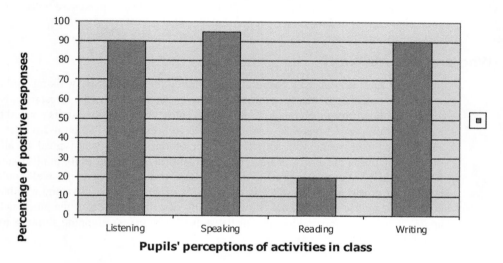

■ **Figure 6.8** Pupils' perception of activities (questionnaire 1)

Skills covered: questionnaire 2

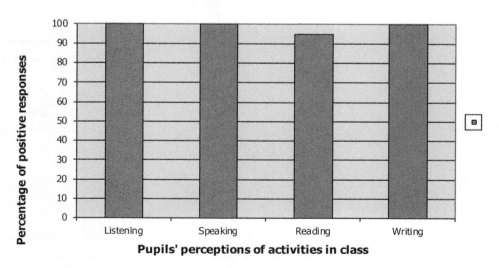

■ **Figure 6.9** Pupils' perception of activities (questionnaire 2)

profile of language learning within the school, but also to provide children with a reason to practise and perfect their language.

The focus on literacy in these projects was deliberate. Edelenbos, Johnstone and Kubanek (2006) suggest that young learners need to be introduced to reading and writing early in their language learning experiences. In the initial questionnaire (see Figure 6.8 on p. 87) only 20 per cent of pupils indicated that they had opportunities to engage in reading activities in French. This project maximised opportunities for pupils to encounter text with a view to developing their willingness to decode and persevere with sometimes quite challenging language (see Figure 6.9).

Who are you, Mr Wolf?

In a small rural school, Key Stage 2 pupils started their project by walking in the local woods: the first clue to their focus was the discovery of a basket on the forest path. Nearby, a red cloak hung from the branches of a tree. On closer examination pupils noticed muddy paw prints on the red material: could a wolf have been there? Pupils discovered a half-eaten cake – the scene was set! The launch of this project was typical of all work undertaken during the term – characterised by plentiful opportunities for pupils to discover first-hand and designed to stimulate learning. Pupils wanted to know if a wolf could have marked the cloak, which led to excited discussion of where wolves live and whether there could be one close to the school. Rowley (2009) describes aspects of the most successful approaches to teaching and learning as those that 'draw upon a stunning stimulus to move children' (p.121).

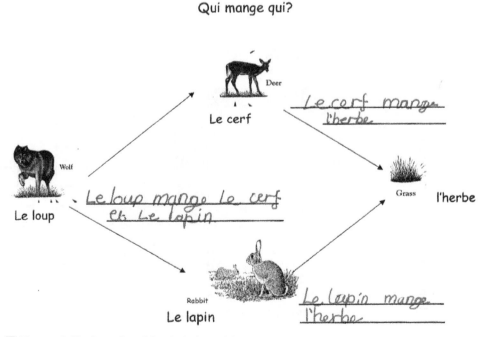

Qui mange qui?

Figure 6.10 Completed food chain activity

Work on habitats and adaptation, food chains and webs developed locality awareness – on a regional and wider European scale, as pupils researched the Mercantour National Park in the South of France, now inhabited by wolves. Much of the science focus in this project was delivered through or at least re-visited in French lessons – even younger pupils could form simple sentences describing where wolves live, having learned a variety of phrases for locations. They were able to give precise details relating to food chains (see Figure 6.10).

The adjective poems created by older pupils to describe the wolves typified the open-ended approaches adopted to engage children in their learning. Cognitive demand was high but language was kept relatively simple; pupils worked with outline models of poems that they adapted and personalised, as can be seen in the opening to this chapter. Experimentation was encouraged, even if outcomes were not always accurate; the teacher's role became one of facilitator. As Kerry (2015) points out:

> Teaching in a cross-curricular context makes the place of the learner central, rather than the place of content, and requires a different kind of approach to teaching in order to be effective. Overall didactic approaches won't do, though at times they may have a place.
>
> (2015:13)

In the wolf project, higher numbers were introduced and revised daily rather than in a single lesson. This little-and-often approach developed greater pupil confidence through regular exposure to language content, reflecting findings from Edelenbos, Johnstone and Kubanek that suggest that frequency of contact raises achievement (2006:25). Numbers were used meaningfully by pupils to talk about aspects of the wolf: length, height, weight, longevity, number of teeth! The teacher used a range of French texts to support and motivate and pupils were fascinated by the popularity of wolves in children's literature in France; this project culminated in a performance of *Le Petit Chaperon Rouge*.

CONCLUSION

The focus of this chapter was not to discuss the role of the non-specialist teacher in the delivery of primary languages, but it would be negligent to omit the essential role class teachers play in embedding the foreign language. Planning support from a languages specialist was indispensable in ensuring teachers' confidence and in securing pupils' linguistic progression. With such support it became evident that non-specialist primary teachers were ideally placed to deliver the foreign language, able to identify and create opportunities for integration into daily activities, recognised by Martin (2000b) and Muijs *et al.* (2005) among others. Teachers were able to draw on the confidence they felt for familiar areas of the curriculum (Tierney and Hope, 1998) to enhance their language teaching.

This project enabled teachers to embed the foreign language firmly in the primary curriculum. The target of 1 hour per week was surpassed: 'This has tripled the amount of French we were doing before' (Year 5 teacher). This included not only direct language instruction but also discussion of culture and use of the context of the foreign country wherever possible. In this way the foreign language enhanced rather than replaced other subjects: 'I'm doing more language but I don't feel it's encroaching on other areas'

(Year 4 teacher). It is not difficult to speculate that such an approach to languages provision in the primary school would go some way to improving the status of the foreign language, perhaps addressing the issue of the lack of priority given to primary languages and the under-achievement of potential identified by Tinsley and Board (2017:39). Certainly the teachers' own enthusiasm for working in this way was clearly evident, with one Year 4 teacher remarking 'I don't know who is more enthusiastic – the kids or me!'; this reflects Greenwood's findings with teacher positivity seen as a 'vital pre-requisite for pupil enjoyment' (2013:452).

The teachers involved in these projects would not advocate that this approach to primary languages teaching is always appropriate. Skelton and Reeves (2009) make the point that integrating any subject can have its pitfalls as well as its advantages and acknowledge that learning can take place within both approaches.

> Both have strengths and weaknesses. Single-subject curriculums enable teachers and children to focus on the learning within subjects . . . but they inhibit the opportunities for children to begin to see the links across subjects . . . Cross-curricular or integrated approaches can help children see the links between subjects but can fail to provide children with the opportunity to study any subject in depth.
>
> (2009:158)

With specific reference to languages teaching, pupils should be able to develop competence in age-appropriate language to talk about themselves and carry out transactional tasks in their interaction with the foreign country. Furthermore, there will be occasions when the context for learning does not lend itself readily to meaningful connections with the foreign language; forcing connections where they do not exist naturally would be artificial and detrimental. Hood and Tobutt remind us of the need to include language for 'survival' (2009:19) and Muir highlights the dangers of diluting the impact of language when embedding (1999:101). Martin (2000b) acknowledges the difficulties of tracking and testing when languages are integrated into the curriculum. Schools adopting such an approach may find that they need to liaise particularly carefully with secondary teachers to ensure that they share both the rationale behind the approach and the language content pupils have experienced. As mentioned previously, it is an approach facilitated by the content-free nature of the National Curriculum (DfE, 2013a). While acknowledging these potential difficulties, it is important to reiterate that these projects did not aim to reject conventional languages teaching or to suggest that discrete languages lessons do not have a place in the primary curriculum. What they aimed to do and clearly achieved was to suggest ways of enhancing languages delivery and increasing subject status and pupil motivation, and, in doing so, show how learning a language can truly be an integrated part of the curriculum.

With thanks to staff and pupils from Eastergate CE Primary School, St Mary's Catholic Primary School, Singleton CE Primary school and all others which were so supportive of and enthusiastic about this project.

REFERENCES

Barlow, C. and Brook, A. with contributions from Shuttleworth, D. and Bowden, P. (2009) 'Valuing my place: how can collaborative work between geography and art help make the usual become unusual?' in Rowley, C. and Cooper, H. (eds) *Cross-curricular Approaches to Teaching and Learning*. London: SAGE Publications.

Cameron, L. (2001) *Teaching Languages to Young Learners*. Cambridge: CUP

Department for Education (2013a) *The National Curriculum in England – Key Stages 1 and 2 Framework Document*. London: DfE.

Department for Education (2013b) *Languages Programmes of Study: Key Stage 2 – National Curriculum in England*. London: DfE

Department for Education and Skills (2005) *Key Stage 2 Framework for Languages, Parts 1 and 2*. London: DfES.

Department for Education and Skills (2007) *Key Stage 2 Framework for Languages, Part 3*. London: DfES.

Driscoll, P., Jones, J. and Macrory, G. (2004) *The Provision of Foreign Language Learning for Pupils at Key Stage 2*. London: DfES.

Edelenbos, P., Johnstone, R. and Kubanek, A. (2006) *The Main Pedagogical Principles underlying the Teaching of Languages to Very Young Learners*. Final Report of the EAC, lot 1 study.

Fisher, R. and Williams, M. (2004) (eds) *Unlocking Creativity – Teaching Across the Curriculum*. London: David Fulton.

Greenwood, R. (2013) 'Subject-based and cross-curricular approaches within the revised primary curriculum in Northern Ireland: teachers' concerns and preferred approaches', *Education 3–13*, 41, No. 4, 443–458.

Hood, P. and Tobutt, K. (2009) *Modern Languages in the Primary School*. London: Sage.

James, S. (1991) *Dear Greenpeace*. London: Walker Books.

James, S. (2003) *My Friend Whale*. London: Walker Books.

Jones, J. and McLachlan, A. (2009) *Primary Languages in Practice – A Guide to Teaching and Learning*. Maidenhead: Oxford University Press.

Kerry, T. (2015) *Cross-curricular Teaching in the Primary School: Planning and Facilitating Imaginative Lessons* (2nd edn). London: Routledge.

Kirsch, C. (2008) *Teaching Foreign Languages in the Primary School*. London: Continuum.

Martin, C. (2000a) 'Modern Foreign Languages at primary school: a three-pronged approach?', *Language Learning Journal*, Winter, No. 22, 5–10.

Martin, C. (2000b) *An Analysis of National and International Research on the Provision of Modern Foreign Languages in Primary Schools*. London: QCA.

Mayhew, J. (2004) *Boy*. Frome: Chicken House.

Minett, E. (2008) 'Getting creative! Embedding Languages in an Enriched Primary Curriculum' *LINKS*, Winter, No. 38. London: CILT.

Modern Languages in the Primary School Initiative – Final Report 1998–2012 Kildare Education Centre www.onevoiceforlanguages.com/uploads/2/4/6/7/24671559/mlpsi_final_report_july_2012.pdf. Last accessed 12 January 2018.

Muijs, D., Barnes, A., Hunt, M., Powell, B., Arweck, E., Lindsay, G. and Martin, C. (2005) *Evaluation of the Key Stage 2 Language Learning Pathfinders*. London: DfES.

Muir, J. (1999) 'Classroom connections' in Driscoll, P. and Frost, D. *The Teaching of Modern Foreign Languages in the Primary School*. London: Routledge

National Advisory Committee on Creative and Cultural Education (NACCCE) (1999) *All Our Futures: Creativity, Culture and Education*.

Ofsted (2011) *Modern Languages: Achievement and Challenge 2007–2010*. Ofsted, no. 100042.

Pommaux, Y. (2002) *Une nuit, un chat . . .* Paris: l'école des loisirs.

Powell, B., Wray, D. Rixon, S., Medwell, J., Barnes, A. and Hunt, M. (2000) *Analysis and Evaluation of the Current Situation Relating to the Teaching of MFL at Key Stage 2 in England*. London: QCA.

Rowley, C. (2009) 'Thinking through environmental values: planning for a long-term cross-curricular theme using local change and partnership – geography, art and science' in Rowley, C. and Cooper, H. (eds) *Cross-curricular Approaches to Teaching and Learning.* London: SAGE Publications.

Rowley, C. and Cooper, H. (eds) (2009) *Cross-curricular Approaches to Teaching and Learning.* London: SAGE Publications.

Sharpe, K. (2001) *Modern Foreign Languages in the Primary School – the What, Why and How of Early MFL Teaching.* London: Kogan Page.

Skelton, M. and Reeves, G. (2009) 'What it means for primary-aged children to be internationally minded: the contribution of geography and history' in Rowley, C. and Cooper, H. (eds) *Cross-curricular Approaches to Teaching and Learning.* London: SAGE Publications.

Starko, A.J. (2014) *Creativity in the Classroom: Schools of Curious Delight* (5th edn). New York and Abingdon: Routledge.

Thorne, K. (2007) *Essential Creativity in the Classroom: Inspiring Kids.* Oxford: Routledge.

Tierney, D. and Hope, M. (1998) *Young Pathfinder 7: Making the Link – Relating Languages to Other Work in the School.* London: CILT.

Tinsley, T. and Board, K. (2017) Language Trends 2016/17 – Language Teaching in Primary and Secondary Schools in England Survey Report British Council.

Williams, M. (2004) 'Creative literacy: learning in the Early Years' in Fisher, R. and Williams, M. (eds) *Unlocking Creativity – Teaching Across the Curriculum.* London: David Fulton.

CHAPTER 7

AHOY THERE, ME HEARTIES! COMBINING FOREIGN LANGUAGES AND DANCE IN THE PRIMARY CURRICULUM

Elaine Minett and Laure Jackson

INTRODUCTION

The introduction of Modern Foreign Languages (MFL) as a statutory element of the National Curriculum (DfE, 2013) may have led many to assume that this would assure their position on the school timetable and accord a certain degree of status to their delivery. Yet the pressure of time in an already crowded curriculum (Barton, Bragg and Serratrice, 2009) – cited frequently in previous years as a major issue preventing the successful delivery of primary MFL (NCCA, 2008; McLachlan, 2009; Legg, 2013, for example) – continues to affect primary languages provision (Tinsley and Board, 2017). Legg's study in 2013 indicated that some teachers felt that time could only be found for MFL teaching at the expense of other subject areas.

Primary MFL is not alone in receiving a sometimes-reduced time allocation in the curriculum, perhaps not helped by the lack of prescription in this area in the National Curriculum (DfE, 2013). The status of dance within the primary Physical Education (PE) curriculum has long been a subject of much debate (Best, 1992; McFee, 1994; Smith-Autard, 2002; Hall, 2008; Siddall, 2010; Cultural Learning Alliance, 2017), partly due to a lack of specialist teaching and time allocated to PE in Initial Teacher Education and also to the value placed upon it in some schools increasingly under pressure from a results-driven curriculum. It was certainly the personal experience of these authors that both MFL and dance were often allocated insufficient time on the primary timetable, making it difficult for pupils to secure consistent progress and perpetuating the status of these subjects as poor relations of the primary curriculum. In reviewing the success of the Modern Languages in the Primary School initiative in Scotland, Crichton and Templeton (2010) referred to the need for a consistent time allocation, along with a recommendation for appropriate links to be made between MFL and other curricular areas.

Combining subjects normally taught separately may create time for both (Barlow and Brook, 2010, cited in Greenwood, 2013) and may provide additional opportunities for effective language learning (Driscoll *et al.*, 2004). Satchwell suggested in 2006 that adopting a cross-curricular approach which linked MFL to other areas of the curriculum had indeed created the space in a busy timetable for languages to be delivered effectively; this was similarly found in the 2005 review of the Pathfinders' initiative which recommended inclusion of cross-curricular elements in language lessons (Muijs *et al.*, 2005) and also in *The Key Stage 2 Framework for Languages* (DfES, 2005). In the *Languages Review* Dearing and King (2007) described this way of working as 'a specifically primary experience of languages' (9), offering a combination which is not always feasible in secondary provision and suggesting that languages could be taught in conjunction with other subject areas such as Sport; 4 years later OFSTED's 2011 report described this combination of discrete language teaching with the integration of languages into other subjects as a feature of curricula in outstanding schools (2011). Coyle, Holmes and King (2009) went further to suggest that Content and Language Integrated Learning (CLIL), an approach where the content of a different subject area is taught through the foreign language, makes 'good use of time since both subject area content and languages are being learned together' (18).

The time issue is a very practical consideration and not an unimportant one. However, there are reasons for combining subjects that extend beyond the purely practical. For example, the Modern Languages in Primary School Initiative (MLPSI) (NCCA, 2008) in Ireland suggests that 'learning in one curriculum subject/area is deepened and enhanced through the child's experiences of discovery and learning in other curriculum subjects/areas' (2008:47); Greenwood (2013:444), citing Barlow and Brook (2010), describes these as 'more cohesive learning experiences'. Not only does this kind of integrative approach enable pupils to make connections across their learning, it also adds status to the subjects involved as they are no longer perceived as 'fringe' subjects (Hayes, 2010:385). According to Sharpe (2001), 'What matters . . . is that teaching within an integrationist environment transforms the significance for pupils of what is learned and can potentially raise standards of achievement and motivation' (17). Additionally, Lamb (2016) concluded that creative methods of engaging pupils in learning language through other subject areas can motivate and capture interest and in an applied context saw increased confidence and less anxiety.

THE RESEARCH CONTEXT

The issues outlined here were addressed through the creation of a pack of teaching materials consisting of 12 lessons designed to combine the teaching of dance and MFL to pupils in both Key Stage 1 and Key Stage 2. The aim of this small-scale research project was two-fold: to investigate the impact of learning languages through the context of dance and to consider pupils' responses to engaging in dance when taught through the foreign language.

The pack was initially created in French and subsequently translated into Spanish. Materials were first piloted with a mixed-age Key Stage 1 and 2 class in a local primary school and were then used in training sessions with undergraduate and postgraduate trainee teachers, as well as with serving teachers. The pack was then delivered in its entirety to two classes of 30 pupils in Year 2 (pupils aged 6–7 years) in a different local mixed primary school and data collected to explore the benefits of working in such a way and the potential to inform future practice. An action research method was considered most suitable (Cohen and Manion, 1994) to investigate the integrated approach of learning languages through the context of dance and to consider pupils' responses to engaging in dance when taught through the foreign language. The researchers acted as visiting teachers and were therefore not known previously to pupils.

Convenience sampling was used to draw data from pupils in one school. Any claims as a short-term case study with a limited number and range of pupils are acknowledged as non-generalisable. For the pupil interviews a purposive sample (Cohen and Manion, 1994) was used to obtain responses from pupils with different ability levels within the two classes. It was seen as important to investigate the effectiveness of the resource with both boys and girls with some range of ability (teacher-selected). Questionnaires, designed to be child-friendly, were given out to pupils before and after the project by class teachers, with the project leads not present; interviews were conducted with class teachers and a mixed-ability focal group of pupils from each class after their participation in the project. In this project questionnaires offered a number of advantages: although they can be difficult to design effectively they do give a relatively quick overview of basic opinions (Edwards and Talbot, 1994), and provide data that can be analysed quantitatively (Anderson and Arsenault, 1998). In this project class teachers read aloud questions for pupils who needed additional support. Using questionnaires in conjunction with interviews ensured that opportunities existed for detailed follow-up and for greater richness of detail and depth in responses.

THE TEACHING MATERIALS – OVERVIEW

This project combined the teaching of dance and MFL. Hayes (2010) points out that the risks of a cross-curricular approach include a lack of rigour in the teaching of individual subjects (2010) and Greenwood (2013) acknowledges the concerns that many teachers express when it comes to combining subjects – these 'tensions which exist between the desire to highlight and celebrate subject distinctiveness while teaching within a "connected learning" context' (2013:444). The lack of prescribed content in the curriculum guidance for both subject areas is helpful in this respect, where the focus is on skills development (DfE, 2013). Consequently, learning may be structured around any focal area as long as opportunities are provided for pupils to develop their understanding. This lack of prescription in MFL signals greater freedom in the primary phase than in secondary.

MFL and dance may perhaps be perceived as making for strange bedfellows, yet MFL has previously been linked very successfully with PE (Lamb, 2016; McCall, 2011), and was a common cross-curricular link found in Cable *et al.*'s longitudinal study of primary MFL provision (2010). Additionally, Graham, Macfadyen and Richards (2012) highlight the performative element that is common to both MFL and PE, along with the 'fairly 'public' display of how well learners have mastered what has been taught in the lesson' (2012:324), which can sometimes lead to anxiety in learners.

The theme of pirates had been previously used as a stimulus for primary dance with students on undergraduate and postgraduate teacher training programmes. It was always likely to appeal to pupils yet also enabled specific opportunities for pupils to engage with spoken and written target language from a variety of sources. The choice of music fitted well with the theme and served as a motivational tool for learning. Combining only two curriculum areas facilitated a tight focus so that both subjects were of equal importance and neither was sacrificed in favour of the other. In this respect the project was illustrative of Montet and Morgan's assertion (2001) that the content of the non-language subject can be acquired through being taught in the foreign language and that pupils can acquire the foreign language when encountering it in those lessons.

This project was not initially devised as an experiment in CLIL, yet it must be acknowledged that CLIL can take many forms. For example, Coyle, Holmes and King (2009) explain that there is no prescribed length for CLIL curriculum models and that they may vary from a few lessons to longer-term provision. Dalton-Puffer and Nikula (2014), while acknowledging a myriad of approaches that come under the umbrella term of CLIL, define typical CLIL as involving the 'use of a foreign language . . .; teaching by subject specialists, rather than language teachers; classes being timetabled as content lessons and taking place alongside language teaching rather than instead of it' (2014:117). Crucially the learning in the subject is new learning, being acquired through the foreign language (Coyle, Holmes and King, 2009). In these respects this experiment fit the CLIL definitions.

THE TEACHING MATERIALS – KEY FEATURES

The lesson sequence (Figure 7.1) shows how lessons were separate yet integrated. Language required for the dance lessons, conducted largely in the target language, was introduced in the language lessons. Language encountered in the MFL lessons was also recycled and extended through the dance activities. Pupils benefited from the opportunity to reencounter language on a regular basis, as suggested by Montet and Morgan (2001). For example, language introduced in the warm-up consisted of a series of pirate instructions such as '*Grimpez vers la voile!*' (pupils would enact climbing the rigging), '*Le capitaine arrive*' (pupils saluted the arrival of the pirate captain), '*Lavez le pont!*' (pupils would scrub the deck), '*Un orage se prépare*' (pupils huddled together to shelter from the brewing storm). During the pirate story used to contextualise the different sections of the dance, pupils encountered the same verbs used in different ways (*les pirates **grimpent vers la voile**,* (the pirates climb the rigging), *les pirates descendent au **pont** inférieur,* (the pirates go down to the lower deck), *les pirates **se préparent** pour la bataille* (the pirates prepare themselves for battle)).

The text in the pirate story intentionally contained unknown language but the collaborative approach adopted in lessons enabled pupils to pool ideas and share strategies for deciphering meaning. Kirsch (2016) acknowledges that this can be a daunting exercise but cites Heathfield (2011) in suggesting the use of strategies such as actions, repetition, intonation and use of props as ways of making the text more accessible. Pupils also became adept at looking for visual clues from the accompanying illustrations. The collaborative approach meant that they were not afraid of making suggestions and possibly translating incorrectly. For example, the first lines of the story are as follows: *Dans la mer des Caraïbes, une bande de pirates part en bateau. Les pirates cherchent du trésor secret.* Pupils were able to recognise *Caraïbes* from the *Pirates of the Caribbean* films;

bateau and *trésor secret* were included on their initial word match activity; *pirates* is a cognate, as is *bande*. *Cherchent* and 'search' were close enough and easily guessed from the context. This approach was very empowering as it gave pupils the feeling that they were able to understand a considerable amount even given their relative lack of French.

The first MFL lesson started with a word bank activity that required pupils to try to decipher the meaning of unknown pirate-related French words for themselves (Figure 7.2, p. 98). In this respect the lesson sequence followed that suggested by Moore and Lorenzo (2015) who suggest that initial tasks should 'gauge learner awareness of topics' (p, 341) and should 'be learner-centred: previous knowledge should be elicited, not presented' (ibid.). Pupils worked collaboratively, using their understanding of word classes and looking for cognates to suggest meanings of the new language. As recommended by Coyle, Holmes and King (2009), pupils were expected to deal with language that was at a higher level than that which they already possessed. The focus was consistently on developing pupils' strategies for learning language:

> CLIL accelerates the development of a range of language learning strategies to support learners in working out the meaning of what they hear and read, including recognising key words and cognates, identifying high-frequency structures and using prior knowledge to predict content.
>
> (Coyle, Holmes and King, 2009:16)

It was also noticeable how many opportunities arose to increase and develop pupils' existing vocabulary in English; by the end of the project many Key Stage 1 pupils were confidently using 'cutlass' rather than 'sword', and had encountered a range of adjectives through the foreign language focus, such as 'content' rather than 'happy', 'timid' instead of 'shy', 'savage' as well as 'wild'.

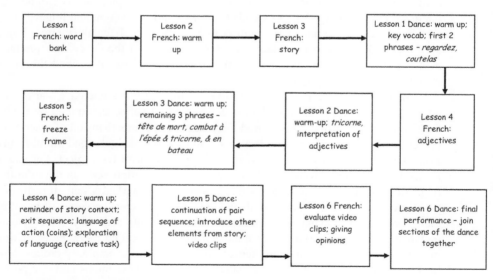

■ **Figure 7.1** Sequence of lessons and activities: Ahoy there, me hearties! Suggested pathway

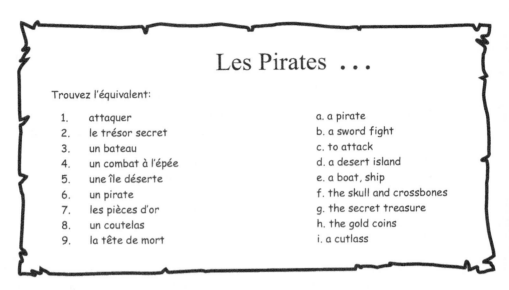

Figure 7.2 Vocabulary matching task

In each MFL lesson, pupils were presented with a 'pirate challenge' that clearly linked to the lesson objectives (for example, can you understand the main points of a pirate story? Or can you use some adjectives to describe a pirate?). The work focusing on adjectives was one of the most successful aspects of the project. Pupils were presented with a series of adjectives in the target language and asked to decipher meaning (using the approach adopted in the text comprehension work). They then created movements to convey these adjectives, moving in the manner of, for example, clumsy, confident, shy or famous pirates. This work was extended for older and more confident linguists to include sentence-level descriptions that applied to both male and female pirates. Pupils then used these adjectives to reproduce the relevant section of the dance, interpreting movements using a range of dynamics, to fit the adjective. They described the movements of others using the target language.

In addition to a focus on adjectives, pupils also completed a variety of tasks which enabled them to develop their understanding of verbs, as required by the National Curriculum (DfE, 2013). This started through pupils' comprehension of a series of commands in the warm-up; verbs were also a feature in both singular and plural forms in the story; and were also used in the creative dance element of the project. For example, in Dance lesson 4 pupils were introduced to a variety of action verbs in the infinitive form (e.g.: run, jump, crawl, roll, fall, strike a pose). This marked a departure from the set phrases of the dance and gave pupils the opportunity to create a series of movements of their own, still following the pirate theme. In the coins task they selected cards that included action verbs, along with number cards that dictated the number of times this movement was to be included in their creative dance. For example, in groups they might have to create a dance phrase that included two rolls, three jumps and one pose. These dances were filmed and evaluated in class; at a basic level pupils were able to suggest verbs to describe the movement they observed, while more able linguists would be able to construct simple sentences using conjugated verb forms to explain what action was taking place (e.g. *ils sautent et ils roulent* – they are jumping and rolling).

FINDINGS

In considering the findings from this project, it is perhaps worth bearing in mind Moore and Lorenzo's thinking that in CLIL classrooms 'the language will always be "real" in the sense that learners are involved in learning the content rather than simply communicating about something for the purpose of communication itself' (2015:337).

In each questionnaire pre- and post-project pupils were asked how they felt about learning French (they were used to having French lessons as a normal part of their timetable). Of the 33 boys who responded in the first questionnaire, just 13 expressed a positive response, with 3 unsure and 17 negative. Girls' responses were similar, although a greater proportion were positive: 13 were positive, 7 unsure and 4 negative. By the end of the project, of the 34 boys responding, 21 were positive (and 18 of these were very positive), with only 8 expressing a negative opinion; of the 24 girls, 14 were positive, 5 were unsure and 5 gave a negative opinion. In the words of Teacher 1, 'It was really positive – I don't think there was any negative feeling from them . . . When asked to reflect, they were really positive about it. They absolutely loved it, I think . . . completely adored it.'

There was clearly an impact on the boys' opinion of learning French, when combined with dance. This may have been for a variety of reasons, one main one being the positive response of the boys to the theme of pirates and the equation of French with active, collaborative working. This choice of theme may have gone some way towards addressing what is described by McCall as the 'feminine space' that is the French classroom (2011:6). Yet, many others have referred to the advisability of choosing topics which are of intrinsic interest to learners (Lamb and Fisher, 1999; McCall, 2011, for example) and in discussing CLIL, Coyle, Holmes and King (2009) recognise the importance of 'choosing relevant contexts for learning which are appropriate to the learners' age, ability and interests and provide meaningful interaction with and through the language' (2009:14). Graham, Macfadyen and Richards (2012) suggest that linking MFL, traditionally perceived to be a more academic subject, with PE, seen as 'a 'fun' subject' (Smith and Parr, 2007, cited in Graham, Macfadyen and Richards, 2012:324) may be beneficial for MFL. In support of this assertion, Lamb and Fisher (1999) found similar responses to MFL learning from both boys and girls when adopting a combined focus on MFL and football. Findings cited in the report *Dance in Schools and Beyond* for Youth Dance England by Siddall (2010:6) suggest that despite a relatively small allocation of time on the timetable, dance remains the second most popular activity for children following football. The unique contribution it offers to the holistic development of children makes it increasingly relevant as a subject, enabling them to find opportunities to express their own identities and cultures. Dance also has the potential to contribute to the building of self-esteem and confidence alongside artistic and social skills. The benefits for improved verbal and non-verbal communication cannot be underestimated (OneDance UK, 2017). In many ways dance offers opportunities for some of the essential elements which appeal to and motivate learners presented by Chambers (1993), cited by Lamb and Fisher (1999), namely the potential for movement around the classroom, the possibility of a concrete outcome, and relevant content.

The choice of pirates as a theme in this project also facilitated the inclusion of discussion centring on cultural aspects of Francophone countries. Pupils were intrigued to discover that there were French-speaking pirates as well as Anglophone; female pirates were presented alongside male counterparts to ensure both sexes were represented. In this respect this project created opportunities for pupils to engage with content through 'another cultural lens' (Coyle, Holmes and King, 2009:16).

This positive response from both boys and girls to foreign language learning is an important one. Although disenchantment with MFL learning may not set in until pupils are older, Enever and Watts (2009) found that primary-aged girls taking part in the Pathfinders' project were already more positive than boys, and suggested that boys' disenchantment with language learning may well start before secondary age as a result of the lack of relevance of MFL. Tierney and Gallastegi (2011) noted that although in Primary 6 both boys and girls were generally positive about MFL, girls were slightly more so; they recognise the significance of maintaining motivation even in the early stages of learning MFL. Tierney and Gallastegi (2011) also point out that at this age and stage in their learning pupils are motivated by the teaching approach and the possibility of using their language on holiday, rather than by any possible future career opportunities, and therefore the need to provide positive learning experiences is paramount. Greenwood (2013) noted that cross-curricular teaching led to greater levels of enthusiasm and involvement.

The very nature of the project, with visiting teachers and protected curriculum time to ensure its delivery, accorded both subjects 'special status' throughout its duration; this meant that pupils had regular access to both MFL and dance and therefore the opportunity to make progress over a sustained period of time. Indeed, when asked in the interview what had helped them to learn French better, one pupil simply answered 'Having lots of lessons'. Teachers, however, remained convinced that the practical applicability of the language proved invaluable for pupils: 'I think it was the way that we weren't just doing French for the sake of it. Here's how you say 'cat', here's how you say 'dog' . . . it was for a purpose' (Teacher 1). Certainly this echoes Mearns's suggestion that 'A suggested reason for . . . demotivation is the lack of ostensible purpose' (2012:178) and supports Tierney and Gallastegi's findings (2011) that desire to learn a foreign language is linked to how useful it is seen to be, as well as Johnstone's (2003) and Doiz, Lasagabaster and Sierra's assertion (2014) that a CLIL approach provides a real need for pupils to learn the language. Dearing and King (2007) perceive this 'real' content as constituting the kind of subject matter that will motivate young learners (2007:15). Doiz, Lasagabaster and Sierra (2014:211) quote Darn (2006:3) in referring to this as 'natural use of language' and describe its positive effect on learners' motivation; this emphasises that the end goal of the learning is not the acquisition of the language, it is the need to understand and be able to use the language to access the content of the subject lesson. Of course it is also possible that working in this integrative way may have provided pupils with the opportunity to take skills learned in one context and apply them to another, thus emphasising their relevance and usefulness, the importance of which is acknowledged by Hayes (2010). This comes close to replicating the 'unifying areas of learning that help young people make sense of the world and give education relevance and authenticity' described by Coyle, Holmes and King (2009:9). 'It makes them use language in other lessons and not just in one lesson, and it is actually useful language that they can use again . . . linking it to dance made a huge difference' (Teacher 1).

Certainly in this project the impact of combining the two subjects was significant. As discussed earlier, pupils were required to use adjectives in the foreign language to describe pirates and the way in which they might be moving to music; this language became part of their everyday vocabulary, even if it was not used exclusively in target language conversations. The class teacher noticed that pupils began to re-use vocabulary from the project in other, often unrelated, aspects of school life. For example, the word '*grincheux*' ('grumpy') was particularly popular:

> They always talk about that. A few of them really clung to that word and loved it. And they use it – oh, he's a bit 'grincheux' . . . They use the words actually, they enjoy it now whereas . . . it was a French lesson on its own, it wouldn't be linked to anything else.

> (Teacher 1)

Driscoll *et al.* (2004) suggest that encouraging pupils to experiment with the language constitutes effective practice. The teacher also noticed that other French words that had been taught prior to the dance project were being used spontaneously by pupils: 'In a piece of work we were doing the other day, they had to describe something, and a boy wrote in French '*gris*' and '*blanc*' . . . And he just [said], "Oh, I wanted to do it in French!"' In this respect the profile of the foreign language had been raised in the most general of terms; this supports Driscoll *et al.*'s finding that pupils were using French in other areas of the curriculum such as literacy (2004).

It is possible that one of the reasons why pupils responded so positively to the project was that it enabled them to feel more confident about their language learning, echoing Lamb's findings in 2016 in a handball and French project. In response to a question asked in the second questionnaire – 'Did the dance project help you learn French better?' – 30 of the 34 boys replied that it had, and 20 of the 23 girls also indicated that it had. This was supported by responses from individuals in both the questionnaire and interviews:

> The dance has helped me remember it [French].

> (Questionnaire response)

> The actions that we did and the dance helped us with the words.

> (Pupil 1, interview)

A month after the project was completed, pupils were able to recall, unaided, lexical items when asked in interview. One Year 2 pupil recalled with perfect pronunciation part of the warm-up language: '*Attention! Il y a une méduse!*' ('Be careful! There's a jellyfish!'). Interestingly, as pupils volunteered various items of vocabulary, they were nearly always accompanied by the action or the gesture that had been used in the dance. One pupil recalled another phrase from the warm-up – '*Le capitaine arrive!*' and immediately saluted, standing to attention. The dance seemed to offer the total physical response (TPR) and level of interaction promoted by Driscoll *et al.* (2004) as effective practice, enabling pupils to '"breathe" the language' (2004:7). It encapsulated the 'exaggerated movements, mime and tonal musicality and visual clues' recommended by Driscoll (2000), cited in Driscoll *et al.* (2004:41). Such a kinaesthetic approach to teaching MFL is not new; indeed, Barton, Bragg and Serratrice (2004) recognised the benefits of such pedagogical approaches for all pupils but particularly for those of lower ability, those with special needs and boys; Porter's study in 2016 considered the benefits of learning French through gesture, suggesting that the enactment of the language was helpful in supporting memorisation and recall, particularly because of the demand for involvement that enacting requires. The longitudinal study conducted by Cable *et al.* (2010) also indicated that teachers value the use of gesture in vocabulary learning for primary-aged learners.

The medium of dance however goes beyond simple hand and facial gestures: 'With the entire body as the instrument of dance, imagine its potential to communicate beyond mere hand gestures!' (Hanna, 2001:41). Hanna (2001) describes the combination of senses and the impact this can have; certainly, when it comes to recall, pupils involved in the pirate dance project were able to draw on visual, auditory and kinaesthetic memories that had been created, rehearsed and performed in both French and dance. Lamb (2016) stressed the importance of the opportunity for experiential learning and in this project it was this powerful combination of both the visual and the physical movement that offered an additional dimension to memory. The opportunity to create movement for themselves (and the importance of actually *doing* the actions as well as *responding* to commands was stressed by Asher, Kusudo and De la Torre, 1974) perhaps goes some way to explaining why pupils internalised the language so effectively. Lamb (2016) found that pupils' learning of French vocabulary was more effective as a result of having the chance to actually use it during the handball lessons. According to one of the class teachers involved in this project this was unusually effective, particularly for some pupils:

> There were some that were quite surprising, they don't always retain a lot of words when we're talking in English, when we're doing reading ... and yet in this particular project they were remembering, if not straight away, as soon as they saw the action, and they were confident enough to join in.
>
> (Teacher 2)

In order to maximise the acquisition of physical skills, much is documented within the field of motor skill acquisition to suggest that it is helped by kinaesthetic movement. According to Magill (2011), the clearer the original visual image made in the learner's mind, the more effective the muscle patterning used to produce the movement. This is an important factor in ensuring success in the learning of movement skills. Porter (2016) supports this further in her study on how the use of gesture enhances the learner's ability to memorise language. She suggests that the memory trace created as a result of using the kinaesthetic cues is more durable (Porter 2016:237), resulting in a higher level of recall of vocabulary and a lower loss.

The model of working memory by Baddeley (2003) identifies the idea that visual and non-visual information can be processed at the same time and what the subject does with the material to be remembered and how meaningful this is, is also critical in the creation of richer memory traces (Baddeley, 1997:107). Porter (2016) asserts that learning is improved from these richer traces, using a combination of visual, kinaesthetic and audio stimuli according to Baddeley and Hitch (1974: 47–90). Porter (2016:236) went on to find that the use of gesture boosts memorisation due to richer memory traces but also due to retrieval cues and a deeper processing. This was found to be particularly effective when the gesture was meaningful. It was also noted by Kelly, McDevitt and Esch (2009) that if speech was used with gestures, not only did it affect recall but it also created a deeper image element of memory trace in a clearer, more meaningful embodied way. Tellier (2008) argued that involving the body in learning creates more effective memory traces and helps with recall. Stern and Schaffer (2012), having researched the effects of teaching Maths through dance, also assert that embodying the idea is 'memorable, it's social, it's creative, it makes the ideas accessible' (Stern and Schaffer, 2012). Tellier (2008) surmised that gesture production acted as a stronger modality than pictures alone, arguing that involving the body in the learning process created richer memory traces and facilitated recall. In the pirate project it was noted how children identified the teacher modelling and the constant replication of the movement images (kinaesthetically) as something which really helped them to learn the target language more effectively.

Retention may also have been facilitated by the constant exposure to the foreign language that was experienced by pupils. French lessons were conducted largely in the foreign language, and key vocabulary was reused in the dance sessions. This related not only to specific topic-related lexical items but also to peripheral language such as commands that were used from the start of the project throughout its duration. In this project pupils had the opportunity to listen and absorb significant amounts of language before having to produce it for themselves (recommended as effective practice by Driscoll *et al.* (2004), among others). Martin (2002) found that pupils of primary school age coped with and responded positively to lessons taught entirely in the foreign language, developing good skills of gist comprehension, and that even younger pupils in Key Stage 1 were not fazed by immersion in the target language as they did not worry if they did not understand everything. In this project, immersion in the target language was accepted quickly by pupils who did not view it as anything out of the ordinary:

> I thought it was interesting that often, when you said things like 'hands down', that sort of thing in French, they knew what you were saying. I've no idea how they knew . . . I guess it was just a natural thing . . . That just seemed completely natural.
>
> (Teacher 1)

> That's a good way of learning – they are absorbing lots of language even if they don't understand it all.
>
> (Teacher 2)

Montet and Morgan (2001) in particular discuss this aspect of CLIL approaches, explaining that pupils' receptive skills can show rapid improvement simply because pupils are largely immersed in the target language throughout the lessons. Although this was true to a certain extent in the pirate dance work, pupils were also involved in speaking the language at the same time and, when asked to recall lexical items after the project, pupils were able to produce them verbally without assistance, and with a high degree of accuracy. Pupils were also involved in evaluating their creative dances and giving simple opinions in the foreign language. Wingate (2016) makes the valid point that listening activity is still usefully communicative if pupils are required to use the language gained in a follow-up activity which requires them to communicate either verbally or in written form.

Of course, immersing pupils of such a relatively young age in the foreign language for large amounts of time did mean that the level of challenge was high and placed considerable demands on them in terms of levels of concentration required. Some pupils acknowledged this in the subsequent interview and admitted that it would have been easier to do the dance in English. However, Wingate (2016) – in a review of MFL teaching (albeit in secondary schools) – refers to the 'culture of low expectations, lack of challenge and light entertainment' (2016:11) prevalent in the lessons observed and suggests that greater challenge may actually engage pupils more successfully than a focus on fun; in a similar vein, Jones and Coffey (2006) warn of the potential dangers if primary MFL is only ever associated with light-hearted relief from the more important focus on core curriculum subjects. Enever and Watts (2009) and Cable *et al.* (2010) similarly highlight the need to ensure that provision stretches pupils who need greater challenge. Certainly one Year 2 pupil involved in the pirate dance project relished the additional demand posed by operating in the target language: when asked if he would have preferred to do the project in English, he replied 'No, because it would then be easy and wouldn't have been a challenge'. Perhaps we should remember that challenge and fun are not mutually exclusive. In the words of one PGCE student who took part in the training session for this dance project: 'If a mature person can enjoy this, I can imagine how enjoyable this must be for children. It's good practice'.

What became quickly apparent, however, was also how little language was actually needed at times, and certainly there was no temptation to speak in the foreign language simply for the sake of practising. This supports the findings of Nikula (2010), cited in Van Kampen, Admiraal and Berry (2016), that teachers teaching CLIL subject lessons adopted simpler, more repetitive language than that used in other lessons. Perhaps in this respect we are acknowledging the importance of both subject areas in this project, recognising that in dance it is not appropriate to give too much aural information alongside early demonstrations (Magill, 2011). It also guards against an unnecessary overuse of the target language that may have a 'demotivating effect' on pupils (Low *et al.*, 1995, cited in Driscoll *et al.*, 2004:41). In the project children tuned into the critical language and focused on the essential content. Certainly the class teachers recognised the benefit of the dance as its physicality, and pupils understood that the physical demonstration often removed the need for language:

Interviewer:	Was there anything the teacher did that helped you with the dance?
Pupil 6:	Teaching us what to do, telling us what to do stuff (sic).
Interviewer:	And how did you understand when she told you what to do in French?
Pupil 4:	'Cause she done it.

Indeed, Martin (2002) suggested that pupils can learn effectively through doing, for example through involvement in a variety of non-verbal activities, and that this can subsequently lead to the development of positive attitudes.

As Coyle, Holmes and King recognise (2009), support for learners can take a variety of different forms; indeed, they make the point that CLIL provision will combine appropriate pedagogical approaches from both subject areas. In the pirate project it was apparent that good practice in dance was not at odds with promoting effective language acquisition in any way. In the words of Teacher 2;

There were lots of opportunities to try things again, to reinforce, and it was good to have the teacher modelling at the front . . . I think that worked very well that they had the visual stimulus at the beginning.

This project set out to investigate the impact of learning languages through the context of dance and to consider pupils' responses to engaging in dance when taught through the foreign language. Pupils were generally positive in their response to the initiative and showed good retention and recall of the language encountered. Combining the two areas ensured provision at least for the duration of the project and undoubtedly added status to the subjects: 'I'm a PE specialist so I love the opportunity to give PE and dance a slightly higher standing than some of the more academic subjects . . .' (Teacher 2). In this particular instance the project was taught by visiting specialists in both areas whereas these are subjects often taught by non-specialist class teachers who may lack confidence to deliver both MFL and dance; these issues of language competency are acknowledged in the MLPSI (NCAA, 2008). Nevertheless this project should raise the possibility of different ways in which to integrate foreign languages effectively into the primary curriculum.

With thanks to staff and pupils from Castle Primary School (Portchester).

REFERENCES

Anderson, G with Arsenault, N. (1998) *Fundamentals of Educational Research* (2nd edition). London: Routledge Farmer.

Asher, J., Kusudo, J.A. and De la Torre, R. (1974) Learning a second language through commands: the second field test, *The Modern Language Journal*, 58:1–2, 24–32.

Baddeley, A. (1997) *Human Memory: Theory and Practice* (revised edition). Hove: Psychology Press.

Baddeley, A. (2003) Working memory and language: an overview. *Journal of Communication Disorders* 36: 3, 189–208.

Baddeley, A.D. and Hitch, G.J. (1974) Working memory. *In Recent Advances in Learning and Motivation*, vol. 8, ed. Bower, G.A. 47–90. New York: Academic Press.

Barton, A., Bragg, J. and Serratrice, L. (2009) 'Discovering Language' in primary school: an evaluation of a language awareness programme, *The Language Learning Journal*, 37:2, 145–164.

Best, D. (1992) *The Rationality of Feeling: Understanding the Arts in Education*. London: Falmer Press.

Cable, C., Driscoll, P., Mitchell, R., Sing, S., Cremin, T., Earl, J., Eyres, I., Holmes, B., Martin, C, with Heins, B. (2010) *Languages Learning at Key Stage 2 – A Longitudinal Study Final Report*. London: DCSF.

Cohen, L. and Manion, L. (1994) *Research Methods in Education* (4th Edition). London: Routledge.

Coyle, D., Holmes, B. and King, L. (2009) *Towards an Integrated Curriculum – CLIL National Statement and Guidelines*. London: The Languages Company.

Crichton, H. and Templeton, B. (2010) Curriculum for Excellence: the way forward for primary languages in Scotland? *The Languages Learning Journal*, 38:2, 139–147.

Cultural Learning Alliance (2017) Imagine Nation, https://culturallearningalliance.org.uk/about-us/imaginenation-the-value-of-cultural-learning/. Last accessed 12 January 2018.

Dalton-Puffer, C. and Nikula, T. (2014) Content and Language Integrated Learning, *The Language Learning Journal*, 42:2, 117–122.

Dearing, R. and King, L. (2007) *Languages Review*. Annesley: DfES.

Department for Education (2013) *National Curriculum in England – Languages Programme of Study*.

Department for Education and Skills (2005) *The Key Stage 2 Framework for Languages*.

Doiz, A., Lasagabaster, D. and Sierra, J.M. (2014) CLIL and motivation: the effect of individual and contextual variables, *The Language Learning Journal*, 42:2, 209–224.

Driscoll, P., Jones, J., Martin, C., Graham-Matheson, L., Dismore, H. and Sykes, R. (2004) A systematic review of the characteristics of effective foreign language teaching to pupils between the ages 7 and 11, *Research Evidence in Education Library*. London: EPPI-Centre.

Edwards, A. and Talbot, R. (1994) *The Hard-pressed Researcher*. Harlow: Longman.

Enever, J. and Watts, C. (2009) Primary Foreign Language Pathfinders: the Brighton and Hove experience, *The Language Learning Journal*, 37:2, 219–232.

Graham, S., Macfadyen, T. and Richards, B. (2012) Learners' perceptions of being identified as very able: insights from Modern Foreign Languages and Physical Education, *Journal of Curriculum Studies*, 44:3, 323–348.

Greenwood, R. (2013) Subject-based and cross-curricular approaches within the revised primary curriculum in Northern Ireland: teachers' concerns and preferred approaches, *Education 3–13*, 41:4, 443–458.

Hall, T. (2008) *The Dance Review. A Report to Government on Dance Education and Youth Dance in England*. London: DCSF.

Hanna, J.L. (2001) The Language of Dance, *Journal of Physical Education, Recreation and Dance*, 72:4, 40–45.

Hayes, D. (2010) The seductive charms of a cross-curricular approach, *Education 3–13*, 38:4, 381–387.

Johnstone, R. (2003) Evidence-based policy: early modern language learning at primary, *The Language Learning Journal*, 28:1, 14–21.

Jones, J. and Coffey, S. (2006) *Modern Foreign Languages 5–11 A Guide for Teachers*. London: David Fulton Publishers.

Kelly, S.D., McDevitt, T. and Esch, M. (2009). Brief training with co-speech gesture lends a hand to word learning in a foreign language. *Language and Cognitive Processes*, 204:2, 313–334.

Kirsch, C. (2016) Using story-telling to teach vocabulary in language lessons: does it work? *The Language Learning Journal*, 44:1, 33–51.

Lamb, P. (2016) Fostering a passion for languages through physical education, *Physical Education Matters*, 11:1, 65–69.

Lamb, T. and Fisher, J. (1999) Making connections: football, the internet and reluctant language learners, *The Language Learning Journal*, 20:1, 32–36.

Legg, K. (2013) An investigation into teachers' attitudes towards the teaching of modern foreign languages in the primary school, *Education 3–13*, 41:1, 55–62.

Magill, R. (2011) *Motor Learning and Control*. New York: McGraw-Hill International.

Martin, C. (2002) Children's views about encountering a variety of foreign languages in the primary school, *Education 3–13*, 30:1, 52–57.

McCall, I. (2011) Score in French: motivating boys with football in Key Stage 3, *The Language Learning Journal*, 39:1, 5–18.

McFee, G. (1994) *The Concept of Dance in Education*. London: Routledge.

McLachlan, A. (2009) Modern languages in the primary curriculum: are we creating conditions for success? *The Language Learning Journal*, 37:2, 183–203.

Mearns, T.L. (2012) Using CLIL to enhance pupils' experience of learning and raise attainment in German and health education: a teacher research project, *The Language Learning Journal*, 40:2, 175–192.

Montet, M. and Morgan, C. (2001) Teaching Geography through a foreign language: how to make text accessible to learners at different levels, *The Language Learning Journal*, 24:1, 4–11.

Moore, P. and Lorenzo, F. (2015) Task-based learning and content and language integrated learning materials design: process and product, *The Language Learning Journal*, 43:3, 334–357.

Muijs, D., Barnes, A., Hunt, M., Powell, B., Arweck, E., Lindsay, G. and Martin, C. (DfES) (2005) *Evaluation of the Key Stage 2 Language Learning Pathfinders*, University of Warwick.

National Council for Curriculum and Assessment (NCCA) (2008) *Modern Languages in the Primary School Curriculum – Feasibility and Futures*, Dublin.

OFSTED (2011) *Modern Languages – Achievement and Challenge 2007–2010*.

OneDance UK (2017) *Dance Education, a Guide for Governors and Trustees Providing High Quality Dance Education in Schools:* OneDanceUK, Arts Council England & National Governors' Association (NGA).

Porter, A. (2016) A helping hand with language learning: teaching French vocabulary with gesture, *The Language Learning Journal*, 44:2, 236–256.

Satchwell, P. (2006) Languages in our primary schools – putting the National Languages Strategy into practice, *The Languages Learning Journal*, 34:1, 47–54.

Sharpe, K. (2001) *Modern Foreign Languages in the Primary School – the What, Why and How of Early MFL teaching*. London: Kogan Page.

Siddall, J. (2010) *Dance in Schools and Beyond – Report for Youth Dance England*.

Smith-Autard, J. (2002) *The Art of Dance in Education*. (2nd edition) London: A & C Black.

Stern, E. and Schaffer, K. (2012) Math dance: Erik Stern and Karl Schaffer at TEDxManhattan Beach. www.youtube.com/watch?v=Ws2y-cGoWqQ. Last accessed 12 January 2018.

Tellier, M. (2008). The effect of gestures on second language memorisation by young children, *Gesture* 8:2, 219–235.

Tierney, D. and Gallastegi, L. (2011) The attitudes of the pupils towards modern languages in the primary school (MLPS) in Scotland, *Education 3–13*, 39:5, 483–498.

Tinsley, T. and Board, K. (2017) *Language Trends 2016/17 – Language Teaching in Primary and Secondary schools in England Survey Report*, British Council.

Van Kampen, E., Admiraal, W. and Berry, A. (2016) Content and language integrated learning in the Netherlands: teachers' self-reported pedagogical practices, *International Journal of Bilingual Education and Bilingualism*, March 7, 1–15.

Wingate, U. (2016) Lots of games and little challenge – a snapshot of modern foreign language teaching in English secondary schools, *The Language Learning Journal*, June 7, 1–14.

CHAPTER 8

TEACHING THE YOUNGEST LEARNERS

Kristina Tobutt and Philip Hood

INTRODUCTION

In this chapter we look at issues surrounding teaching languages to the 'youngest children' and naturally the first point is to define what we mean by that target group. If we consider the term 'early childhood education' we will already find discrepancies between, for example, the Organisation for Economic Co-operation and Development (OECD) (up to 8 years old) and England (up to 5 years old). As the book is intended to be relevant to more than a UK readership we will use the OECD definition and so the chapter will refer also to the first 2 years of compulsory education in England, in other words up to 7 years old. This is the age group that in England and Wales is not subject to the National Curriculum specification regarding language teaching. In Scotland language learning is recommended from 5 years old while in Northern Ireland primary language learning is recommended rather than required.

HOW DOES THIS AGE GROUP LEARN?

At any age, but especially in the first years of life, we should always start from the child and consider their learning needs as a whole, not just by subject. We should recall as Fisher points out (2013:1) that:

> Before starting statutory schooling at the age of 5, young children have developed a range of skills, knowledge and understanding at a speed that will never again be repeated in their lives.

What does a teacher intending to introduce active and creative second or foreign language teaching to a 4 year old need to put at the heart of the pedagogy? We will consider this in terms of language learning shortly but initially it is vital to think beyond that. At the heart of any learning by young children is the need for a special blend of guidance and independence, of connections and tangents (which are personal connections for individuals), of multimodal experiential learning. And at the centre of all of those is a set of highly positive and warm teacher-child and child-child relationships. Attachment theory (Bowlby 1999) makes very clear how young children will usually develop a secondary attachment figure after a prime carer and how an Early Years practitioner is very likely to become such a person. Gillanders (2007:48), researching the integration of Spanish-speaking children into an English medium class, noted: 'During the course of the study, I found that Sarah was concerned primarily with establishing a positive relationship with the children.'

Children do not hold subject-based timetables in their schematic view of how they spend their time but react to what is stimulating, engaging and therefore enjoyable moment to moment. Although UK government guidance on Early Years' education currently tends towards greater formalisation, for example as in Bold Beginnings (DfE 2017), there is still a strong belief among many practitioners that the classroom week should consist of more child-initiated than teacher-led activity. This makes planning a complex activity as teachers need to decide how best to create a learning environment where child-initiated activity will be positive, fruitful and developmental and not simply by default turn into teacher-directed tasks. Young children like to know where they are, who they are with and what they are doing in a sense that they feel a secure base within which they can explore and be creative. The continuum that operates from fully teacher-centred, teacher-led to completely child-initiated has many steps and shades of steps. Within this context Fisher (2013:6) points out a need for routine and repetition according to what we know about brain-based learning:

> In the early years of education, it is crucial that young learners have opportunities for the constant reinforcement of experiences, skills and understandings in order for repetition to forge secure pathways of learning in the brain.

This means that a mixture of fresh stimulation (i.e. the new) and safe reinforcement (i.e. the familiar) are both important to young children. Continuous provision as well as enhanced resources and the use of hooks to ensure surprise and challenge help to make this blend of the two main modes of operation more subtle.

Additionally, alongside the Areas of Learning and Characteristics of Effective Learning (Early Education 2012), which effectively make up the early childhood education curriculum, the facilitation and nurturing of the skills of self-regulation is seen by all involved as a significant element both of development and preparation for more formal learning. In fact the importance of developing self-regulation for children aged 2 to 5 years unusually unites all involved in the phase: policy makers, practitioners and researchers; the OECD even includes this in its scheme for an Early Years Programme for International Student Assessment (PISA)-style testing programme, itself a deeply contentious issue as is assessment for this age range in general. We will address this theme later in the chapter. The skill of creating structures and routines for children while in school but not making over-rigorous or rigid timetables is a key element of good practice. In a research inquiry report Robson (2016) shows that children's skills of self-regulation and metacognition can benefit from both teacher and child-initiated modes but that (ibid.:780) 'Child-initiated activities very often provided the richest opportunities for children to both develop and display their self-regulation and metacognition'. This element certainly impacts on the daily lives of practitioners as they address issues that arise from emotional self-regulation. Routines provide a very fruitful way of creating what we call 'natural repetition' also of content and conceptual items as well as of skills. They also make behaviour management easier to keep in the background and not to be juxtaposed with the more creative agenda.

All of the above is the core of the provision for the age group, whatever they are learning and we should remember this when moving to address language learning specifically,

WHAT DOES THIS MEAN FOR LANGUAGES IN THE CURRICULUM?

We should underline, therefore, that, in the light of the first sections of this chapter a teacher is a teacher of those children rather than a teacher of French or Spanish or German. Supporting this linking, The European Commission (2011) produced a report on pre-school language learning and concluded (ibid.:7): 'Young children's second/foreign language acquisition is similar in many ways to the acquisition of their first language/mother tongue, which is natural and effortless.' They also stated (ibid.:10): 'Experience shows that young children acquire languages in an intuitive way (unconscious learning), for example through listening and creative exploration stimulated by curiosity.'

The Goethe Institute produced a document in 2010 known as the Nürnberg recommendations, which in a translation provided by Scottish CILT (www.scilt.org.uk/ Portals/24/Library/oneplustwo/Key%20messages%20for%20Primary_Nuremberg.pdf) includes the following that is worth quoting in full:

> Children's spontaneity and lack of inhibition make them exceptionally capable of enthusiasm and quick to join in playful activity. Their normal abundance of curiosity, their urge to explore, readiness to learn and capacity to absorb should all be turned to good use in the form of practical, activity-oriented learning and experimentation.
>
> Children are strongly focused on the here and now, on direct, tangible experience. In a non-target language environment they need to be motivated in ways that make sense to them.
>
> If children are to understand, material must be presented to them in terms of tangible realities that they can visualise. Until they have reached a certain age, they cannot cope with abstract concepts. Situational and action-linked stimulus material and learning procedures are accordingly of key importance for their learning attainment and their pleasure in learning.
>
> Children are able to concentrate for short periods; playful means should be sought to address and further develop their usually good memory powers.
>
> Children's fundamentally open-minded attitude invites an engagement with intercultural topics.

This leads naturally into the themes we have noted above; taking, first, the teacher- and child-initiated issue, we might conclude that if we consider language learning to be more strongly balanced in the teacher-led direction, we already have a dilemma! Of course the children need to 'meet language' (Hood and Tobutt 2015) and this is probably organised by the teacher. But whether it needs to be highly structured by the teacher, using say and repeat techniques perhaps centring on single word items such as numbers, colours, family members, parts of the body etc., is open to question and for this age group probably inappropriate. We spoke above of 'natural repetition' that is also explained for language learning in Hood and Tobutt (2015). The kinds of repetition that we sometimes associate with language learning may not fit with this and we will be looking at what comprises a more subtle model throughout this chapter. It follows also that we are not talking about a discrete skills model either. The rather innovative Key Stage 2 Framework (DfES 2005, 2007) notably identified the three strands: oracy, literacy and intercultural understanding as its core elements. The first and last of these are the key aspects to emphasise in early language learning, as literacy skills will follow when children are individually ready.

HOW MIGHT THIS LOOK?

We can illustrate some of this thinking through two practice examples. The first is of a class of 18 children aged 2 to 3 years old starting a school setting in January and attending afternoons only. After 6 weeks they start to learn French. What is the first activity? Perhaps surprisingly the experienced teacher opts to use the commercial DVD *Mon Âne* (Le Notre 2012) (www.folimage.fr/fr/production/mon-ane-86.htm) and so the children watch, hear and gradually make some global sense of an authentic French children's song (*Alouette*). While they watch it they smile, laugh, point things out to each other, and, where they can, begin to join in with the song. They ask to watch it again a couple of times because they really like it and so they begin, to differing degrees, to start forming French words in near native pronunciation because they are imitating and know no different. This is all completely age-appropriate and even relatively at their own cognitive level.

In the second example, children of 4–5 years old who are still well within their first year of French listen to an authentic French picture book (*Va-t-en, Grand Monstre Vert*, Emberley 1996) being read by the teacher and they gradually join in, even hearing and beginning to use two grammatically different ways of saying 'Go away!' (*Va-t-en* and *partez!*). This draws in various parts of the head and face as the monster is built up and then dismantled. Later, on the same afternoon, they assemble a face for a dragon mask associated with Chinese New Year and start to use the face/head vocabulary for themselves (while also practising where things go on a face!) before making one for themselves around a table with the teacher who only uses French for all of the instructions.

In this second example, by the end of this sequence of activities the children are no longer conscious of whether they are hearing French or English. They hear language, make sense of it and act on it. The analogies we made in the second chapter of this volume apply especially to this age group.

WHAT IS THE BACKGROUND TO THIS APPROACH?

If we now think specifically about examples of second language acquisition research that appear to have influenced mainstream language teaching, then possibly the work of Krashen will be central either because of what he said or as a result of what was argued against him. Cameron (2001), Pinter (2006) and Kirsch (2008) all address the role of the use of target language and what Krashen (1982) named 'comprehensible input' (i.e. purposeful and meaningful messages). This links to the debate about how close foreign language learning is, or is not, to first language acquisition and indeed Krashen (ibid.), although working more in a bilingual and second (rather than foreign) language context, explored the difference between acquisition and learning as two different processes, a distinction that we are actively referring to in this chapter. Taking the first of those threads we can say with near certainty that the drivers of first language acquisition (intense curiosity, a desire and in fact a need to make meaning and to communicate) can usefully be aroused also in second or foreign language learning. Writers on language learning usually consider that the target language can be used as the major means of teaching as long as it is used in that purposeful way, as we showed in Chapter 3 of this book. The challenge came to the Krashen (1982) view that, simply by doing that, acquisition would be enabled when others (e.g. Swain 1995, 2000) researched the role that language production (oral or written) has in securing the language in long-term memory. In other words acquisition occurred when learners both met and used/produced the language.

All of the above points towards an approach that does not centre on small discrete blocks of vocabulary taught as 'topics' such as colours or numbers. In the 2–5 years age range in nursery or school settings these topics when handled in first language are contextualised. Teachers do not hold up objects or blocks of colour and ask for the colour, but are more likely (if they do at all) to ask a child to choose a red object relating to a broader topic they are engaged in, or look around the room for something blue. While numbers as visual figures may need to be practised and memorised, real counting needs to be done for a reason and involve a mathematical process not just a recitation of words. This points more towards locating any such language themes inside activities such as singing and storytelling, and inside connected sentences rather than word lists. The other principal area and a major route into early language learning are the *routines* that we referred to as being a core element of learning for these children. An important part of what they do is contribute to the development of self-regulation (e.g. Pintrich and Zusho 2002; Whitebread *et al.* 2009) that would include skills such as turn-taking and empathy, which language learning can support. Additionally routines are about healthy reinforcement of knowledge, skills and behaviours. Good Early Years practitioners intuitively understand the blend of regular repetition, especially of social routines (that are inevitably teacher-led/imposed), and activity that leads to the development of independence and creativity – just as children like the re-reading of favourite stories so they feel secure and safe in the context of a familiar start to a day, a repeated aspect of timetable such as snack time or tidy-up time, of a shared and rotated responsibility such as special person, of weekly events such as the sharing of a 'family-box' of items of importance to the child whose turn it is to share. All of these form the fundamental structure of the curriculum and the collaborative shared life of the class and have a sense of meaning and depth beyond just the classroom instructions/management language that also forms part of the routines element. And all of this, in terms of the teacher language at least, can be slowly moved into the additional language to a greater or lesser extent and over time because it is part of the fabric and children will have quickly internalised it almost as bilingual children do from birth.

Bruner's (1966) separation of modes of learning into enactive, iconic and symbolic is especially relevant here both because of the age of the children and of the nature of language and its development. This points to using real objects and staying with concrete concepts, using visual material to scaffold extended talk and especially any more abstract ideas, and avoiding unsupported written language. It also echoes a little Piaget and Cook's (1952) developmental stages, which although challenged (e.g. Baillargeon and DeVos 1991) in terms of their rigidity to ages, nevertheless represent a linearity that supports our work with younger children, notably warning against too much abstraction with our age range. In fact, most of what a practitioner does with young children is simultaneously visual and non-verbal as well as strongly verbal in a consciously fashioned way, as this is how comprehension is assured and a good model of language given. So it follows very naturally that the 'normal' way of behaving and making shared meaning with the class fits admirably in an additional language (as Chapter 2 demonstrated).

SOME PRACTICE EXAMPLES OF THE ROLE OF ROUTINES

Consider a 3 year old starting school and encountering the notion of tidying at the end of the morning for the first time as this has not been identified as a shared task at home. As the teacher asks the class to start tidying and perhaps sings a song or plays a piece of music that regularly accompanies this daily event, the child will be learning the concept of tidying along with the word for it. It is wrong to assume that a child needs to know a concept first in L1 before gaining the word in L2. It can happen in the opposite direction. If something like the song *'Faut ranger!'* is used (obtainable from French Pinterest at https://fr.pinterest.com/pin/443112050807878481/), then at first the music will be associated with the new idea of tidying and gradually the individual words. If the teacher mimes while singing and encourages children to imitate this will also be comprehended and may later become active.

This is likely to be a daily task so repetition in a positive way is assured and there does not need to be a time limit on when aspects of this are learned. Certainly in terms of more active productive use this will vary enormously across classes of 3–5 year olds,

All teachers tend to use a range of strategies to gain attention and these can involve clapping rhythms, counting down or simple signals such as a raised arm. The Spanish class routines available at www.pinterest.es/pin/302022718744640864/ can be turned into songs quite easily and share a format for different types of class activities, e.g. coming to the carpet. The important (if rather obvious) rationale of using the additional language for the very mundane regular routines of the classroom is clear: by definition these occur regularly so the repetition is entirely natural and expected; the frequency also fixes the language initially as a 'set phrase' but with skilful slight variations the teacher can start to make children think about more subtle meanings as they sense a difference and notice it; and, above all, because these are meaningful/purposeful (if sometimes resented!) messages, so the language has the status of being a necessary communication tool and not just a 'thing to learn'.

THE ROLE OF SONGS

Earlier in the chapter we mentioned stories and songs and the supply of these is virtually limitless. When we talked to children across a primary school after 3 months of learning French once a week (they had all started learning French at the same time after the appointment of a languages teacher for PPA cover), the Reception focus group patiently answered the researcher's questions but asked rather insistently if they could sing some of the songs they had learned for him. And once they had started they didn't want to stop. Why do music and perhaps especially the use of songs enable language learning? In a doctoral dissertation (Lowe 2000) from a Canadian setting, a small experimental group made significantly more progress in both French oral and reading skills as well as in the Music curriculum when the subjects were combined. de Groot (2006) found that for some learners vocabulary was learned better when the process was accompanied by background music. In an interesting article addressing very young children's language acquisition, Schön *et al.* (2008) established that songs enable language acquisition perhaps because of the emotional/motivational factor but also because, through their structuring of the lines of the song, they help to show the gaps between words, i.e. identifying what are separate words within the flow. There is also the element of emphasis and intonation helping to shape this structure. They state (ibid. 982): 'Therefore, learning a foreign language, especially in the first learning phase wherein one needs to segment new words, may largely benefit from the motivational and structuring properties of music in song.' Kao and Oxford (2014) documented a personal experience of using music to learn language. Very recently researchers in Finland (Alisaari and Heikkola 2016, 2017) have looked in depth at the support given by singing (as opposed to listening to songs) and found that it enabled better receptive learning of structures and even increased written fluency. The vignette about the Reception children wanting to sing to the researcher shows how motivating they had found singing and probably how purposeful it seemed; they clearly benefited from exposure to connected text rather than single words. Interestingly, the Finnish researchers also found that teachers believe singing to be effective even if they do not always use it much in their practice. In the light of that last finding they argue that singing should be emphasised more in teacher training for language teaching. In our experience too, young children enjoy singing enormously and it might sometimes be teacher reluctance or lack of confidence that inhibits the greater use of this aspect of musical support for language learning. In all of this it is important that songs and stories are authentic, from target language-speaking countries and, as long as they are visually supported, do not need any vocabulary pre-teaching. This is the best way to encourage children to start to use the language actively.

However, there is a jump between singing simple songs such as children's nursery rhyme-equivalents and using more challenging and possibly age-appropriate material with the children in KS1. For the first set, clearly, a search of sites such as YouTube using the additional language search term is the most effective way of locating simple song material quickly. For example for German the song *Backe Backe Kuchen* www.youtube.com/watch?v=gtGHoYldnME contains a three times repetition of a nine-line song, is subtitled (although in uppercase letters) and is visually clear. In the case of this example the song actually underpins a topic (baking cakes and the ingredients needed). It also starts a mix of similar songs aimed at young children if you subscribe without charge to that channel. These songs are very quick to learn and many are familiar. Similarly, http://emp3i.down load/play/950AAFXgivk/un-elefante-se-balanceaba-canci%C3%B3n-infantil-heykids.html has a set of songs in Spanish for younger children with the lyrics on screen as subtitles – this does require some effort from the teacher to interpret where would be good for a 'joining in' sequence, but again will prove popular with some children who will start to 'read' the words from the screen and sing along more independently. This material can also be downloaded as mp3 for audio only or as mp4 video.

If we then wish to move beyond the nursery rhyme format then other searches can equally easily quickly produce material that will be popular. You can do this by topic or by name of story, film, song, author etc. For example, www.youtube.com/watch?v=3f BvwINDEcE is a Spanish version of the 'I'll Make a Man Out of You' song from Disney's

Mulan for the 7 year olds while www.youtube.com/watch?v=PoKMn2Pk0Dc is 'Let it Go' from Disney's *Frozen* for younger children who are usually very impressed that Elsa knows Spanish too! We are not suggesting that the children will learn these songs off by heart or will understand them word for word of course, but the lyrics are obtainable too (e.g. for *Frozen* see http://lyricstranslate.com/en/%C2%A1sueltalo-let-it-go-let-it-go-let-it-go.html) and the teacher can choose a chorus line or something else that is manageable for joining in. The more able/interested will find ways of doing more if encouraged.

www.youtube.com/watch?v=0UPoBSvmzuo features a song ('*C'est les vacances*') recorded a long time ago by a French 11-year-old, Ilona Mitrecey, and which would be a good one for the summer term of Year 2. The lyrics are here and contain some very good vocabulary and some useful repetition:

www.allthelyrics.com/lyrics/ilona_mitrecey/cest_les_vacances-lyrics-836502.html.

Again this also leads into a mix of songs by the same artist, all of which are challenging lyrically but have memorable melody lines and are mostly very lively and generate enthusiasm from children listening to them.

READING, WRITING AND PHONICS

If we think about other aspects of children's language and literacy development at the age of 2 to 5 years and then forward to 7 years, one constant feature is phonics teaching. It is not that phonics should provide a model for foreign language learning and certainly not that we should 'do phonics' in the foreign language at this time. Indeed, given that 'English is the most inconsistent language in the world in terms of the consistency of letter–sound correspondences' (Goswami 2005:281), we could argue that doing phonics in another language simultaneously would be unhelpful to the overall process of learning to read as a technical skill. But because phonics teaching is ever present it does provide one model for the intense pacey interactive but teacher-led style of activity that is often associated with language teaching and learning. Additionally, and more importantly in our view, it consists initially of a lot of activity centred on phonological awareness about which Kirby, Parilla and Pfeiffer 2003:453 state: 'There is considerable evidence that phonological awareness (PA), the awareness of the sound structure of words and the ability to manipulate sounds in words, is a key component in the development of reading ability.'

This site, http://enseignant-ados-autistes.over-blog.com/pages/La_phonologie-5835568.html, also first accessed via French Pinterest, has sets of visuals (mainly of animals) that split these common vocabulary items. Although this does not use a synthetic phonics approach, the setting up of the onsets of each word means children can focus on producing an accurate first sound and may (with crab, tiger and snake) lead to some guesswork about the completion. The matching, although simple visually, will enable the children to 'discover' the complete word with a focus on the reading and pronunciation (with teacher support). This is appropriate for the top end of our age range, who at 7 years will have mostly completed their phonics stages in English, and shows that reading can involve some fun and simple problem-solving. Although we would not want to overdo the technique, it clearly can be used again with other sets of words as the children encounter new topics.

CROSS-CURRICULAR INITIATIVES

As we have said throughout the chapter (and the book), rooting the language learning in the child's whole experience is the best way to show pupils that additional languages belong to life and can be part of theirs. The linking with active subjects that allow children to move or create is a strong model in the early stages as this does not require them to produce language. For example, children enjoy 'making' activities (e.g. mask making) and also engaging in physical activities, e.g. following a trim trail, and all of these can be triggered by instructions in the target language that they will internalise quickly as they are applied to real actions and outcomes. In this way their exposure to language is entirely authentic, purposeful and simple, but also natural language can be used at all times, constituting a good model of Krashen's comprehensible input. Some children will start to respond in L2 but this is not something teachers of young children need to 'push', but to notice and encourage when it occurs.

The European Commission report from 2011 identified good practice projects – one of which, from Oviedo in Spain, the 'CLIL Collaborative Project Work at Early Ages' (which won European Language prizes in 2005 and 2009), summarised itself as involving:

■ Use English in everyday school life as a usual way of communication.
■ Learn language and content in an integrated and holistic way, making the projects cross-curricular.
■ Work through collaborative projects of very different kind (Opera, Dinosaurs, the Space, Health, We're the same/different, Books, Plants, Bread, Potatoes, Milk, etc.).
■ Promote autonomous and active learning.
■ Bring the world into the classroom and take the classroom out into the world.

KEY ACTIVITIES

Photo books – related activities, songs, rhymes, chants, TPR activities, art and craft activities
Ángela Álvarez-Cofiño Martínez: C.P. Bilingüe (Bilingual Public School) Ventanielles – Oviedo – Asturias
http://ec.europa.eu/dgs/education_culture/repository/languages/policy/language-policy/documents/ellp-handbook_en.pdf

Linked to this is the use of what we refer to elsewhere as simple decision-making tasks that help children engage with material in the foreign language and do something with it (no matter how simple) that involves thinking. As thinking is the basis of learning, a simple decision about something they see is the best starting point. A commercial resource that features this approach, and which was mostly aimed at Year 3/Year 4 but can be adapted for KS1, is *A La Française* (originally published by Authentik, now obtainable from Little Linguist). The simplest item in that collection is a PowerPoint in which the children must identify likely places for a butterfly to be on the French-speaking island La Réunion. Each slide asks *Où est le papillon?* The children only need to say they think it is there (in a house, on the beach, in the volcano!) or not. This exercise makes them familiar with some key vocabulary connected to an islands topic and also involves them looking at a map of the island, so underpinning their Geography in English curriculum. One class using these materials produced some quite accurate maps of the island and some labelled some of the sites mentioned in the PowerPoint. The intercultural understanding strand of the previous KS2 Framework mentioned earlier is a very important part of language learning although with younger children we always need to consider their life experience and their difficulty in understanding more abstract material including distance and very different contexts. Sometimes looking for similarities across cultures is the best starting point and the video material contained, for example in the *Early Start* packs (available in French, German and Spanish), give short simple child-centred views of everyday life in a range of countries where the languages are spoken. Even if conversation about this happens in English, this is still valuable exposure to other ways of shopping, eating, playing, living. The ideas behind Content Language Integrated Learning (CLIL) (Coyle, Hood and Marsh 2010) are usually thought to be for use with older children but if we consider the first language development of young children and the way they learn language while learning about other things and the second language development of young children who are learning two sets of ways of talking about the phenomena that interest them, then this is the same as CLIL. Or CLIL is the same as these processes.

WHAT ABOUT 'NORMAL' LANGUAGE TEACHING APPROACHES?

It may seem strange to leave the more conventionally 'expected' types of activity to late in the chapter but it was important to foreground whole-language and language-rich approaches as the mainstay of early provision. Nevertheless, of course there is room for some more discrete activity based on the topics teachers feel children should learn and in which (we hope) the children also express an interest. This is not to say we should simply teach repetitively a set of single word colours, numbers, animals, foods etc. but clearly such items need to be known and can sometimes be the content of simple games. These should be as interactive as possible and can form the type of sequence as follows:

Teacher starter activity:

T – *Les couleurs en français – qui ici connait une couleur?*
C – (Children suggest any colours they know in French – if they have already learned to say *je voudrais* then they can be scaffolded to say *je voudrais dire 'blue'* and can be given the French for this).

[NB Teacher regularly uses a 'memory' whiteboard in French (with an elephant at the top to remind children that's what it's for) – she or he writes colour words here emphasising the initial sound/grapheme only – this is not a reading expectation, but a quick way of operating a checklist. Teacher can organise these in different ways, for example as a rainbow, in alphabetical order, colours a dog can or cannot be etc.]

> T – *Ma couleur préférée est le bleu. Et toi, Chantelle?*
> P – *(Le) rouge* [sentence not expected but praised if given] + others volunteer.
> T – *OK, faisons un graphique (un diagramme en bâtons) pour les couleurs préférées de la classe.*
>
> After this has been created and commented on, children do pair work – guess the favourite colour of three other children.

This is structured so the focus is very much on the single word colours but it is wrapped up in richer (but still very simple and manageable) talk from the teacher. The children are asked to think, remember, notice and it should be considered completely acceptable for them to learn what they can and what they wish to at this early stage.

ASSESSMENT

Earlier in the chapter we mentioned assessment. This is a rather challenging area for the age group and there are a number of discussions current at the time of writing that may have been resolved by the time the chapter is read, but essentially an ongoing disagreement between different factions highlights the reliability issue of any kind of testing other than observation over time for the 2–5 years age group. This certainly holds true for second language learning. Children of this age sometimes remember things and sometimes forget them, are sometimes tired and sometimes intensely focused. Second language acquisition should be seen as a gradual progress over time with observational noting of what children say, understand, ask, engage with and do (for example, in child-initiated play including role play). A child who independently asks peers to say '*Merci*' rather than 'thank you' when she distributes fruit, using the French words, has internalised aspects of the language and that is meaningful. A child who independently reads a foreign language book he has heard being read by the teacher, even if no real decoding is happening (and even if the book is upside down!) is demonstrating engagement with the notion of additional languages; his experience of the book and his meaning construction of the story has been through using that other language, not through English, and that represents successful contact with it. It is probably unnecessary to say this to Early Years/primary practitioners but this should certainly *not* lead to a vocabulary test on the topic vocabulary! Games with visuals such as 'Guess the next card' or 'Beat the Teacher' games (where the class repeats a word or phrase if it matches a visual but is silent if not and the first to five points wins) will be very popular with KS1 and can be tried with Reception Year small groups as well. It may be difficult to contemplate that we are not talking about a checklist of vocabulary, skills and defined 'knowledge' as an outcome of early language learning, but rather a demonstration of engagement, interest, pleasure in learning and a willingness to construct meaning and sometimes express it. All of these are competencies that can be noted in the Early Years Foundation Stage (EYFS) Learning Journey format and illustrated with photos, sound or video recordings or examples of 'work'. All of these are the features of a foundation for further learning as the child grows older. For this age group, playing with the additional language is likely to be a strong indicator of potential motivation to engage a little more formally during KS2. Talking in a first language about cultural experiences with the additional language is also of great importance and should also be logged as evidence of achievement in the languages area of learning.

CONCLUSIONS

It may have been surprising to read in this chapter that we should start with whole-language and not with isolated vocabulary with the youngest learners, but we hope not. Children of this age are intensely curious and open-minded and spend their whole days constructing meaning from the multitude of messages they receive. Dipping into a flow of communication and coming out with new ideas, new ways of saying something, new opinions and often with more to add to their repertoire of humour is their natural way of being. This is why we must offer them chances to experience combinations of tastes and textures and not single dishes to bite on with the advice that eating it will do them good. This is not the easy ride for the teacher that more focused vocabulary-based topics would give, but when did teachers of the 2–7 years age range ever have an easy ride?

REFERENCES

Alisaari, J. and Heikkola, L.M. (2016). Increasing fluency in L2 writing with singing. *Studies in Second Language Learning and Teaching* 6(2), 271–292.

Alisaari, J. and Heikkola, L.M. (2017). Songs and poems in the language classroom: Teachers' beliefs and practices *Teaching and Teacher Education*, 63, 231–242.

Baillargeon, R. and Devos, J. (1991). *Object Permanence in Young Infants: Further Evidence. Child Development*, 62(6), 1227–1246

Bowlby, J. (1999) [1969]. *Attachment. Attachment and Loss (vol. 1) (2nd ed.).* New York: Basic Books.

Bruner, J.S. (1966). *Towards a Theory of Instruction.* Cambridge, MA: Harvard University Press.

Cameron, L. (2001). *Teaching Languages to Young Learners.* Cambridge: Cambridge University Press.

Coyle, D., Hood, P. and Marsh, D. (2010). *CLIL: Content and Language Integrated Learning.* Cambridge: Cambridge University Press.

Department for Education (2017). *Bold beginnings: The Reception curriculum in a sample of good and outstanding primary schools.* www.gov.uk/government/publications/reception-curriculum-in-good-and-outstanding-primary-schools-bold-beginnings. Last accessed 9 January 2018.

Department for Education and Skills (2005). *Key Stage 2 Framework for Languages, Parts 1 and 2.* London: DfES.

Department for Education and Skills (2007). *Key Stage 2 Framework for Languages, Part 3.* London: DfES.

Early Education (2012). Development Matters in the EYFS. London: Early Education. www.foundationyears.org.uk/wp-content/uploads/2012/03/Development-Matters-FINAL-PRINT-AMENDED.pdf. Last accessed 9 January 2018.

Emberley, E. (1996). *Va-t-en Grans Monstre Vert.* Paris: Kaleidoscope.

European Commission (2011). Language learning at pre-primary school level: Making it efficient and sustainable: A policy handbook. http://ec.europa.eu/dgs/education_culture/repository/languages/policy/language-policy/documents/ellp-handbook_en.pdf. Last accessed 9 January 2018.

Fisher, J. (2013). *Starting from the Child.* Maidenhead: Open University Press.

Gillanders, C. (2007). An English-speaking prekindergarten teacher for young Latino children: Implications of the teacher-child relationship on second language learning. *Early Childhood Education Journal*, 35(1), 47–54.

Goswami, U. (2005). Synthetic phonics and learning to read: A cross-language perspective. *Educational Psychology in Practice*, 21(4), 273–282.

de Groot, A.M.B. (2006). Effects of stimulus characteristics and background music on foreign language vocabulary learning and forgetting. *Language Learning*, 56(3), 463–506.

Hood, P. and Tobutt, K. (2015). *Teaching Languages in the Primary School (2nd ed.).* London: Sage.

Kao, T, and Oxford, R.L. (2014). Learning language through music: A strategy for building inspiration and motivation. *System* 43, 114–120.

Kirby, J.R., Parrila, R.K. and Pfeiffer, S.L. (2003). Naming speed and phonological awareness as predictors of reading development. *Journal of Educational Psychology*, 95(3), 453–464.

Kirsch, C. (2008). *Teaching Foreign Languages in the Primary School.* London: Continuum.

Krashen, S. (1982). *Principles and Practices in Second Language Acquisition.* Oxford: Pergamon.

Le Notre, P. (2012). Mon Ane, DVD. www.folimage.fr/fr/production/mon-ane-86.htm. Last accessed 12 January 2018.

Lowe, A. (2000). The integration of music into the Core French second-language program: What can be achieved? *The Canadian Music Educator*, 41(3 & 4), 21–31.

Piaget, J. and Cook, M. (1952). *The Origins of Intelligence in Children.* New York: International University Press.

Pinter, A. (2006). *Teaching Young Language Learners* (Oxford Handbooks for Language Teachers). Oxford: Oxford University Press.

Pintrich, P.R. and Zusho, A. (2002). The development of academic self-regulation: The role of cognitive and motivational factors. In A. Wigfield and J.S. Eccles (Eds), *A Vol. in the Educational Psychology Series. Development of Achievement Motivation* (pp. 249–284). San Diego: Academic Press.

Robson, S. (2016). Self-regulation, metacognition and child- and adult-initiated activity: Does it matter who initiates the task? *Early Child Development and Care*, 186(5), 764–784.

Schön, D., Boyer, M., Moreno, S., Besson, M., Peretz, I. and Kolinsky, R. (2008). Songs as an aid for language acquisition. *Cognition*, 106(2), 975–983.

Swain, M. (1995). Three functions of output in second language learning. In G. Cook and B. Seidlhofer (Eds), *Principle and Practice in Applied Linguistics* (pp. 125–144). Oxford: Oxford University Press.

Swain, M. (2000). The output hypothesis and beyond: Mediating acquistion through collaborative dialogue. In J. Lantolf (Ed.), *Sociocultural Theory and Second Language Learning.* Oxford: Oxford University Press.

Tobutt, K. and Roche, C. (2007). *A La Française.* Dublin: Authentik.

Whitebread, D., Coltman, P., Pino Pasternak, D., Sangster, C., Grau, V., Bingham, S., Almeqdad, Q. and Demetriou, D. (2009). The development of two observational tools for assessing metacognition and self-regulated learning in young children. *Metacognition and Learning*, 4(1), 63–85.

| CHAPTER 9 | # CREATIVITY AROUND TRANSITION |

Katherine Richardson

INTRODUCTION

Many schools have identified transition as an area for development and, while many schools work very hard at their general transition practices, they have been facing much more complexity recently as the links between neighbourhood families of schools have become less fixed in the new educational climate. For both primary and secondary schools languages transition is a relatively new but growing issue as the number of primary schools teaching languages in the first decade of this century expanded. There is much diversity between primary schools (and often within primary schools) even to the point where the languages taught may differ between neighbouring schools. Good practice in transition benefits both children and also teachers who can gain professionally from collaborative work across both sides of the transition point. This chapter addresses common challenges to effective transition in creative ways both in terms of the structures which benefit the process but also through suggesting a range of exciting cross-phase projects which inspire children and show their receiving secondary schools their true capability.

BEING CREATIVE AROUND TRANSITION

Schools can work effectively to ease transition between phases and to develop teachers professionally by sharing practice. The chapter addresses commonly experienced issues in creative ways and suggests cross-phase projects that inspire children and show their receiving secondary schools their true capability.

Chapter focus

Creativity in this chapter is mainly conceptualised as being 'creativity in approach' at a macro level. Though the chapter provides some examples of creative approaches exemplified through transition activities, the chapter's understanding of creativity relates to the creative ways in which the primary to secondary school transition for languages is and might be organised and managed. To do this, first we take a moment to consider the broad issue and challenges of the primary to secondary school transition before exploring transition for languages in terms of research, policy and practice. The chapter adopts a positive approach, sharing a selection of examples from schools that range from steps taken by individual teachers to larger-scale initiatives involving a cluster or group of schools. It also seeks to encourage you, the reader, to probe and reflect on the practice you have observed in school and to consider what role you might play to support young learners as they make the transition from the primary languages classroom to the secondary languages classroom.

Some may think: 'that's all very well but why is transition such an issue?' The next section explores that very point, considering the general landscape of transition – namely, the challenges of the primary to secondary transition for all subjects before focusing on transition for languages.

CONTEXT: WHAT ARE THE ISSUES SURROUNDING THE PRIMARY TO SECONDARY SCHOOL TRANSITION?

Before we explore transition for languages and approaches to ensuring a smooth transition for students in languages, let us first consider transition in the broader sense to contextualise the situation for languages.

The research suggests that transition can be a stressful period for pupils (Evangelou *et al.*, 2008; Sutherland, 2010) and adversely affect both their social-emotional well-being and academic progress (Sutherland, 2010). Transition appears to be a problematic and challenging issue across the curriculum including PE (Capel, Zwozdiak-Myers and Lawrence, 2007) and music (Marshall and Hargreaves, 2008). Of course, the timing of the primary to secondary school transition clashes with adolescence and the hormonal and socio-emotional developments/challenges this brings, as highlighted again in a recent study (Burns, 2016).

One landmark study of transition was the government-funded 'Moving Classrooms project'. The study focused on pupils' progress at the Key Stage 2–3 transition but also considered the Key Stage 1–2 transition in the core subjects: English, Maths and Science. A key finding related to pupil performance: up to 40 per cent of pupils in the study experience a drop in motivation and a hiatus in progress in the year following their transfer to another school (Galton, Gray and Rudduck, 1999). In addition to a lack of pupil progress and a fall in motivation, often the result of repetition of content and insufficient cognitive challenge, the study identified boys as being more susceptible to experiencing a drop in attainment. It also makes a strong case for focusing on transitions between year groups in addition to those between key stages. As Hood and Tobutt (2015) argue, if this were the case for languages, with the well-documented challenges of boys' participation and attainment in languages (Barton and Downes 2003; McCall, 2011), this would be a very worrying prospect indeed.

The researchers in this seminal study identified a range of problems caused by ineffective transition that included the challenge of providing curriculum continuity and they also observed a discontinuity of pedagogy that they articulated as shift from the child-centred approach of the primary school to the subject-centred approach of the secondary school. This difference in pedagogical approach was later described by Sutherland *et al.* (2010:74) as a consequence of the fact that teachers from the two different phases originate from 'two tribes'.

WHAT ABOUT TRANSITION FOR LANGUAGES?

As explored below, the transition for languages appears to be particularly tricky. This section seeks to deepen understanding of transition in languages, through considering the context and exploring the complexity of the issue. The experiences of four children are used to illustrate this.

Recent reports and research have flagged up the primary to secondary transition (and some also the transfer between year groups or key stages) as an area of concern. One of the most recent of these was the Ofsted report: 'The Wasted Years' (2015). Some may think that transition for languages is a relatively new issue given the relatively recent introduction of languages as a compulsory subject in the National Curriculum (DfE, 2013) – though, importantly this does not extend to academies or free schools which are not obliged to follow the National Curriculum and may, therefore, chose not to offer their pupils the opportunity to learn a language.

Transition for languages was identified as an issue back in the 1960s when the primary French pilot projects, such as 'French from Eight' were undertaken. A research team commissioned by the National Foundation for Educational Research evaluated the project (Burstall *et al.*, 1974), comparing the attainment in French of two groups of pupils at age 16: those learning French since the age of 8 years and those who began their French studies at secondary school, aged 11 years. This was a pivotal time for the future of languages in England as the outcome of the report was to determine whether the project be continued, perhaps leading to the introduction of languages in all schools, or its demise. The authors concluded that beginning to study French at an earlier age did not confer any significant long-term advantage over starting to learn French at secondary school. It also highlighted inadequate progression and a lack of continuity of learning between the two phases as contributory factors. As a result, in the overwhelming majority of cases, the primary language pilot projects ended and languages did not become part of the compulsory curriculum in primary schools in England until September 2014 – 40 years after the publication of Burstall *et al.*'s report.

However, the picture is not completely bleak. In the intervening years, primary languages continued to be taught in some corners of the country and, over time, the enthusiasm for languages teaching grew, providing more children with the opportunity to learn a language (or in some cases several languages as part of a multilingual approach – as those documented by Jones, Barnes and Hunt (2005) and Barton, Bragg and Serratrice (2009)). Research suggests that a language awareness or multilingual approach can provide a successful introduction to language learning or a valuable addition that comple-ments the study of one language by aiding pupils to develop language awareness and transferable language skills. For example, by learning to look for contextual clues (such as the layout, visuals, author and date of publication), cognates, grammatical patterns (e.g. word order) and similarities with 'known words' to support their understanding of a new text. (An accessible and informative overview of the challenges and research can be found in Hood and Tobutt (2015)).

HOW CAN WE CREATE A POSITIVE TRANSITION EXPERIENCE?

This section explores a range of approaches and activities that might be used to smooth the transition for pupils moving from primary to secondary school for languages.

Many of them can be applied also to transfers between year groups and to other areas of the curriculum.

Galton and colleagues analysed responses to a survey of the transition activities in 215 schools carried out by the Centre for the Study of Comprehensive Schools (Galton, Gray and Rudduck, 1999). They then grouped the transition activities into five areas:

■ bureaucratic/managerial
■ social and personal
■ curriculum
■ pedagogic
■ managing learning.

Conceptualised as a series of five transition bridges, the researchers found that the majority of activities undertaken by schools to support pupils' transition related to the bureaucratic bridge, and that the social and personal bridge was also in place in the majority of schools. However, the data suggested that the other three bridges (curriculum, pedagogic and managing learning bridges) were in place in only a minority of schools. This means that many pupils were not making a smooth transition between schools. Table 9.1 provides examples of the types of activity that may be associated with each of bridge.

Given that successful transition requires all five elements, consequently, this might be a helpful framework to analyse and evaluate current transition provision and may lend itself well to being used as part of a cross-phase meeting to map current provision and to identify those aspects that may require additional support or development. This might begin with colleagues noting each transition activity and then sorting them, or better still, placing them on the bridge. This approach promotes discussion and collaboration and can reveal interesting and valuable pockets of activity that might be replicated or adapted to schools and classrooms.

■ **Table 9.1** The Five Bridges: examples of activity (based on Galton, Gray and Rudduck, 1999:28–29)

Transition bridge	Examples of activity
Bureaucratic/managerial	Cross-phase meetings, transfer of administrative information, pupil information, test data (e.g. SATs scores), parents' evenings.
Social and personal	Induction events, open evenings, peer mentoring, buddying programmes.
Curriculum	Sharing curriculum information, sharing schemes of work, joint projects (e.g. bridging units), planning for curriculum continuity, building on prior learning.
Pedagogic	Cross-phase lesson observations (e.g. Y7 teacher observes a primary lesson), team teaching.
Managing learning	Pupils supported to manage their learning, 'Learning to learn' programmes, pupils actively involved in the transition process (making suggestions, choices).

To provide a context, Galton, Gray and Rudduck (1999) observed that the social-emotional and personal aspects of transition were often met but the academic aspects (such as progression and providing curriculum continuity) were not – hence this chapter's focus on the academic aspects.

The 'Five Bridges' approach might also be used in another way to explore the transition journey of one particular pupil or group of pupils. The teachers chart the various transition activities and mechanisms the pupil has experienced and sorts these into chronological order. They then use this list and colour code it according to the nature of each activity (for example, by using Galton's 'Five Bridges', detailed above). This might then be analysed to consider the personal experience of the child and can be compared with the journey for other subjects or from a child from another school. This activity can generate valuable discussions at transition meetings within local school networks – especially if the feeder primary schools and the receiving secondary school complete the activity independently, compare responses and use it to generate discussion about how both phases can work more closely to support the various aspects of transition and ensure that all are addressed.

It is of course important for us to consider the reasons why transition is worth developing and the impact of effective transition on learning. To date, pupils arrive at secondary school with very mixed experiences of learning languages ranging from those with very limited experience to those who have learned a language (sometimes more than one!) throughout Key Stage 2 and perhaps even longer. Though the diversity of experience of a Year 7 class is likely to be broad, following the introduction in September 2014 of languages in the National Curriculum (DfE, 2013) as a compulsory subject for all children in Key Stage 2 (aged 7–11 years), most children joining secondary school might have experience of learning a language. This means that transition in languages is a real issue for all pupils and teachers and that plans for supporting transition need to be fluid and flexible to accommodate the increasing diversity of pupils' prior learning. Of course, it is noteworthy that the National Curriculum (DfE, 2013) is not compulsory in academies and free schools, which make up a growing proportion of the country's schools, though in the latest edition of the annual 'Language Trends' survey (Tinsley and Board, 2016), of the 556 primary schools completing the survey, almost all reported that they 'now provide at least some teaching of languages to pupils throughout Key Stage 2' (2016:8) and 37 per cent of the primary schools participating in the survey stated they provide the National Curriculum (DfE, 2013) entitlement teaching a language to all pupils throughout Key Stage 2. This underlines the urgency in addressing issues of transition in languages to ensure that appropriate structures and mechanisms are in place.

Learners' experiences of languages at primary school and of transition are very mixed. Below are the experiences of transition in languages shared by four children in the same Year 7 Spanish group to provide an insight into the process:

Joe learned French in his final year at primary school and felt he was making good progress. He enjoyed French lessons and was looking forward to learning more French. When he participated in an interview in the autumn term of Year 7, he revealed that he was studying Spanish as he was not in one of the Year 7 classes timetabled to learn French.

> Jade enjoyed studying Spanish in Years 5 and 6 at primary school but would have preferred to learn French as her mother speaks French. She requested to learn French in Year 7 but is continuing to study Spanish at secondary school and feels she is repeating what she has learned at primary school.

> Lewis studied Spanish for a term in Year 5 but did not enjoy his language lessons. He describes his Year 7 Spanish lessons as 'boring' at secondary school and would rather learn Polish so he can speak to his Polish friends and neighbours.

> Noemi speaks fluent Spanish and speaks English as an additional language. She enjoyed supporting her classmates at primary school to learn Spanish but is enjoying secondary Spanish lessons more as she finds the content more interesting and challenging, though she sometimes feels a little isolated doing work different to her peers.

The views of these four children illustrate the diversity of their prior experience and provide a small insight into the scale of the challenge of providing effective transition from primary to secondary school for languages.

HOW CAN WE ENSURE A SMOOTH TRANSITION FOR PUPILS?

The challenges presented by transition, and in particular, transition for languages, are well documented and extensive. However, there are examples of creative practice that have supported pupils throughout the transition period.

Through a group of schools working together and adopting a unified approach, the section below outlines a case study of effective and creative practice from one secondary school and its main feeder primary schools.

A CASE OF EFFECTIVE TRANSITION

This formed part of a larger study exploring pupils' and teachers' experiences and perceptions of transition (Richardson, 2014). Twelve schools participated in the study: eight primaries and four secondaries. Pupil and teacher questionnaires and interviews were administered at three points: the summer term of Year 6, the autumn term of Year 7 and then the summer term of Year 7.

Over the course of the study, a more positive picture emerged from one of the 'cases' (of one secondary school and two of its feeder primary schools). Initially, the primary pupils' enjoyment of language lessons was less than in the other cases with 55.4 per cent (24/44) pupils agreeing with the statement: 'I enjoy language lessons', compared to a mean average of 61 per cent (149/244) across all four cases. However, as shown in Table 9.2, this situation changed.

■ **Table 9.2** Percentage of pupils agreeing with the statement: 'I enjoy language lessons'

	Y6 summer	Y7 autumn	Y7 summer
All 4 cases	61% (149/244)	72.2% (65/90)	55.1% (54/98)
Case 2	54.5% (24/44)	73.1% (19/26)	84.6% (22/26)

As shown in Table 9.3, pupils' self-efficacy was also higher in this case. Although levels were slightly higher in Case 2 than in the other cases initially, this rose so that a year later in the summer it was even higher for Case 2 despite falling – albeit slightly – across all four of the cases in the study.

■ **Table 9.3** Perecentage of pupils agreeing with the statement: 'I am good at languages'

	Y6 summer	Y7 summer
All 4 cases	64.5% (58/90)	63.3% (62/98)
Case 2	65.4% (17/26)	73% (19/26)

In another question relating to self-efficacy, the levels increased for Case 2 but declined in all other cases. This is an immensely positive and interesting finding which raises the question of what it is that this school did to promote such levels of self-efficacy. The interviews revealed that these children believed languages to be valuable, wanted to learn languages and considered themselves to be successful language learners.

■ **Table 9.4** Percentage of pupils disagreeing with the statement: 'Most people in my class are better than me at languages'

	Y6 summer	Y7 summer
All 4 cases	48.9% (44/90)	44.9% (48/98)
Case 2	50% (13/26)	73% (19/26)

Why was the picture of transition for languages in Case 2 more positive?

The profile of the Case 2 schools (for example, the Pupils Premium data) was similar to the other cases– so the results suggest the differences were due to the approach or actions that the Case 2 schools were taking.

▪ Shared aims: the primary and secondary teachers met to agree the aims of primary languages and ensured that these were embedded across all the primary schools in the cluster and that they were aligned with those of the secondary school. A situation where the aims of the primary and secondary schools are not aligned presents a significant barrier to effective transition. Ideally, these ought to be agreed at a national level to provide the basis of practice in all schools.

▪ Developing self-efficacy: one approach taken in Case 2 was that although the teachers aimed to make language lessons enjoyable and engaging for the pupils, an attempt was made to defer pupils' immediate gratification from unassessed, 'fun' activities and to create opportunities for them to focus on tracking their own progress, building up a picture of their progress over the long-term progress and developing pupils' self-efficacy in languages.

▪ Role models: attempts were made to expose the pupils to positive role models, including older pupils who were pursuing their language study, teachers, parents, other members of the school community and, where possible, celebrities (e.g. posters and video clips of footballers promoting languages or speaking in another language). This relates to one of the tenets of Bandura's Social Learning Theory (1977): that pupils learn from observation of others. This is difficult to achieve when children do not have positive models around them and are often surrounded by monolinguals.

▪ Opportunities: pupils were presented with real-life opportunities to use the target language and experience the target language culture: ,You do a lot more in secondary school. We got to go to Paris -we spoke to the waiters, asked them how they were' (Year 7 pupil).

▪ Cross-phase liaison: this was perceived by primary and secondary teachers alike as a priority.

▪ Conceptualisation: transition was considered a shared issue for primary and secondary colleagues, with collaboration and shared ownership of the transition for languages.

▪ Collaboration: cross-phase observations and teaching took place regularly from Year 5 in the primary school. Schemes of work were planned jointly and where possible, meaningful cross-curricular links were made. Some lessons were team taught by the primary class teacher and a secondary languages teachers.

▪ Profile of languages throughout the transition period: unusually, the secondary school's transition work was led by the Languages Department. This included hosting a conference for Year 5 pupils and a Year 6 transfer day – both with a language focus. This included a range of activities including language lessons and an intercultural arts project.

▪ Personal commitment of teachers: this was felt to be a determining factor in the success of the pupils' transition for languages. This came at a personal cost – for example, some of the secondary teachers gave up their PPA time to visit and teach in the primary schools and one teacher gave weekly language class to teachers from the main primary feeder schools (which the primary teachers attended voluntarily). In a climate of ever-mounting work pressures, this raises the issue of sustainability.

QUESTION TIME

You might wish to consider, perhaps with colleagues from both primary and secondary schools:

1   How do these findings relate to your experience?
2   What examples of effective practice have you experienced?

POSSIBLE APPROACHES

The following section shares some examples of activities, many of them creative and innovative, which have been used successfully to support transition.

Film project

Year 7 pupils created film tours of their secondary school (in the target language) which were sent to the primary school for the primary pupils to view, discuss and identify questions. A group of the Year 7 filmmakers and the secondary school's Year 7 leader visited the primary school to meet with the Year 6 children and discuss queries and concerns. This was very well received and provided reassurance for the pupils prior to transition in addition to useful information to the secondary school that was used to shape their transition programme. In addition to discussing language lessons at secondary school, the discussions spanned out to include other aspects of the transition. These included progression, the level of difficulty of the work, homework, teachers' expectations and also related to non-academic aspects such as making friends, navigating around the school, school uniform, school dinners and extra-curricular activities. Following the visit, the Year 6 children revisited the videos, using them as a resource for finding out additional information about the school.

Buddying

In a different school, another project that related to buddies was also found to be very successful in terms of supporting pupils' transition to secondary school in languages but the benefits were also felt more broadly. The project involved the use of e-penpals. First, the Year 6 pupils were each allocated a Year 7 buddy. Using email, the Year 7 pupils wrote (in the target language) to their buddy to introduce themselves and share some of their work from secondary school. The Year 6 pupils then responded by introducing themselves and sharing information about their hobbies and interests. This supported the pupils in building up a relationship with their buddy and was felt to have a positive effect on the social and emotional aspects of transition, in addition to the transition in languages.

Storytelling

This project promotes progression within the primary school, liaison between year groups and collaboration within the school with the older children supporting the learning of the younger children. The Year 5 children create their own versions of a traditional fairy-tale (this also brings a cross-curricular element and links to work in English) and the project culminates in a storytelling event where the children read their stories to the KS1 children. These are filmed and the recordings used for peer and self-assessment. The children spoke very positively about this experience: 'Normally only our teacher reads our work but I felt really proud and excited when I read my story to Mrs X's class' (Year 5 pupil).

The project has been extended to become a cross-phase primary/secondary project and form a bridging unit. The secondary pupils made videos in their Computing lessons, narrating them in Spanish. This also included a popular film awards event 'Oscar' style, including a nominations process and acceptance speeches in Spanish. The award-winning films are presented to Year 6, who assume the role of film critic and review them.

Video-conferencing

This formed part of an initiative to introduce languages to primary schools. The secondary languages teacher taught the lessons to the primary pupils from the secondary school via a web-cam and, in the primary school, the class sat down at the same time each week for their languages lesson. They were supported by their class teacher who participated in the lesson along with her class and also created opportunities throughout the week for language work to be integrated throughout the week (i.e. opportunities for practice) and other areas of the curriculum. The aims of this were two-fold: to enable to the primary teacher to work with the class throughout the week between language lessons to practise their Spanish and to support the development of the primary teacher's subject knowledge and pedagogical knowledge for teaching Spanish and, very importantly, increase her confidence in teaching languages and, in the longer term, to create a more sustainable model of language teaching where the primary school children will be taught Spanish by the class teacher. This relates to a European project that explored video-conferencing as a method of teaching languages in primary schools without a specialist language teacher (Pritchard, Hunt and Barnes, 2010).

Exercise books

Activities to support transition do not necessarily require significant investments in time or finance. For example, one secondary academy in Nottinghamshire and its five main feeder primary schools agreed at a liaison meeting that Year 7 pupils would keep their Year 6 French exercise books and continue to use them in their Year 7 lessons. This means that not only can the pupils use them as a resource to refer to their prior learning but it also means that the teachers are able to refer to them too. When marking work, the teachers felt that through taking a moment to flick through the exercise book to the Year 6 work, they were able to see the pupils' work from Year 6 which helped them take into account prior learning when planning lessons.

Stars

This activity is a simple way for pupils to share key information (six items, each written in the 'point' of a six-pointed star) about themselves and their language learning with their Year 7 teacher. For example, this might include the language they are learning in Year 6, the learning activities or lessons they enjoy and the language learning strategies they use. An effective alternative might be to use 'stop, start, continue' whereby pupils note two aspects of their primary languages lessons they would prefer to stop/change, two they would like to be included in future lessons and two they would like to continue.

Sharing work

Some primary school pupils create a portfolio of work or select a piece of work to share, which they bring to their first Year 7 language lesson – or, better still, beforehand (such as to a transition day) so that it can be used by the secondary school to inform planning for their Year 7 classes.

Teacher collaboration

In addition to the valuable contribution to the children's experience of language learning across the primary-secondary school transition, transition activities can bring benefits to teachers in both sectors. These result from collaboration and liaison with colleagues working in the 'other' sector. This might be on a school-by-school basis or from working as part of a cluster or group of schools – perhaps a geographical grouping or from being part of a Teaching School Alliance or Academy chain.

Other professional development opportunities include those facilitated by universities such as the University of Nottingham's Language Education Research Group (LERG) – a group of Initial Teacher Education (ITE) mentors, students, teachers (both primary and secondary), tutors and researchers.

You might arrange a transition event (perhaps a TeachMeet) with primary and secondary colleagues to share ideas and showcase good practice? Perhaps pupils could be invited too to share their experience and their languages work.

WORKING IN PARTNERSHIP WITH UNIVERSITIES

In addition to providing opportunities for beginning teachers to teach and experience language lessons in both the primary and secondary phases – for those training to teach in either phase to experience the other, ideally over the course of a sequence of lessons, a range of other opportunities are available.

Universities often act as a vehicle for drawing together teachers from across their partnership (commonly spanning a wide geographical area and a broad range of schools). Events such as partnership meetings and subject focus groups provide valuable opportunities for everyone to share good practice, explore issues and identify opportunities for collaboration with each other and with the university tutors and students. The LERG at the University of Nottingham is an example of this and provides a forum for discussion and collaboration. Universities welcome the opportunity to work in partnership with schools and often seek opportunities for collaboration, which might include teachers and pupils speaking and working with beginning teachers about their experience and practice, special events (perhaps be involved in transition events) and engagement in research projects (ranging from large-scale funded projects to working with students and staff engaging in action research closely aligned to their teaching).

CONCLUSION

This chapter has explored the challenge of transition for languages and its background. It has also highlighted a range of transition activities and approaches to transition from simple activities to larger projects.

Key to the success of pupils' transition in languages is for colleagues in both the primary and secondary phases to adopt a unified approach and conceptualise transition as a shared challenge for which the two phases are jointly responsible. Related to this is having shared aims for primary languages so that primary and secondary provision can be aligned.

Through a greater focus on transition from both the primary and secondary phases, with a shared approach, it is hoped that primary languages can mark the beginning of pupils' life-long language learning and provide a positive and valuable experience on which pupils can build at secondary school and beyond. As Graham *et al.* (2016) argue: 'In England, the likelihood of the primary modern languages initiative having a positive impact on learners' motivation for the subject at secondary school is perceived to be threatened by problems surrounding the transition between the two phases of education' (Graham *et al.*, 2016: 683).

FURTHER INFORMATION

Association for Language Learning (ALL)

The languages subject association welcomes members from across the language teaching community, including both the primary and secondary colleagues. The annual Language World conference is an excellent opportunity for cross-phase collaboration and learning from colleagues' experiences from the classroom and research. The association also publishes a regular magazine *Languages Today*, weekly e-bulletins and access to the *Language Learning Journal* and *all* resources: www.all-languages.org.uk/.

REFERENCES

Barton, A., Bragg, J. and Serratrice, L. (2009). 'Discovering Language' in primary school: an evaluation of a language awareness programme, *The Language Learning Journal*, 37(2), 145–164.

Barton, A. and Downes, P. (2003). Differentiation and gender: boys and language learning. In T. Lamb and M. Raya (Eds), *Differentiation in the Modern Languages Classroom*. Frankfurt am Main: Peter Lang.

Burns, J. (2016). Teenage hormones 'turn pupils off school for three years'. BBC. [Online] www.bbc.co.uk/news/education-37375278. Last accessed 16 September 2016.

Burstall, C., Jamieson, M., Cohen, S. and Hargreaves, M. (1974). *Primary French in the Balance*. Windsor: National Foundation for Educational Research.

Capel, S., Zwozdiak-Myers, P. and Lawrence, J. (2007). The transfer of pupils from primary to secondary school: A case study of a foundation subject – physical education, *Research in Education*, 77(1), 14–30.

DfE (Department for Education) (2013). Languages programmes of study: Key Stage 2 and 3. National Curriculum in England. [Online] www.gov.uk/government/publications/national-curriculum-in-england-languages-progammes-of-study/national-curriculum-in-england-languages-progammes-of-study Last accessed 12 January 2018.

Evangelou, M., Taggart, B., Sylva, K., Melhuish, E., Sammons, P. and Siraj-Blatchford, I., (2008). *What Makes a Successful Transition from Primary to Secondary School? Effective Pre-school, Primary and Secondary Education 3–14 Project (EPPSE 3–14)*. London: Institute of Education.

Galton, M., Gray, J. and Rudduck, J. (1999). *The Impact of School Transitions and Transfers on Pupil Progress and Attainment.* London: DfEE Publications.

Graham, S., Courtney, L., Tonkyn, A. and Marinis, T. (2016). Motivational trajectories for early language learning across the primary–secondary school transition. *British Educational Research Journal*, 42(4), 682–702.

Hood, P. and Tobutt, K. (2015). *Teaching Languages in the Primary School*, 2nd Ed. London: Sage.

Jones, N., Barnes, A. and Hunt, M. (2005). Thinking through languages: a multi-lingual approach to primary school languages. *The Language Learning Journal*, 32(1), 63–67.

Marshall, N. and Hargreaves, D. (2008). Teachers' views of the primary–secondary transition in music education in England. *Music Education Research*, 10(1), 63–74.

McCall, I. (2011). Score in French: motivating boys with football in Key Stage 3, *The Language Learning Journal*, 39(1), 5–18.

Ofsted (2015). KS3: The wasted years? [Online] /www.gov.uk/government/publications/key-stage-3-the-wasted-years. Last accessed 12 January 2018.

Pritchard, A., Hunt, M. and Barnes, A. (2010). Case study of a videoconferencing experiment in primary schools, teaching modern foreign languages. *The Languages Learning Journal*, 38(2), 209–220.

Richardson, K. (2014). *The Primary-Secondary School Transition for Languages: Pupil and Teacher Experiences and Beliefs*. [Unpublished PhD thesis] Coventry: University of Warwick.

Sutherland, R., Ching Yee, W., McNess, E. and Harris. (2010). *Supporting Learning in the Transition from Primary to Secondary Schools*. Bristol: University of Bristol.

Tinsley, T. and Board, K. (2016). Language trends 2015/16: The state of language learning in primary and secondary schools in England. Reading: Educational Development Trust and the British Council. [Online] www.britishcouncil.org/sites/default/files/language_trends_survey_2016_0.pdf. Last accessed 12 January 2018.

CHAPTER 10

THE NEXT STAGE OF A JOURNEY?

Lessons learned from Scotland

Lynne Jones and Fhiona Mackay

INTRODUCTION

We turn now to an example of a coherent, planned policy initiative that has made real progress and which is ongoing. This is in a familiar context, a predominantly English-speaking country, part of the UK and therefore one with similar language learning issues to England. To develop primary languages and to make learning creative and fulfilling, a degree of government commitment is needed, along with trust in professionals and experts to implement it. This chapter consists of a full case study written by colleagues at Scotland's National Centre for Languages (SCILT) of their coherent policy to increase and enhance the language curriculum from 5 years old and to make for a continuous provision up to the end of the secondary phase. Scotland began this journey in advance of England and Wales and in the 1990s committed a large sum of money to launching a full-scale primary languages programme. The case study that appears here updates us as to where they are currently and gives a model for other contexts to consider when planning provision. There is not at present in England and Wales such a coherent, government-backed and funded Key Stage 2 languages development programme as there is in Scotland, as we will see from the case study. In Wales and Northern Ireland, as in Scotland, the devolved government responsibilities include education, but neither of these two countries have a large focus on languages as part of that. While the population sizes differ greatly between England on the one hand and the three other home nations on the other, and this would have implications for funding, we can say that without a coherent policy such as the one the Scottish Government are working towards, there is not much hope for a consistent emerging policy or practice across the primary schools of England.

THE SCOTTISH CASE: ENGAGING WITH PARTNERS AND STAKEHOLDERS TO ENCOURAGE CONSISTENT DEVELOPMENT

Setting the scene

Let us start with a brief exploration of the Scottish context. Education is completely devolved to the Scottish Government who in turn shares responsibility for its governance with the 32 local authorities. After the publication of the Worton Report (2009), the Scottish National Party (SNP) included a commitment to language learning in their 2011 manifesto.

> Over the course of two parliaments we will introduce a norm for language learning in schools based on the European Union 1 + 2 model – that is we will create the conditions in which every child will learn two languages in addition to their own mother tongue.
>
> (SNP, 2011: 24)

As the SNP were returned to government in May 2011, *Language Learning in Scotland: A 1+2 Approach* (the 1+2 Report) was commissioned and a working group comprising representatives from Scottish Government, Her Majesty's Inspectorate (HMI), Scotland's National Centre for Languages (SCILT), local authorities, teachers, parents, universities, teacher education institutions (TEIs), teaching unions and directors of education was set up to consider how a 1+2 approach might look in Scottish schools.

The last 10 years have borne witness to a radical rethink of the Scottish education system known as Curriculum for Excellence (CfE). It is against this background of unprecedented educational change that the 1+2 approach was formed. The group took into consideration, among other publications, the findings of the Modern Languages Excellence Group (SCILT, 2011). It also identified, among other factors, a £0.5 billion deficit in the Scottish economy caused by a lack of language skills (Foreman-Peck, 2012). The recommendations of the report received broad cross party support for what has become known as Scotland's 1+2 language policy.

Although it is the ambitious nature of the report and its recommendations that have made headlines, the recommendations go much further than that. The 1+2 approach actually marks a fundamental change in how languages are taught and who teaches them. By 2021 the expectation is that every learner should learn two additional languages from ages 5–15 years. As such, it calls for an absolute reinvigoration of this curriculum area, in line with the design principles of CfE. Its successful implementation requires the upskilling of the teaching workforce in all sectors.

Languages are not new to the Scottish curriculum and have been supported by SCILT since 1991. Another organisation supporting language learning, Cultural Organisations and Local Authorities (COALA), has held regular meetings involving Scottish Government since 1995. However, prior to the 1+2 policy, a decreasing number of local authorities were actively participating. As a result of the policy, this collaborative has grown and diversified to include HE and other members of the wider languages education community. It has rethought its structure and purpose and regrouped as the Languages Network Group Scotland (LANGS).

Since the early 1990s, Modern Languages in the Primary School (MLPS) had been routinely taught by specialist trained MLPS teachers, chiefly but not exclusively, in the last 2 years of primary education. The MLPS approach had its own set of strengths; specialist teachers had the language skills and confidence to lead the learning. However, there were often issues around workforce planning and if a primary school lost its language teacher, then often it could be left with no language provision at all and children would lose their entitlement to learn an additional language. Similarly, because the additional language was most commonly taught by a 'drop in' specialist, there was little chance of consolidation and practice from one week to another, making progression slow. Furthermore, it became evident that if language learning was left confined to the latter stages of the primary curriculum then it was never going to be considered 'the norm' and would continue to be seen as a 'bolt-on' rather than an integrated and core part of the broad general education (BGE) from age 5 to 15 years.

The 1+2 report, therefore, advocated a change particularly in how languages are taught in primary schools, moving away from the timetabled 'slot' delivered by a specialist in favour of a more integrated approach that embeds language learning in the wider curriculum. This effectively means that all primary teachers are responsible for language teaching in the same way that they are expected to deliver on all other areas of the Scottish curriculum.

However, it is not just the primary sector that is affected by the policy. In order to achieve successful implementation the recommendations range across all sectors, calling for better cluster planning to ensure continuity between primary and secondary schools, more flexible pathways for youngsters to follow to qualification level in the senior phase and cross-sectoral engagement between schools, further and higher education and the business world. It is clear then, from the report, that if we want to win hearts and minds, a galvanised cross-sector approach is necessary; one that engages with wider society as well as education, creating a team of teams, that work locally and autonomously, but that are connected, sharing and collegiate.

2012–2014: early stages of implementation

Essential to the early stages of implementation was strong leadership from Scottish Government. Responsibility for oversight of the policy was given to the Minister for Learning, Sciences and Scotland's Languages, himself a native speaker of Scots and learner of Gaelic and Norwegian. The Minister was a powerful advocate for language learning who championed the policy in its early stages and underlined publicly the importance of languages for our society (Allan, 2014). This effectively provided the high-level message that allowed the policy to be seeded.

Furthermore, in order to 'create the conditions' that supports implementation; Scottish Government committed to give the local authorities both time and money. The date for full implementation of the recommendations of the report was set at August 2021, effectively two parliamentary terms. Between 2013 and 2018, local authorities received an extra £24.7 million,[1] vital in order to build enough capacity to realise the ambitious nature of the policy. This substantial funding allocation allowed local authorities to tailor their 1+2 strategy and develop their practice. This sent out a clear signal that 1+2 was not 'just another initiative' but a serious attempt to change the languages landscape in

Scotland. Local authorities committed to provide a strategy and associated action plan to Education Scotland, which is continuously updated.

An extensive review of Scottish teacher education undertaken by the Chief Inspector HMI highlighted the need for the provision of high-quality professional learning for teachers.

> The strong uptake of high quality training given by bodies such as . . . SCILT in modern languages is indicative of a wider need. Immediate priorities might be the teaching of modern languages in primary schools, science, aspects of mathematics and Gaelic.
>
> (Donaldson, 2011: 104)

In this climate, the SCILT team was extensively enlarged in order to be in a position to support its local authority partners effectively. In 2012, the Confucius Institute for Scotland's Schools (CISS) joined SCILT. CISS provides the strategic leadership to all of Scotland's Confucius classrooms, ensuring that the Confucius programme helps local authorities to include Mandarin in their 1+2 strategies. Enhanced funding for SCILT meant there was capacity to localise initiatives that had already proven to be successful in the rest of the UK. Inspired by Routes into Languages, SCILT launched Scottish versions of the Spelling Bee in 2012 and the Adopt a Classroom initiative in 2014. The Spelling Bee pilot was adapted to become Word Wizard[2] and Adopt a Classroom became Language Linking, Global Thinking.[3] Similarly, inspired by the CiLT Cymru model, SCILT began to develop a Business Language Champions (BLC) scheme[4] which links schools with local businesses.

In order to give the national steer, government established the Strategic Implementation Group[5] to develop an engagement strategy and oversee delivery of the 1+2 policy commitment. The group, jointly chaired by Education Scotland and Association of Directors of Education in Scotland (ADES) with representatives from SCILT, the General Teaching Council of Scotland (GTCS), teaching unions, school leaders, parent organisations and local authorities, jointly hosted a series of five engagements between 2012 and 2015. The group was later expanded to include representation from teacher education and HE. A subsequent sub-group looked at wider engagement.

As 1+2 funding became available, local authorities seconded development officers to lead the implementation of the policy. As a result active participation in COALA grew exponentially. It became an important forum for a widening range of stakeholders and partners including development officers, Higher Education (HE) and Initial Teacher Education (ITE), consular staff to meet and collaborate. As attendance rose, it became evident that the format was no longer fit for purpose. In 2016 COALA was rebranded as Languages Network Group for Scotland (LANGS)[6] The meetings now have a theme and include interactive workshops led by members of the group.

In line with Recommendation 5 of the 1+2 Report, a total of 11 schools in all sectors agreed to undertake national pilots between 2012 and 2015 and were accorded additional funding and support from Education Scotland and SCILT. Each pilot had a different focus; all projects aiming to positively contribute to the learning and teaching of languages. Creative approaches were encouraged. The primary school pilots included introducing/embedding an L2 into the life of the school; establishing progression in language learning; developing literacy skills across several languages; using IT effectively to support primary language learning and developing interdisciplinary contexts for language learning. The secondary school projects focused on contextualised language learning to suit local employment opportunities and alternative qualification pathways for a variety of learners.

Each project was evaluated by an HMI Inspector. The individual evaluations and a document detailing the overarching themes that emerged were published (Education Scotland, 2014). In 2013–2014 four regional learning events were held around Scotland in partnership between Education Scotland and SCILT. The events focused on the 1+2 pilot projects and the creative, solution-focused approach of school management, teachers and learners. A second round of regional events was organised in 2014–2015. This time the focus was on approaches to L3 in all sectors and means of effecting positive uptake in secondary schools.

In autumn 2012, a working group was set up by the then HMI national specialist for languages at Education Scotland with a view to developing a progression framework for second and third level of CfE (P5 – S2/3, age 9–14/15 years) that would encourage a common understanding of assessment standards across stages, levels and sectors. The resulting framework was published in December 2013 with further refinement and exemplification published in 2015. In response, the Council of Europe ratified a Scottish version of the European Language Portfolio.[7]

In 2013 Education Scotland recruited a Senior Education Officer for Languages and Literacy who convened a further four working groups between 2013–16 comprising practitioners and development officers from SCILT and local authorities. These resulted in the publication of:

▨ a comprehensive online resource with written guidance, video exemplification and vocabulary lists with audio files in six languages to support the earliest steps of primary language learning;
▨ curricular descriptors for first level CfE (earlier stages of primary school);
▨ a progression framework for first level CfE.

As a one-stop shop for language learning and teaching, SCILT developed a new, independent website (www.scilt.org.uk/Home/tabid/1069/Default.aspx) that launched in October 2012, with a specific 1+2 area clearly identified on the landing page. Over the following few years SCILT also produced information leaflets for parents about the 1+2 policy in general, about the entitlement for all learners and about the impact of language learning on literacy.

2014–2017: middle stages of implementation

During this period, the University Council for Modern Languages Scotland (UCMLS) developed a network of local hubs aimed at increasing engagements between university to school, creating fora for cross-sector dialogue and raising the profile of languages education.

In 2014/15 SCILT's budget was increased, allowing us to further expand the team and develop new activities such as an annual series of business brunches,[8] led by business leaders and taking place across the country that aim to convince young people of the importance of languages as a key employability skill. In addition SCILT was able to develop much more support for community and heritage languages, including the national roll out of a Routes into Languages inspired poetry competition Mother Tongue, Other Tongue.[9]

A national languages leadership programme was launched by Education Scotland and SCILT in 2014.[10] Beginning with a week-long summer school, the programme provided an introduction to early language learning pedagogy, new online guidance resource, giving access to professional learning providers, networking and collaboration. This professional learning opportunity aimed to build capacity and contribute to local 1+2 implementation strategy. This Masters-level programme has professional accreditation from the GTCS, the independent professional body for teachers. Subsequent iterations of the programme have a much sharper focus on leadership and aim to create agency and advocacy for language learning in the local authorities.

In 2015 questions about language learning included in the Scottish Survey of Social Attitudes (Scottish Government, 2016b) revealed that the vast majority of those interviewed thought that language learning was very important for their children. As a result of these kinds of activities, government felt that it was increasingly important to harness the opinions of the business world and society in general in order to make the case for the policy. As a result, the initial Strategic Implementation Group (SIG)[11] was split into SIG (education) and SIG (wider engagement). This has been an important move in that SIG (education) continues to provide the high-level steer in terms of the recommendations of the policy while the SIG (wider engagement) provides the forum for collaboration and inter-connection. This group comprises representatives of wide and disparate sectors of society who will help create the climate in which languages are valued, challenging the mind-set that English is enough.

Coming from discussion in the SIG education group, ADES collaborated with the University of Edinburgh to produce *A Review of Progress in Implementing the 1+2 Language Policy* (Christie *et al.*, 2015). The findings of this report were important not just in giving a greater understanding of how the recommendations of the policy were being realised in eight local authorities across the country, but also in highlighting important areas for development that informed SCILT's strategic plan 2016/2017. The conclusions called for greater clarity and guidance around L3, more consistent approaches to cluster planning that include the secondary sector and more inter-authority collaboration and sharing of ideas.

On a positive note, it indicates that almost all local authorities are set to be able to fulfil the recommendations by 2021 and that the majority have the recommendations for L2 in place, or are currently rolling out the strategy that will allow them to achieve the entitlement for L2 for learners from age 5 to 15, by the expected date. The researchers also found that the 1+2 policy was welcomed by most stakeholders including learners and their parents and that it represented 'a positive aspect of broad general education and one where the enthusiasm of teachers, parents and learners is demonstrated' (ibid.: 6).

During discussions of the SIG (education) group's response to the report it became evident that a plan was needed to join up the efforts of each member organisation. As a result, the SIG (education) strategic plan (Scottish Government, 2017a) was published in December 2016. This was followed by the cross-sector plan from UCMLS (2017) in March 2017, and a new SCILT strategic plan in April 2017. Overall, this has fostered a much more cohesive, multi-agency approach to supporting the policy and marks an important step forward.

Also in March 2017, further curriculum guidance in the form of the Modern Languages Benchmarks was published by Education Scotland along with benchmarks for the majority of other curricular areas. The Benchmarks incorporate previous publications and progression grids that have been developed across the policy implementation period so far.

In May 2016, a cabinet reshuffle led to the loss of the ministerial brief for Learning, Sciences and Scotland's Languages on one hand, with the Deputy First Minister becoming Cabinet Secretary for Education on the other hand. This marked a major refocus on closing the attainment gap, literacy, numeracy and health and wellbeing in Scottish education. At first it was perceived that there was a pulling back from 1+2. Subsequently, the publication of the Scottish Government's *Delivery Plan for Education* (Scottish Government, 2016) underlined the importance of developing the provision of language skills within education:

> We will take action to help young people develop the skills and knowledge they will need in the workplace in particular in the areas of STEM, digital skills and languages.
>
> (Scottish Government, 2016: 9)

Furthermore, the Deputy First Minister clearly and publically demonstrated his commitment to 1+2 and to language learning as a core part of the curriculum and a benefit to society.

Looking forwards: 2017 and beyond

Most local authorities have chosen to concentrate on embedding L2 before turning their attentions to L3. However, as we move past the halfway stage, L3 is now beginning to present its own set of challenges. Timetabling issues in the secondary school have constrained how L3 can be realised in the secondary sector and also have implications for flexible pathways leading to national qualifications in the senior phase. Several schools have resorted to taking time away from L2 in order to offer L3, but this approach has implications for attainment. Concerns have been voiced that learners are not having sufficient time to develop the skills in L2 that will underpin their learning and enjoyment of L3 and support progression. SCILT has, therefore, developed a series of case studies with attendant curriculum maps that provide exemplification and guidance for school leaders on how some schools have creatively introduced L3.[12] Crucial to the support offered by SCILT and Education Scotland, is a series of professional learning events across the country that bring language teachers and their school leaders together, to discuss examples, case studies, etc. and plan a way forwards that best suits their local circumstances. Building on the success of UCMLS school to HE partnerships, a similar network for further education has recently been established with a view to reenergising languages in the college sector.

In the interests of sustainability, we hope all stakeholders and partners will turn their gaze beyond the recommendations of the policy itself towards creating the climate where language learning becomes 'the norm'.

NOTES

1   Breakdown of 1+2 funding to the 32 local authorities in Scotland: 2013–2014 £4 million; 2014–2015 £5 million; 2015–2016 £7.2 million; 2016–2017 £5 million and 2017–2018 £3.5 million, with some level of funding guaranteed until 2020–2021.
2   In 2012–2013 the Spelling Bee Scottish Pilot featured 3 languages (German, French and Spanish) and involved 16 schools. By 2016–2017 the rebranded Word Wizard competition featured 5 languages (Gaelic, German, French, Spanish and Mandarin) and involved 55 schools across Scotland.
3   Language Linking Global Thinking: 2014–2015, a partnership between SCILT and the British Council Scotland, involved four undergraduate students from one Scottish university on their year abroad in France connecting with schools in two local authorities. By 2017–2018 the scheme was a partnership between SCILT, British Council Scotland, Project Trust, CISS, the National Union of Students and four Scottish universities with undergraduates and volunteers living and working in a variety of European, African, South American and Asian countries connecting with schools in nine local authorities.
4   Business Language Champions In 2012–2013 the initiative began with 4 projects, by the end of 2016–2017 there were over 100 registered BLC projects. www.scilt.org.uk/ Business/Developinglanguageskillsfortheworldofwork/tabid/1597/Default.aspx.
5   Strategic Implementation Group www.gov.scot/Topics/Education/Schools/curriculum/ LanguageLearning/SIGremitandpurpose.
6   Languages Network Group Scotland (LANGS) formerly COALA www.scilt.org.uk/ Partnerships/LANGS_exCOALA/tabid/2098/Default.aspx.
7   Scottish version of the European Languages Portfolio www.scilt.org.uk/News/NewsView/ tabid/1311/articleType/ArticleView/articleId/4515/European-Language-Portfolio-ELP. aspx.
8   Business Breakfasts 2015 became Business Brunches in 2016. More information www. scilt.org.uk/Business/BusinessBrunches/tabid/6095/Default.aspx.
9   Mother Tongue Other Tongue multilingual poetry competition in Scotland www.scilt.org. uk/MTOT/tabid/5841/Default.aspx.
10   Between 2014 and 2017, 4 cohorts numbering 148 participants undertook the national languages leadership programme with representatives from 31 of the 32 local authorities and 2 of the 7 TEIs. www.scilt.org.uk/BeyondSchool/LanguageLinkingGlobalThinking/ tabid/5388/Default.aspx.
11   Strategic Implementation Group www.gov.scot/Topics/Education/Schools/curriculum/ LanguageLearning/SIGremitandpurpose.
12   L3 case studies on SCILT website www.scilt.org.uk/A12ApproachtoLanguageLearning/ Fromprimarytosecondary/tabid/2248/Default.aspx.

REFERENCES

Allan A. (2014) *Video Message about Scotland's 1+2 Languages Policy for the Language Leaders' Summit at Westminster*, 17 October. www.youtube.com/watch?v=rmFt2zVPKrI (accessed 6 July 2018).

Christie, J., Robertson, B., Stodter, J. and O'Hanlon, F. (2016) *A Review of Progress in Implementing the 1+2 Language Policy*. www.gov.scot/Resource/0050/00501993.pdf (accessed 6 July 2018).

Donaldson, G. (2011) *Teaching Scotland's Future. Report of a Review of Teacher Education in Scotland*. www.gov.scot/Resource/Doc/337626/0110852.pdf (accessed 6 July 2018).

Education Scotland (2014) *Language Learning in Scotland: A 1+2 Approach: 1+2 Pilot Projects: Key Messages and Next Steps*. www.scilt.org.uk/Portals/24/Library/oneplustwo/ pilot%20evaluations/Report%20pilot%20evaluations.pdf (accessed 6 July 2018).

Foreman-Peck, J. (2012) *Talking the Talk, So That Scotland Can Walk the Walk: A Rapid Review of the Evidence of Impact on Scottish Business of a Monolingual Workforce.* www.gov.scot/Resource/0039/00393436.pdf (accessed 6 July 2018).

SCILT/Scottish Government (2011) *Modern Languages Excellence Report.* www.gov.scot/Resource/0039/00393437.pdf (accessed 6 July 2018).

Scottish Government (2012) *Language Learning in Scotland: A 1+2 Approach.* www.gov.scot/Publications/2012/05/3670 (accessed 6 July 2018).

Scottish Government (2014) *Curriculum for Excellence: Addition of 1st level CfE Experiences and Outcomes.* https://education.gov.scot/scottish-education-system/policy-for-scottish-education/policy-drivers/cfe-%28building-from-the-statement-appendix-incl-btc1-5%29/Experiences%20and%20outcomes#lang (accessed 6 July 2018).

Scottish Government (2016a) *Delivering Excellence and Equity in Scottish Education. A Delivery Plan for Scotland.* http://www.gov.scot/Resource/0050/00502222.pdf (accessed 6 July 2018).

Scottish Government (2016b) *Attitudes Towards Language Learning in Schools in Scotland in Scottish Survey of Social Attitudes 2016.* www.scilt.org.uk/Portals/24/Library/research/SG_2016_ScottishSocialAttitudesSurvey.pdf (accessed 6 July 2018).

Scottish Government (2017a) *Language Learning in Schools – Strategic Plan for Implementation 2017-2021.* www.gov.scot/Resource/0051/00514755.pdf (accessed 6 July 2018).

Scottish Government (2017b) *CfE Modern Languages Benchmarks.* https://education.gov.scot/improvement/curriculum-for-excellence-benchmarks (accessed 6 July 2018).

Scottish National Party (2011) *Scottish National Party Manifesto 2011.*

Swinnie J. (2016) www.youtube.com/watch?v=mMf9NTYbahc&list=PLXe6vDlHtEF8MvvXGjEccfgmiu6Z3IS9P (accessed 6 July 2018).

University Council for Modern Languages Scotland (2017) *1+2: Looking Back and Moving Forward. To 2020 and Beyond for Scotland's 1+2 Language Policy.* www.scilt.org.uk/Portals/24/Library/FEandHE/1plus2%20ActionPlanfinal30march17.pdf (accessed 6 July 2018).

Worton, M. (2009) *Review of Modern Foreign Languages Provision in Higher Education in England.* HEFCE. http://www.hefce.ac.uk/media/hefce1/pubs/hefce/2009/0941/09_41.pdf (accessed 6 July 2018).

THE NEXT STAGE OF A JOURNEY?

Lessons learned from this book

Philip Hood

In the final chapter we will review the main messages from the book, considering both what we said in Chapter 1 were the important issues and where we could sensibly and above all creatively move next. We want this to be a forward-looking and positive conclusion that asks teachers to take these initiatives and approaches forward and make them their own.

WHAT HAVE WE LEARNED?

We noted in Chapter 1 the need to address certain pressing issues that were:

- The rationale for using the children's own contexts and interests to determine the content of the language learning and how best to explore one's own culture and the culture of others.
- The importance for motivation and thinking skills development of creative approaches to teaching and to teaching children to be creative in the primary language classroom.
- The importance of authenticity and credibility in the materials we use – this includes all platforms as paper, video, audio and screen are all equally valid and each can be creative and mundane, stimulating and restrictive.
- The difference between learning language/s and using language to learn – both strands are important but the second has a more obvious immediate purpose that will appeal to children as it will locate what they are doing in what they know and are interested in. But for the first we need to remember the importance of creative approaches in the emergence of grammatical understanding and the use of language learning strategies.
- The knowledge and skills of the workforce that enable all of the above to become a reality over time. This is a factor that cannot be ignored and for which we need to show as much creativity if we want teachers to feel they can be successful.

What has emerged through the nine chapters that make up the core of this book is that we ignore at our peril children's normal everyday experience of being at school and learning in general. Foreign language learning cannot sit quietly in the corner of a disconnected weekly half hour, perhaps taught by a relative stranger as part of a PPA arrangement (the facility that allows teachers to have free time for planning and assessment and where the class is covered by another teacher). It cannot occupy a unique flat model of a carousel of topics all taught at beginner level with no real linking and no real progression. In every other curriculum subject there is a degree of specified content for the primary phase. In language teaching this is and can be legitimately different, but at all times we as teachers need to remember that children exhibit interest in what is unknown. For children in Key Stage 2 basic elements such as, for example, what are colours and what are they called, how do we add and subtract simple one and two digit numbers are for the most part extremely well known. Vocabulary listing, i.e. this is the Spanish, German, French for this noun, adjective, verb is not in itself enormously stimulating especially if it is the normal learning diet. This links the second and third bullet points above that speak of thinking and cultural authenticity. So it is not enough to have a café menu in isolation as a purpose of teaching. We can argue that this is vocabulary that is usually dropped into dialogue frames such as ordering and this moves us on to the bullet point about using language to learn. But if it is just single words dropped into single rote-learned sentences, then it does not move far enough. As a minimum the 'set phrases' need to include supplementary questions from a waiter or issues of availability (which represents reality rather than an unlikely ideal café dialogue). Work has been done, for example by Sussex Local Authority (see also Chapter 6), to ensure that children work out the meanings of vocabulary rather than have then presented to them and a menu is a very appropriate context for this. Children will have favourite items which may or may not be available in another country and they can learn to ask about these as well as to clarify what something is or contains or if it is appropriate to allergy conditions. This needs careful building but it is entirely representative of *why* we might learn another language and so must be part of the programme.

Materials such as those contained in the publication *A La Française* (Tobutt and Roche, 2008) show for example that we can teach simple colours and animal names in another language through drawing on pieces of art, in this case the collages of Matisse. This material has a simple question/answer format involving choosing between options of animals, naming primary and secondary colours, and comparing elements of the artwork. Nothing here is too difficult yet all of it requires children to think and make decisions. It builds on prior knowledge and adds to that base (for example by introducing complementary colours which are often not as well known as primary and secondary colours as a classification). It uses creative material (the artwork) to motivate and thereby introduces vocabulary while evoking interest in the content.

There are a host of ideas in this volume and in many others that have been published over the last 15 years and it is urgent that we 'normalise' language learning where it is still not properly implemented and do that in a way that fires enthusiasm. While we hope that more and more new primary teachers will feel keen and well-equipped to teach a language, we cannot ignore our final bullet point above, that at present many teachers do feel under-skilled and that creativity is a long way down the queue which has bare survival at its head. For this reason Languages as a subject needs resources and senior leaders should prioritise the buying at least of some electronic audio/visual material that will support teachers and offer a taste of real lives in real target-language speaking countries. Go-to places include, as specific support websites for language learning, the extensive

SCILT resource at www.scilt.org.uk/Home/tabid/1069/Default.aspx and The Association for Language Learning site at www.all-languages.org.uk/, which has a resources links section for primary languages and which has been running a cross-curricular initiative called FLAME (search the site for the latest material). There is also a resources section of the Network for Languages London site at www.networkforlanguageslondon.org.uk/resources/.

We placed the chapters in an order deliberately. We wanted to start from a place that is familiar to many teachers who daily create positive learning experiences for children who have other languages than English in their lives and who may have less rich and developed English as a result. While this is different from teaching a foreign language to a class where most children are roughly equal beginners, there are many messages about learning language by learning something *in* a language that are important for both contexts. Teachers can be creative about how children meet the foreign language through varying stimulus across audio, visual and textual platforms, using print and electronic media. We introduced material that raised issues of keeping up target language use by teachers and children, issues of accuracy in speech and writing while using a creative platform, ways to integrate other subjects such as mathematics and dance, ways to show how 'texts', whether read, watched or sung can inspire children especially the younger pupils in our schools, to find languages both pleasurable and purposeful. We have previously mentioned the case of a 3 year old, picked up early from Nursery by his mother, having a tantrum on the way out of the classroom and shouting 'I want to do French'.

DARE TO BE DIFFERENT

Although acronyms can be rather tired in the current climate we are concluding with one. DARE is going to be applied to both teachers and learners in turn with two slightly different variants. This is in keeping with the aim of the book and the series to foster independent creative learners as well as creative teacher-made or -found approaches, resources and tasks.

We are urging teachers to be **direct** about the whole language learning process. This includes a range of approaches:

■ Be open with children about why we learn languages and how for the majority of children on earth it is quite normal to be aware of more than one. Use the bilingual children in your own class/school to show how useful it can be. Susan Jones' chapter, which linked English as an Additional Language (EAL)/bilingual teaching to foreign language learning, highlighted how important this was.
■ Whatever your capabilities, use them as fully as you can – talk in the foreign language but show the children as well that you often use a dictionary because you don't know everything. Use Colin Christie's survival kit and guidance to de-mystify how to create a language-rich classroom. Always let the additional language appear to be a language, not an add-on to English that can only work when it's mixed. Short, purposeful and comprehensible messages, rather than words are the really vital units to work in.
■ Be direct also about what might be difficult and compare what they are learning to English or other languages known to the class.

■ Ensure that the children are always **active**. Listening is an important skill but we need to do something with what we hear. When planning continually ask yourself the question: 'and what are the children doing at this point?' Think about how careful you are in other lessons to move away from too much passive time in the classroom and hand over tasks to pairs and groups so the learners engage actively with resources or ideas, whatever they are. Go further and ensure they are actively thinking, deciding, discovering and not just 'actively repeating' (which is not really an active act!). Chapters in this book by Claudine Kirsch, Sarah Lister and Pauline Palmer, Elaine Minett alone and with Laure Jackson and Kristina Tobutt all emphasised the activity that children can engage with when using the approaches and resources they proposed. Primary age children need concrete and visual stimulation and hands-on collaborative tasks that go beyond imitation and repetition even in game format. Language learning should always involve as real communication as possible. If we review those chapters we see a whole range of stimuli for this; in some cases it involved the use of technology-based devices while in others it was simply about singing together or in groups or even alone.

As teachers we need to be **responsive** to children when they express any and all emotional or cognitive feedback on what they are expected to engage in. This response might be to repeat something that is highly enjoyed and valued or to revise what we offer to take into account creative and innovative suggestions they make or problems they might be encountering. The Tobutt chapter highlighted that the youngest children will engage with visual, physical, emotional stimuli first and language next. They will not learn language just because we present it to them, but will show pleasure, interest and engagement and then start to construct meaning and absorb words and structures if we notice and respond to their responses. This does not change completely as they grow older.

It should always be our intention to **enhance** the learning that we plan and organise. This enhancement can link back to the responses we have had from the children and involve using techniques we know to be successful from previous language work or from other subjects, but in a new way; or it can be a conscious extension of the learning in a direction in which we have seen the children's interest. The Richardson chapter about transition showed that giving the learners more active ownership over the transition tasks and enhancing their normal experience by siting work in a partner school and with different age students, they were given insights into how their learning could develop and be enhanced in the future. The transition activities also enhanced the knowledge of the primary teachers where that was of benefit to them.

But the children need to DARE too. They will need to be encouraged to play out their own version of the acronym. This is another dimension of the teachers' role of being *direct* in that they need to signal clearly to the children that language learning is heavily dialogic in all its senses. The children's four aspects are all closely linked.

Language lessons should always be about **discovery** and it is ultimately the responsibility of both teachers and learners to make this happen; the projects involving technologies, physical tasks, research, discussion, creation as epitomised in the central six chapters of the book by Kirsch, Lister and Palmer, Minett and Jackson, Tobutt and Richardson all involve children coming out of activity having controlled their own learning to some extent and having discovered something that means something to them as individuals, (which might be something subtly different from the other children in the class).

The learners need to **ask** – for words that they want to know; for extension to themes especially if the language learning is linked to class topics that run through the rest of the week; for more of a certain type of resource or more time to pursue activities that they have started; for opportunities to show off their knowledge, for example through assemblies; or simply for clarification of more difficult aspects of language.

The children also need to be encouraged to **research** all and any aspects of the target language communities that interest them and to seek opportunities to meet new language in the process. This does require some care on the part of teachers who will of course carry out their safeguarding duty in offering suggestions for legitimate research sites. The TV-based sites in other countries can be a useful resource on a visual level (although of course the language will normally be too difficult) and some are accessible through YouTube.

Finally, they need to know they can **experiment** with language. On one level this is just substituting words in songs and, if they are really advanced, re-rhyming where they can. But this can grow into using an interview format to others with assumed identities or adapting it for different topics. Further on in time it can be developed into using drama-based activities such as hot-seating or conscience alley initially with pre-learned lines that can be collaboratively extended and amended. The Kirsch chapter shows how children enjoy being creative with the language they know and how this in time develops their capabilities. Other core chapters in this volume also encourage the movement from limited building blocks to freer structures, showing the power of motivation generated by content and activities that capture interest.

A BOX OF LANDSCAPES

We conclude the book by taking the image, appropriately, of two Scottish artists, a poet and an illustrator (Thomas A and Laurie Clark) who together produced literally a box full of fragments of writing and drawing which showed tens of pathways towards reflecting aspects of landscapes. The items contained there are different in form and content but create a consistent and coherent whole both within the box and when they are extracted and viewed. This book has presented a similar menu of academic arguments and reports, snapshots from classrooms, signposts to resources and advocations to approach language teaching from specific pedagogical stances. It is not an instruction manual but a collage of thoughts that requires all readers to ponder and make sense for themselves of their own personal take on language learning and teaching. In harmony with the principles of both book and series, it offers creative ideas but asks the practitioners to become creative themselves in making them real and alive in classrooms. It asks them also to ensure that the children they teach do likewise. Children want to be creative as their energy levels mean they will become bored with over-rigid frameworks and moulds, over-use of repetitive techniques, with an imposed belief that there is only one way. The education policy makers in England have too often believed that there are simple solutions and that we can 'crack' any problem with a prescription and a framework. It is actually much harder than that and the most creative people we have to ensure progress and success in our young people are to be found more among teachers in schools than among those who work in ministry offices. This is how it should be, but it requires the restoration of a level of trust in the pedagogical understanding and capabilities of the teaching workforce that is currently lacking if it is to mean anything tangible for schools and classrooms.

There is no doubt that if we want to teach languages creatively books like this might be helpful, but in reality we need to trust and promote those who actually do it day after day.

REFERENCES

Tobutt, K. and Roche, C, (2008) *A La Française*. Dublin: Authentik.

INDEX

Locators in **bold** refer to tables and locators in *italics* refer to figures.